THE PALESTINIAN REGIME
A "Partial Democracy"

To
my mother Su'ad
and my father Fayyad

The Palestinian Regime

A "Partial Democracy"

———

AS'AD GHANEM

sussex
ACADEMIC
PRESS

BRIGHTON • PORTLAND

2 4 6 8 10 9 7 5 3 1

First published 2001
in Great Britain by
SUSSEX ACADEMIC PRESS
PO Box 2950
Brighton BN2 5SP

and in the United States of America by
SUSSEX ACADEMIC PRESS
5824 N.E. Hassalo St.
Portland, Oregon 97213-3644

British Library Cataloguing in Publication Data
A CIP catalogue record for this book is available from the British Library.

Library of Congress Cataloging-in-Publication Data

Ganim, As'ad
The Palestinian regime : a "partial democracy"/ As'ad Ghanem.
p. cm.
Includes bibliographical references and index.
ISBN 1–902210–68–9 (alk. paper)
1. Palestinian National Authority. 2. Munaòòamat al-Taòrar al-Filasòanayah.
3. Democratization—Palestine. 4. Palestine—Politics and government—1948–
I. Title.

JQ1830.A58 G36   2001
320.95695'3—dc21   00–140213

Typeset and designed by G&G Editorial, Brighton
Printed by TJ International, Padstow, Cornwall
This book is printed on acid-free paper

Contents

Foreword by Naseer Aruri

Much has been written about the transition to democracy in post-colonial societies and the problems they encountered in social and economic development, power distribution and consensus-building, among other issues related to the process of nation-building. Palestine would not be a typical case, inasmuch as it is one of the few societies that had the misfortune of being re-colonized in the age of de-colonization. In the aftermath of their dispersal, dispossession and fragmentation, Palestinians never ceased to struggle for normalcy and a dignified national existence. With the establishment of Israel, statehood was denied to the Palestinians, who became either stateless in their own land, refugees in neighboring Arab states, or an oppressed minority inside Israel.

Decades of struggle have failed to produce an autonomous existence, let alone a measure of independence and democratic governance. The uprising (*Intifada*) of 1987–91 seemed for a while their only hope, in utilizing the grassroots nature of their movement and its egalitarian character to establish a viable alternative to the occupation. Ironically, however, the *Intifada* was exploited by the Palestinian leadership as a bargaining chip to secure a qualified Israeli recognition of the PLO and a vague promise that statehood would be attainable after an interim phase of limited self-rule. It was not only a deal in which the achievements of the *Intifada* were sacrificed at the altar of the Oslo process, but it was also a terribly unequal exchange, in which the prospects for independence and democracy were given up for instant gratification – ruling over a collection of disconnected bantustans, while awaiting what, by the process itself, has been effectively rendered unattainable .

Neither independence nor democracy could possibly emanate from the Oslo "peace", which made "security" an overarching principle that governed the entire process and its substance. "External security" was vested in Israel, making it impossible for any Palestinian state to control its borders and exercise sovereignty over the points of exit and entry. Similarly, democracy was precluded by the terms of the "reciprocal" arrangements obligating the Palestine Authority (PA) to replace the occupation regime as gendarme and assume the role of sub-contractor for the Israeli occupation.

"Reciprocity", which was coined by Netanyahu, and incorporated in the Hebron Protocol of January 15, 1997, was also reiterated in the preamble of the Wye Memorandum of October 1998, both of which predicated further redeployment on the "assumption of responsibility for public order and internal security by the Palestinian police". Every single redeployment was made contingent on PA compliance subject to CIA verification, with specific "security" and "reciprocity" requirements. Thus the first redeployment of a mere 2 percent from Area C to Area B, and a change of status from B to A affecting 7.1 percent, was to take effect only after a Palestinian "security work plan" shared with the US was accepted by bilateral and trilateral security committees and implemented by the PA.

Perhaps one of the most humiliating aspects of these agreements for the Palestinians was the scarcely veiled incongruity of the security needs and "security actions" described in Section 2 of the Wye Memorandum. The preamble of that section refers to mutual security needs and obligations, hence both parties were expected to "take all measures" to "prevent acts of terrorism, crime and hostilities" and to "prevent incitement against each other". The scarcely-hidden agenda, of course, was taking "measures" to suppress free speech, free press, assembly, curricular development, and other forms of free expression.

In addition, the PA was expected to apprehend specific individuals on Israel's wanted list and to transfer (but not extradite, due to the sovereignty connotation of the term) them to Israel. The PA's decree against incitement, required by the Wye Memorandum, was delivered to the Israelis as Order Number 3 entitled "Emphasizing National Unity and Preventing Incitement". Not only is there no definition of the term "incitement", but there is also no distinction between incitement and legitimate political opposition. The decree cites as precedents a repressive British Mandate law of 1936, and a Jordanian law of 1960. In pursuance of eliminating "incitement", the PA was also required to participate in a trilateral committee (with the US and Israel), whose members would include "specialists" in media, education, and law-enforcement areas.

Moreover, democracy suffered again under the Wye rules, which stipulated that the CIA, through bilateral and trilateral watchdog committees with the PA and Israel, was expected to act as some kind of umpire verifying that the PA in fact engaged in arresting, holding trials, collecting arms, criminalizing incitement (i.e. political dissent), and acted in good faith to carry out its contractual obligations.

Ironically, Arafat declared the agreement a significant step toward the realization of "an independent nation having a lot of democracy" and of "the Palestinian dream of geographic unification" between the West Bank and Gaza, in addition to the promise of security, "particularly for the

Israeli people". After three more agreements and attempted agreements at Sharm al-Sheikh, Washington and Camp David, his expectations have gone up in flames and destruction, as Israel continues to wreak havoc on Palestinian civilians, their homes, property and economic well-being.

Thus, while Oslo I and II have divested the Palestine question of its pivotal elements, the Wye Accord extended the damage to the Palestinian psyche, consciousness, and even to the collective memory of the Palestinians and Arabs. It demanded of the Palestinians an effective renunciation of a crucial part of their history and a virtual apology for more than half a century of struggle for national liberation. Furthermore, it put them on notice that any form of resistance is now punishable under CIA supervision. This, indeed, was the price set by Netanyahu for redeployment from a small percentage of West Bank land.

The PA could not fulfill its mandate, which was clearly enunciated in such agreements drafted by Talmudic professionals in the Israeli foreign office, and at the same time pretend to govern democratically. No amount of separation of powers, internationally-supervised elections, or universal suffrage could outweigh the iron-clad commitments undertaken by the PA to protect Israel's interests in the occupied territories, including its territorial designs, settlement security, demographic imperatives, water needs, and its overall hegemonic framework steeped in Zionist ideology.

The PA could, therefore, waive the trappings of statehood, symbols of independence and façade of democracy, but the facts on the ground could never conceal the built-in conditions of dependency, the daily Israeli killings *inside* the domain of Yasser Arafat, whose autocratic rule has been tailor-made for Israel's "security" needs as enshrined in the Oslo agreements. This book demonstrates that the lack of democracy in Arafat's regime is linked not only to the prescriptions and exigencies of Oslo, but also to serious deficiencies within Palestinian society and its leadership. The building of the Palestinian polity in 1994 was hampered by crippling factors inherent in the PLO body politic, which were transplanted to the politics of the West Bank/Gaza enclaves. The task of building democratic institutions remains until now a casualty of archaic decision-making practices, haphazard appointments, lack of accountability at both the political and economic levels, and a total absence of an efficient, rational and consultative policy-making process, in order to guarantee unqualified control at the top.

Moreover, broad segments of the West Bank/Gaza elites and intelligentsia, who were engaged in a valiant struggle against the Israeli occupation, were easily co-opted by Arafat's regime and made to acquiesce in its autocratic practices, in exchange for positions and prestige. For many in the ruling factions, "revolution" has become a source of employment and livelihood. The system of patronage over which Arafat had presided for decades in the Fakhani and elsewhere is in full operation in his realm today.

That dynamic, egalitarian and vibrant society, which had emerged in the West Bank and Gaza in response to the Israeli occupation, is in danger today of losing its progressive and pluralist character under the culture of "security" fostered by Israel and the PA.

The "self-rule" regime, as the product of the so-called peace process, has utterly failed to enhance grassroots institutional development and to promote rational economic planning and the necessary socio-political change in Palestine. Unless this product of the "peace process" succeeds in permitting the re-emergence of a vibrant civil society, and unless the new ruling class, which has displaced the earlier notables of the British and Jordanian eras, is held to the test of accountability and transparency, the final outcome might well be either destructive indifference or chaotic violence.

The outcome of these agreements between Israel and the PA cannot amount to more than a fragmented bureaucratic entity, whose control over resources, borders and external security would be circumscribed by the agreements themselves. This is particularly significant in view of the fact that these agreements now are considered by the United States and Israel as having superseded the instruments and provisions of international law relevant to the Palestine question. In the words of Madeleine Albright, all United Nations resolutions on Palestine are now considered "contentious, irrelevant and obsolete".

And yet, Arafat's regime continues to derive its legitimacy from the United States and Israel, but not from its Palestinian constituents. In fact, Arafat has boxed himself in to the extent that he has no alternative strategy to this "peace process". It is his "only game in town", and to abandon it would automatically mean to concede power and influence to his rivals in the nationalist-leftist sector and/or to the Islamist factions. The "peace process" has become a one-way street for Arafat, but it cannot possibly lead to any destinations of which Israel disapproves. Much of what is normally associated with sovereign existence, democratic politics, and rational planning is excluded from the Israeli agenda for the new Palestine.

Thus, the economic and social dimensions of the Oslo agreements are undermining the potential for long-range political and economic development, and consequently democratic rule, by perpetuating dependency and leaving unresolved issues, such as the movement of goods and labor, the lack of a fiscal regime and participatory politics, among others. Palestinian sovereignty can never become a reality as long as the Oslo Accords sidestep the important issues of occupation, settlements, Jerusalem and refugees; and as long as Israel is not constrained by these accords from expropriating vast areas of agricultural land and allocating water resources in such a way as to suit its expansionist policies. International aid can neither guarantee the survival of the Palestinian people forever in the absence of real development (precluded by Oslo) nor sustain indefinitely the "peace process" and the pretense of diplomacy. The existing arrangements produced by Oslo, which exclude the Palestinian Authority from any controlling power over land, resources, fiscal policies, employment and external security, render terms such as autonomy, statehood – let alone democracy – superfluous. The combination of cronyism, corruption and repression have sustained the "peace process", which, in turn, curtailed the ability and/or the willingness of the PA regime to achieve the requirements for integrated socio-political development, democratic governance and rational economic planning.

As'ad Ghanem's study reveals that the PA leadership continues to seek institutional survival while relegating the broader interests and human and national rights of the Palestinian people to the sidelines. A fairly well developed civil society with voluntary associations and grassroots NGO organizations had given the first *Intifada* a nation-building character, but the political committees and NGOs which catered to the social and economic needs of a captive society during that uprising were placed under tight control after much of their funding was re-channeled to the PA.

Ominously, PA control has also been extended through the promotion of factionalism, as an opportunistic measure to insulate the peace process from a real public debate and demands for accountability. The notable cliques and civil servants of the British Mandate and Jordanian rule periods failed to integrate the society and build national and democratic institutions. Now their successors in Arafat's regime are using factionalism to protect the existing political order in order to escape their responsibility to develop an independent and democratic polity.

In summary, that previous failure to implement democracy, together with the current Israeli vested interest in Palestinian fragmentation as well as Israeli manipulation of the various Oslo agreements to suit its own interests, translates into authoritarian rule, parasitic politics and a crippling dependence. Constitutional and legal issues are thereby neglected, and this in turn leads to a strangling of democratic development. Regime insecurity has led the ruling elite to cling tenaciously to power and to treat any dissenting behavior as a form of treason. Not only does such a policy close the door to viable alternatives to the PA, but it stifles opposition and reduces the capacity of alternative groups and institutions to provide social services, economic benefits and democratic rule to a society that has never ceased to struggle for such benefits during most of the last century.

Naseer Aruri
Chancellor Professor Emeritus, University of Massachusetts Dartmouth
23 December 2000

Preface

This book analyzes the history of the Palestinian regime and the quality of the regime that currently controls the Palestinians in the West Bank and Gaza Strip. Between April 1994 and September 2000 I collected information and statistics about the performance in the field of the Palestinian leadership, which is used here to survey and analyze various aspects associated with the leadership. The situation is extremely grave and attests to the existence of a tyrannical and harsh system that controls the Palestinians and their national movement.

The peace agreement, and the movement toward a Palestinian national state, facilitates a historic process of democratization in the future; but a great effort and much courage will be needed to achieve this. As a scholar, as a Palestinian, and as a human being I deem it my duty to paint the picture of political repression as I see it. While I accept that many issues of the Palestinian past and present may have escaped my view, the outrages and incompetences presented in this book truly reflect the current situation.

The Palestinians in the West Bank and Gaza Strip lived under a harsh and brutal Israeli occupation, which acted in every way possible to neutralize the Palestinians and make them suffer. The Oslo Accords heralded the start of a new path – an end to the occupation and the building-up of an independent Palestinian state. The Accords should also have presaged the beginning of a new age with regard to the regime under which Palestinian citizens would live in the future – but this hope was soon shattered. Today, every observer who follows events in the field is aghast at the strong-arm tactics of the Palestinian regime *vis-à-vis* its citizens. Frequently there is no culpability or reasonable explanation for acts of intimidation and repression. This is the dark and oppressive side of the "partial democracy" that prevails in the Palestinian regime. But not all is darkness: there are social and political organizations in the field that fight against the violence of the Palestinian regime and against corruption, albeit with little success to date. But the courage shown in confronting the regime of political violence indicates that there is nevertheless a basis and a hope for the construction of an enlightened and democratic system in the future.

Six chapters analyze the Palestinian experience with democracy, and a final seventh chapter concludes by discussing the contradictions within Palestinian democracy. **Chapter 1** is a theoretical introduction that offers a concise background for the topic covered, namely a summary of the scholarly background to the study of processes of democratization and a consideration of the relevance of this background for the Palestinian regime and especially for its leaders' performance in impeding or promoting the process of democratization. **Chapter 2** reviews the history of the Palestinian national movement and its struggle to establish a Palestinian state, beginning in the 1920s. This chapter presents a concise description of the main events traversed by the Palestinian national movement until the signing of the Oslo Accords with Israel and the establishment of the Palestinian National Authority (PNA).

Chapter 3 describes the pre-PNA Palestinian experience, with democracy on the one hand, and with centralization and one-man rule (by Arafat) in its political, social, and economic life, on the other. The central argument advanced here is that the Palestinian experience with democracy and pluralism has been a two-way street. In one direction, in the organs of the Palestine Liberation Organization (PLO), which began operating in the mid-1960s and received an injection of energy after the selection of Yasser Arafat (Abu Amar) as chairman of the PLO executive committee in 1969, there was a slow process whereby power was concentrated in Arafat's hands. He increasingly exploited the problems associated with running a campaign of national liberation, in the conditions faced by the Palestinians, in order to tighten his control over the PLO as a whole, including bodies and organizations that were considered to constitute the internal opposition to Arafat. In parallel, among the Palestinians who fell under Israeli occupation in 1967, the struggle was concentrated in an attempt to set up an independent state in these territories (the West Bank, Gaza Strip, and East Jerusalem); their inhabitants constituted the core of the Palestinian national movement. Despite harsh treatment by the Israeli occupiers, there emerged within Palestinian society institutions and procedures that attested to a high degree of political awareness and a disposition toward political and social pluralism, and the basic adoption of democratic methods of decision-making.

Chapters 4 and **5** present the basic structure of the formal political system inaugurated in the PNA since its founding in 1994. According to the agreements with Israel, and in keeping with public declarations by the Palestinian leadership before that time, an ostensibly democratic system of government was established in the PNA, based on a separation of powers, a presidential regime and free, proportional, and fair elections of those who make the decisions in the Palestinian government. **Chapter 4** centers on an analysis of the main components of the political system. In addition to the presidency, whose incumbent is elected in country-wide elections, three branches were set up in the PNA as the three pedestals of the regime: the legislative, the executive, and the judicial, with a formal fundamental separation between them. **Chapter 5** presents the basic principles of the electoral system, the legitimacy of the elections, and the final results of the elections for president and the legislative council, held on January 20, 1996. **Chapters 4** and **5** sketch the structure and functions of the three branches of the Palestinian government since 1994 and the procedures for their election or nomination. This structure is an important and even essential (formal) component of the "partial democracy" set up in the PNA.

Chapter 6 advances a basic analysis of the nonformal system that prevails in the PNA, such that the Palestinians in its jurisdiction live under a centralized regime run by Arafat and his confidants. This system is based on three main elements of control: concentration of power (and decision-making), intimidation (the use of violent means against Palestinian citizens and institutions), and bribery (of elites, intellectuals, families, and the political opposition). These methods are intended to preserve Arafat's exclusive control over the totality of Palestinian life; taken together, they constitute a complete system that operates parallel to the formal structure surveyed in **chapters 4** and **5**. The nonformal system examined in **chapter 6** is dominant and most relevant for the Palestinians who live under the PNA. It constitutes the second part of the "Palestinian democracy", which supplements and parallels the formal structure.

Chapter 7, the concluding chapter, summarizes the arguments presented in the book about the existence of a "partial democracy" for the Palestinians since Arafat's takeover of the principal organs of the PLO in the late 1960s. The presentation differentiates between the periods before and after the establishment of the PNA. At the end of the chapter there is a brief presentation of the basic and minimum conditions that could lead in the future to a normal process of democratization in the Palestinian state.

Also included in this volume are four appendixes: The Political Program of the PNA, published after its founding in 1994; the Basic Law passed by the Legislative Council; the bylaws of the Palestinian Legislative Council; and the draft law on the independence of the judiciary. I wish to thank Ghassan Khatib, Director of the Jerusalem Media and Communiations Center (JMCC), for permission to reproduce these documents.

Many persons have assisted me while I was researching and writing this book, and I would like to express my gratitude to all of them. I would like to thank the Institute for Peace Research at Giv'at Haviva and the Tami Steinmetz Center for Peace Research at Tel Aviv University, for their financial support in the first stages of the research. In particular I would like to thank Professor Moshe Ma'oz, of the Truman Institute at the Hebrew University of Jerusalem, and Muhammad Bheiss, both of whom read the manuscript and offered many helpful comments. I would like to express my heartfelt appreciation to the research assistants who helped me amass material: Aziz Ka'id of the Center for Palestinian Research and Studies in Nablus and A'alia Siksik of the Palestinian Human Rights Monitoring Group, based in Jerusalem. Special thanks are due to all those who gave me of their time and thoughts during the interviews I conducted in the field. I thank Hanan Sa'di, who typed part of the material, and Lenn Schramm, who edited most of the book. Finally, all my love and appreciation to Ahlam my wife who was always there during the process of writing this book.

Ultimate responsibility for what is written here remains, of course, with me.

As'ad Ghanem
October 2000

1

Introduction: Political Development and the Transition to Democracy

The need for a state is important and understandable; it derives chiefly from the urge to create a protected space for all members of a particular group. A society without a state is characterized by traditional loyalties to a lord or to the tribe, or by a group identity based on blood ties or primordial sentiments. The establishment of a state reorients a society's energy and interest toward the new framework, to which citizens contribute and from which they expect to receive in return security, assistance, welfare, and the like. National development reflects the transition from an agrarian and tribal society to a modern society; as part of this transition, traditional units that impede national cohesion are destroyed, while demands that transcend tribal and regional affiliations are formulated.[1]

The establishment of new states in the Third World during the second half of the twentieth century was generally accompanied by processes of modernization, national awakening, the appearance of new elites, and a struggle for democratic regimes.[2] The Palestinian regime that emerged from the peace agreements with Israel reflects the political experience of the Palestinians, especially after the establishment of the Palestine Liberation Organization (PLO). In the present study I locate the Palestinian National Authority (PNA) along the axis that runs from political democracy at one end to an authoritarian (centralized) regime at the other; alternatively, it can be defined as a hybrid that includes elements of both extremes or embodies characteristics of both at the same time. In addition to examining the official structure of the Palestinian regime and the minimal formal democracy (democratic processes) – as proposed by classical theoreticians such as Dahl,[3] Huntington,[4] and others[5] for classifying states and regimes – I shall also refer to sociologists who advocate a more stringent definition of democracy; drawing on events in South America, Eastern Europe, and Asia, they have created a new and original body of knowledge about democratization processes and about regimes, states, and societies in transition.[6] They have also included, as appropriate, references to substantive components of democracy such as equality, freedom, human and civil rights, and protection of minorities and of citizens with limited means or connections. Relying on these scholars, I define democracy as a system based on the following elements: (1) equal citizenship and civil rights shared by all; (2) popular sovereignty and universal suffrage; (3) defense of minorities and of citizens with limited means; (4) free and regular elections; and (5) separation of powers among legislative, executive, and judicial branches.

The issue of democratization processes is intimately linked with the classification of regimes in the Third World. This is because political systems and regimes are dynamic and change in response to diverse circumstances, including the individual dispositions of leaders, and global processes.[7] Hence the necessity of first discussing issues of democratization in the Third World and the Arab world, and then viewing the regime of the Palestinian National Authority in the light of the practices of other regimes.

In recent years, much has been written about political change and democratization processes in Third World countries. The field gained momentum after the collapse of the Communist bloc and the appearance of new (or old/new) countries with democratic regimes. Advocates of the functional model emphasized the existence of prior cultural and economic conditions that led to processes of democratization, such as income level, mutual tolerance, and so on.[8]

According to Samuel Huntington, global democratization processes were the result of five key factors: (1) the legitimacy problems of authoritarian regimes; (2) significant economic growth in the 1960s and 1970s; (3) changes in the perception of the role of the church; (4) changes in the positions and policies of the Soviet Union, the United States, and Europe; and (5) the expansion and diffusion of democratic ideas and concepts from traditional democratic states to the Third World.[9]

According to Lipset, who is the chief representative of the functionalist approach, three structural factors combine to produce the basic conditions that lead to a process of democratization. The first of these is economic level and development. In his opinion, the prospects for democratization are enhanced in affluent countries with minimal poverty, because affluence allows people to go beyond their daily search for bread and cultivate a desire and ability to participate in politics and the democratic process. The second factor is educational level: a literate population with a higher level of education is better equipped to further the democratic process. For Lipset, education expands horizons and makes it possible to understand the importance of tolerance, self-control, and resistance to demagogs and charismatic figures who rely on anti-democratic methods and means. Widespread education strengthens the middle class, which has an interest in reinforcing democracy as the system that enables it to wield maximum influence. The third factor is the legitimacy of the system: the system's need for public legitimacy is crucial for change in the direction of greater democracy. Stability in the face of processes of change depends not only on the effectiveness of the change processes and regime, but also and chiefly on the legitimacy of the system and the change process itself. Reinforcement of the system's legitimacy as perceived by the public depends on the system's capacity to involve and absorb new forces from the general population and to make them willing to defend it. Political systems that prevent new forces from entering the centers of decision-making and power impede the broadening of the system's basis of legitimacy as perceived by the general public.[10]

Unlike Lipset, Rustow used the conflict model to explain the transition to democracy. For him, the level of economic and educational development is a marginal factor in the transition to democracy – perhaps an outcome rather than a precondition. Rustow emphasized the great variation among societies in the course of democratization but was able to distinguish a number of key stages in the transition: national unity, struggle, compromise, adaptation, and democracy. In the stage of national unity, most of the citizens must be confident of their membership in the political community. The struggle stage begins after all citizens accept the system and the changes that entail rejection of the existing order; it is manifested chiefly by the growth of a new elite that seeks to introduce previously weak and marginal forces into the political process. Conflict itself is a process that generates a new mix of division and integration that replaces the former status quo. The compromise stage is when the traditional forces and the new forces decide to conduct the system on the basis of compromise or majority rule; that is, the political leadership decides to accept the existence of domestic disagreements and the need to implement solutions that take account of the opinion of the other side. Hence, the turn to democracy requires the agreement of the political leadership of both camps. The adaptation stage means the broadening of support for the principle of compromise and the provision of appropriate rational justifications for it – including learning from, and public rectification of, mistakes. The success of the compromise and the process of learning from mistakes can encourage forces that formerly rejected democracy to adopt it. By the same token, failure can undermine the system and spark a return to an undemocratic system. In the last stage, democracy, including a commitment to the political processes it generates, becomes the common heritage.[11]

Nancy Bermeo considered processes of democratic transitions in conditions of violent struggle, or under the threat of the eruption of a violent struggle, between different sectors of the civil or political system. She rejects the argument, found in the literature, that there cannot be a democratization process accompanied by the threat or use of violence that pressures the system and causes it to react in a brutal fashion and repress every manifestation of freedom and democracy. Bermeo cites the cases of Spain and Portugal and maintains that pressures from below can in fact encourage a transition to democracy. Moderation is not necessarily a condition for democratic transition; on the contrary, the lack of moderation and threats of the use of force can catalyze the transition. The ruling elites may give in to demands for greater democracy in three cases: (1) if the cost of suppressing the demands from below is too high and does not justify the repression itself; (2) if the elites believe that the change processes will not destroy them or that the transition to democracy will perpetuate rather than put an end to their control; (3) if the elites believe that democracy will not lead to the victory of the extremists and to a fundamental revision of the norms and rules of society.[12]

It is argued here that the proponents of both the functional approach and the conflict model have not given sufficient weight to the most important factor inducing democratization processes around the world; namely, the appearance, in societies and states that have experienced processes of democratization, of a stratum of activists and local or national leaders who emphasize individual, civil, and human rights and equal competition among equals as the essence of the political process and as a goal worth fighting for. This process took place thanks to modernization, globalization, the development of the mass media, and familiarity, gained by various means, with the quality of life in developed (democratic) countries as opposed to less developed (and undemocratic) countries. This factor (leaders with democratic orientation) is crucial for understanding the opposite process of transition from competitive democracy to an authoritarian centralized regime – which is what has taken place in the Palestinian National Authority.

During the course of the Israeli occupation, especially during the *Intifada*, a new Palestinian leadership emerged and crystalized in the West Bank and Gaza District. This leadership agreed upon an unwritten pact that made it possible to maintain a balanced and competitive system (which operated in conditions of pressure because of the occupation) and reached its acme in its demonstrated ability to lead the uprising by the Palestinians in the West Bank and Gaza Strip against the Israeli occupation, to guide and generally control the lives of the Palestinians under occupation, and even to reach a consensus about representative institutions and personalities. This was given formal affirmation by the Oslo Accords. By contrast, the Palestine Liberation Organization signed the agreement with Israel and, after the establishment of the Palestinian National Authority, returned to the country and began setting up a power structure under the close control of Chairman Arafat, in a fashion appropriate to the pre-

Accord period. It set up a power structure parallel to that which had grown up in the field, and which was frozen by the Oslo Accords; this new structure is undemocratic and non-competitive (on the actual as opposed to the declarative level); everything is centralized and under the watchful eye of social, political, and military mechanisms subject to the direct authority of the chairman. In practice, the system has two levels or, more simply, is really two systems. One of them – that which developed locally – is democratic, with separation of powers and ostensible safeguards for full civic equality and the defense of human and civil rights. The other, imposed by Arafat and his close assistants, is undemocratic, and is run arbitrarily and with maximum centralization; essentially, it is similar to other regimes in the Arab world. The first lives in the shadow of the second, which dominates the political structure and process.

On the theoretical level, it can be argued that the Palestinian regime is a unique example of "partial democracy", where "partial" means not only the incomplete adoption of democratic principles, but also their selective adoption, in which a segment of the political structure – the regime, the entity (state), and the society – is democratic or at least experiencing processes of democratization, while another segment is undemocratic, authoritarian and centralized, and "advances" toward reinforcement of its undemocratic aspects.

2

The Palestinian National Movement: A Historical Overview

Until the establishment of the Palestinian National Authority (PNA), after the signing of the Declaration of Principles and Interim Agreement in 1993, the Palestinians' demand for the establishment of an independent state went through several major stages. Similarly, the Palestine Liberation Organization (PLO) knew many vicissitudes and processes, of which the most important was that of moderation – from dogged adherence to a maximalist position that called for the liquidation of Israel and its replacement by supporting compromise and the establishment of a Palestinian state alongside Israel in the West Bank and Gaza Strip. What follows is a general survey of the stages in the development of the Palestinian national movement from its beginnings through to the establishment of the Palestinian National Authority.

The Palestinians Awaken to a Crushing Defeat

The first steps in the development of the Palestinian national movement were taken in the early twentieth century and were strongly influenced by the Zionist movement and the Jews' aspirations to establish a state. They emerged from the Emir Feisal's abortive attempt to establish a state of "Greater Syria" and the subsequent institution of the British Mandate over Palestine, as provided for by the Sykes–Picot agreement that allocated Syria and Lebanon to France and "Southern Syria" (Jordan and Palestine) to Great Britain. This political separation helped reinforce Palestinian national consciousness at the expense of Pan-Syrianism. During the 1920s and 1930s real attempts were made to establish national institutions and develop organizational structures for the movement. Special efforts were invested in founding Muslim–Christian societies in the larger cities and, later, nationalist societies, which were considered to be "more advanced" forms of organization than the confessional societies. Various bodies were established to represent all or most of the Palestinian population. The first of these was the "Palestinian Arab Executive Committee", in 1920, soon followed by the "Palestinian Higher Committee", headed by Haj Amin al-Husseini. These organizations made a serious contribution toward crystalizing the early ideological lines of the Palestinian national movement and its arguments for the existence of a Palestinian people with a right to a Palestinian homeland.[1]

Violent disturbances against the Jews and the Zionist movement, as well as against the Mandate, broke out in 1929. The first serious steps were taken toward the formation of Palestinian political parties. These parties, with the exception of the "Independence Party" (*Hizb al-Istiqlal*), reflected the clan structure of contemporary Palestinian society: the Husseini family and its allies versus the Nashashibi family and its supporters.[2] During the 1930s, because of events in Europe and the rise of the Nazi power in Germany, there was massive Jewish immigration to mandatory Palestine; the pressures created by this immigration and by the British mandatory government led to the outbreak of the 1936–9 revolt, which included extended strikes and demonstrations. These events were a further step toward the appearance of the Palestinian national movement. But from the Palestinian point of view the results of these events were disappointing, epecially after the massive intervention by Arab leaders from neighboring countries to end the strikes and disturbances. This intervention, which widened in subsequent years, marked the beginning of the "Arabization" of the Palestinian problem, which subsequently had a significant impact on the course of the Palestinian problem and the evolution of political activity among the Palestinians.

The disappointing results of the 1936–9 revolt and later events caused the political strength of the Palestinian national movement to wane; a considerable part of its leadership went into exile. Haj Amin al-Husseini moved to Beirut and then to Baghdad, from where he did his best to frustrate all attempts to establish an alternative leadership within the country. The Zionist movement became stronger economically, politically, and militarily. Immediately after World War II it realized that, given the changes in the international balance of power, it needed to move its focus of activities from London to Washington and win the support of the Soviet Union as well.[3] These events culminated in the adoption of General Assembly Resolution 181, which called for the partition of mandatory Palestine into two states, one Jewish and the other Arab, and set the stage for the establishment of the State of Israel. The Palestinians' natural political development until 1948, similar to that in other Arab countries and of many Third World peoples, was disrupted by the outcome of the war and the establishment of the State of Israel.

On the eve of Israel's establishment, close to two million persons were living in mandatory Palestine – two-thirds Arabs and one-third Jews. A majority of the Arabs (close to 940,000) and almost all the Jews lived in the region that became the State of Israel. As the result of mass expulsions and flight, only 160,000 Palestinians (10% of the total) remained there when the fighting ended. Nearly 780,000 became refugees in the West Bank, the Gaza Strip, and the neighboring Arab countries.[4] In 1952 there were about 1.6 million Palestinians, of whom only 11 percent (179,300) lived in Israel; 18 percent (about 300,000) lived in the Gaza Strip, and 47 percent (about 742,300) in the West Bank. The balance, some 380,000, lived in neighboring countries: 114,000 (7%) in Lebanon, 83,000 (5%) in Syria, 150,000 (9%) in the East Bank, and 3% elsewhere.

The dispersion of the Palestinian population disrupted political and social processes that had been at work in the Palestinian community before the war. Many communities had been completely destroyed; others had been partially demolished, and some residents had left the country or moved elsewhere within Israel; the latter came to be known as "internal refugees".[5] Many families were divided across hostile borders. The incipient industries and social structures in Arab communities were also devastated. Worst of all, the processes that should have led to the formation of a Palestinian political entity were disrupted or halted in their tracks.

One result of the dispersal of the Palestinian population was the concomitant dispersal of the leadership that could have provided the center for the formation of a Palestinian entity, which had only just begun to recover from the events of the 1936–9 revolt. In the absence of an agreed-upon Palestinian leadership, the Arab countries decided to send the prime minister of Syria, Jamil Mardam, to Palestine to attempt to put together a Palestinian delegation to participate in the Arab countries' discussion of the Palestine question in Alexandria in October 1944. Mardam's attempt to constitute a consensus delegation of the Husseinis and the heads of the Independence (*Istiqlal*) Party failed. Instead, he nominated Mussa al-Alami, who was an official of the British Mandate, as the Palestinian representative.[6] Mardam's failure testified to the intensity of the differences among the Palestinians, and the Husseinis' refusal to cooperate in any matter not subject to their full control.

Alami failed as the Palestinian representative because of the opposition to his activities by both the Independence Party and the Husseinis. Trying again, in November 1945 Mardam set up the "second" Arab Higher Committee. This attempt, too, did not yield a joint Palestinian leadership because of the Husseinis' domination of the committee and their exclusion from it of Alami and the representatives of the Independence Party. When the British allowed Jamal al-Husseini to return from exile in Rhodesia in 1946, he established the "third" Arab Higher Committee. But this committee, too, encountered problems in its attempt to represent all Palestinians, especially after the founding of the rival Supreme Arab Front by the Independence Party and representatives of other parties, in cooperation with the National Liberation Front (*Asbat al-Tahrir al-Watani*) and the Arab Workers' Union, two organizations that were controlled by the Arab Communists.

Only after June 1946, as a result of massive intervention by the Arab League, founded in 1945, was the "fourth" Arab Higher Committee, sometimes called the "Higher Arab Executive Committee", established. This body was composed of representatives of the Husseini-controlled Arab Higher Committee and the Higher Arab Front. Jamal al-Husseini was elected deputy chairman; the position of chairman was reserved for Haj Amin al-Husseini, who was still in exile in Cairo and Beirut and barred from the country by the British authorities. In the course of time representatives of other bodies were added, including the National Arab Fund, the Reform Party (*Hizb al-Aslah*), and several other groups. These additions reinforced the Husseinis' hold on the Arab Committee and Haj Amin's leadership.[7]

The British declaration, in February 1947, that they intended to surrender their Mandate over Palestine and refer a decision on the country's future to the United Nations, intensified the preparations by both the Arab League and the Arab Committee to frustrate any attempt to establish a Jewish state in part of mandatory Palestine. In October 1947, the Arab League decided to set up an army, under the command of Ismail Safwat, to take up attacking positions along the borders of Palestine. In December of that year, almost a month after the passage of the UN Partition Resolution, the Arab League resolved to establish the Liberation Army (*Jaish al-Anqad*), which was composed of volunteers, and dispatch it to Palestine to prevent the establishment of the Jewish state. Two months later, the League decided to establish a joint command of the armies of Egypt, Transjordan, Iraq, and Lebanon, headed by an Iraqi officer, Nur ed-Din Mahmud, also to be sent to Palestine. Later, the Emir Abdallah became the supreme commander of the Arab armies that crossed the border into Palestine.

The League's measures were opposed by Haj Amin, who feared for his position and the future of the country in the wake of such massive Arab intervention. Independently of the Arab League's measures, he decided to establish the Army of the Sacred Jihad (*Jaish al-Jihad al-Muqadas*), made up of Palestinian volunteers. There was not even minimal coordination between the Liberation Army and the regular Arab armies, on the one side, and the Jihad force, on the other. Subsequently this made it easier for the Jewish army to occupy broad stretches of the country, including regions allocated to the Palestinian state by the partition plan. Elsewhere in the country, the combined Jordanian–Iraqi forces occupied "Central Palestine", later known as the West Bank, including eastern Jerusalem. The Egyptian army occupied the Gaza Strip. The army established by Haj Amin collapsed and the heads of the Arab Higher Committee fled for their lives.

When he reached Gaza, Ahmad Hilmi Pasha, the treasurer of the Committee, immediately convened a "Palestinian National Council" of Palestinian representatives. This assembly met in Gaza, declared an independent state of Palestine in all the territory of mandatory Palestine, and established an "All-Palestine" government (*Hukumat Umum Falastin*). Hilmi was elected prime minister of this state; Haj Amin was named its president. Abdallah, who was interested in annexing the West Bank to his kingdom, prevented this government from operating in the West Bank and Gaza Strip under his control, thereby denying it all contact with a considerable proportion of its putative citizens (about 47% of all Palestinians). Israel, of course, prevented any contact between this government and the Palestinians who remained in the West Bank and Gaza Strip (about 10% of all Palestinians) controlled by the Jewish army. Palestinian government's activities were thus limited to the Gaza Strip. In 1959, its offices in the Gaza Strip were closed by order of the president of Egypt, Gamal Abdel Nasser.[8]

Local leadership, which was to a great extent linked to the national leadership, although it had come into being earlier and constituted the seedbed from which the national leadership developed, began to emerge in the form of clans, especially in the larger cities. In the mid-1940s, most towns and their hinterlands were dominated by one or two clans, who made extensive use of social, economic, and religious instruments to guarantee their control.[9] The members of these extremely well-to-do families, drawing on their financial resources and family ties in neighboring countries, began leaving the country immediately after the adoption of the UN partition resolution, apprehensive of coming to grief at the hands of both the Jewish army and the Arab volunteers. The departure of so many members of the moneyed class – most of them principals and teachers, physicians, lawyers, and the like – paralyzed public life in the cities. This situation, which created tremendous pressures on the middle and lower classes, who feared that they would be left alone to face the "Zionist enemy" after the British left, facilitated the mass departure and flight of April–June 1948.[10]

From Dispersion to Taking the Initiative

The results of the 1948 war, and especially the dispersion of Palestinians and their subjection to regimes that were generally hostile to the idea of

Palestinian nationalism and the establishment of the Palestinian state, inaugurated a period of almost total paralysis of Palestinian initiatives to highlight their distinctiveness and national affiliation (aside from a few actions taken by the "Government of all Palestine").[11]

The Israeli occupation of the Gaza Strip in 1956 and the atmosphere that accompanied this operation, including the Israeli decision to withdraw from the Strip and the appearance of Gamal Abdel Nasser as a militant pan-Arab leader committed to solving the Palestinian problem, led to a period of pan-Arab and Palestinian awakening about the Palestinian problem and the first appearance of distinctly Palestinian organizations or pan-Arab organizations dominated by Palestinians. In 1957 the "Palestinian National Liberation Movement", known as Fatah, was established, initially in Kuwait, by a number of Palestinian activists who were living or working there, including Yasser Arafat, Khalil al-Wazir, Salah Khalef, Farouk Kadoumi, and others.[12] Fatah presented itself as a Palestinian national movement that focused on the Palestinian issue and its solution, even though it did not turn its back on the pan-Arab dimension. Fatah unequivocally demanded that the Arab world invest more than it had in the past to liberate the occupied land and provide financial and military assistance to the Palestinian people to overcome its difficulties.[13]

Around the same time as the founding of the Fatah, several of the founders of that organization established a Palestinian student organization in Cairo known as the General Union of Palestinian Students. The Union, which included student committees from Cairo, Damascus, Beirut, and Alexandria, declared itself the representative of all Palestinian students and set political objectives in addition to providing assistance to Palestinian students and graduates.[14] Yasser Arafat, who completed his civil engineering studies in Cairo around that time, was elected the first chairman of the Union of Palestinian Students.[15]

Palestinians who had remained in Israeli territory also began demonstrating an interest in participating in activities at the pan-Palestinian level. In 1958 some of them established the Arab Front.[16] On June 6, 1958, meetings were held in Nazareth and Acre to proclaim the establishment of the Front. Two separate meetings were required because the military government prevented people from Nazareth from traveling to Acre. The participants decided to publish a joint manifesto and elect representatives to function as the secretariat of the Arab Front.[17]

The Front employed various methods to promote its guidelines and objectives; taken together, these were meant to constitute an appropriate response to their demands and situation in the field. The Front sponsored regional and country-wide meetings, mainly in cities such as Acre and Nazareth, to discuss the Arabs' demands and ways to achieve them. The most important country-wide conferences, of which there were four, met with a hostile response from the military government, which took various measures to disrupt them, such as forbidding delegates to travel to the site of the conference.

The most important elements in the new body were affiliated with two currents in the Arab street of those years – the Communists and the Nasserite nationalists. This dichotomy was subsequently the main factor in the disintegration of the Front, when the representatives of the nationalist stream quit the group and established al-Ard, against the background of the rift between the president of Egypt, Gamal Abdel Nasser, and president of Iraq, Abdul Karim Kassem, who was close to the Communists.[18]

The nationalist group that remained or seceded from the Arab Popular Front after its dissolution, led by Mansour Qardosh and Habib Qahwaji, announced its intention to continue to function as an Arab group. They proclaimed the establishment of *Osrat al-Ard* (the Family of the Land), which came to be known as the al-Ard movement – a name selected to symbolize the strong bond between the Palestinians in Israel and their land.[19] The Israeli authorities evinced strong hostility to the movement's activity.[20] Alleging that the new organization was Nasserite and intended to incite the Arabs against the state, they issued orders restricting the movement of its activists. At the same time the Communists worked openly against the new movement because they considered that al-Ard's call to the Arabs to boycott Knesset elections was addressed chiefly to potential voters for the Party.[21]

In the wake of al-Ard's request to register as a political party, the authorities acted vigorously to "deal with" the movement once and for all. The Haifa commissioner issued an order banning the organization on the grounds that it "harmed the existence of the state of Israel".[22] Al-Ard appealed to the High Court of Justice, which upheld the commissioner's decision and ruled that al-Ard was an organization "hostile to the state and its existence". Immediately thereafter some of its leaders were arrested; the defense minister announced that in accordance with his authority under the Emergency Defense Regulations he was declaring al-Ard and its commercial arm illegal organizations, an action that led to steps against members and supporters of al-Ard. Later, in 1965, when members of al-Ard set up the Socialist List to contest the elections for the Sixth Knesset, this order was exploited to ban the list. This led to the final breakup of al-Ard.[23]

In addition to the establishment of Fatah, the Union of Palestinian Students, and the frustrated endeavors by Israeli-citizen Palestinians, there were other initiatives, such as the formation of the National Liberation Brigade (*Fouj al-Tahrir al-Watani*). Palestinians in Gaza established the Palestinian Arab National Union (*al-Atihad al-Qawmi al-Arabi al-Falasteni*), active under close Egyptian supervision as the representative of the Palestinians in the Gaza Strip.[24]

The zenith of the institutionalization of the Palestinian national movement and culmination of the process of its consolidation and independence from the patronage of the Arab states was the founding of the Palestine Liberation Organization (*Munadamat al-Tahrir al-Falasteniya*), known as the PLO. This organization was founded as the result of initiatives taken at the Arab summit meeting in January 1964, which authorized the Palestinian representative, Ahmad Shukeiry, to establish a "Palestinian entity" to represent the Palestinian refugees. Some Arab countries, like Egypt and Syria, supported the idea enthusiastically, while others, especially Jordan, were opposed. But Shukeiry persevered, and within a few months, in May 1964, he convened the first session of a Palestinian congress, which resolved to turn into the Palestine National Council (PNC). The congress was attended by representatives of all Palestinians, except those living in Israel, and in practice represented the entire Palestinian people. The congress delegates ratified the original text of the Palestine National Covenant (*al-Mithaq al-Qumi al-Falastini*) and elected Shukeiry as chairman of the conference and of the PLO.[25]

The outcome of the June 1967 war catalyzed the crystalization of the Palestinian national movement and its independence as a deliberate step toward the establishment of a Palestinian national entity. In particular, the war significantly undermined the status of the Arab regimes that had asserted their patronage over the liberation of Palestine, in the eyes of their own citizens and especially of the Palestinians. At the same time, confidence in and support for the *fedayeen* organizations, who supported the armed struggle and an all-out war of liberation against Israel, grew among those Palestinians who had fallen under Israeli occupation as a result of the war.

The major outcomes of this alteration in the prestige of the *fedayeen* organizations were to challenge Shukeiry's one-man control of the PLO and its institutions, and to promote Fatah. These changes had major implications for the future of the Palestinian national movement. The members of the PLO executive committee and the *fedayeen* organizations like Fatah and the Popular Front for the Liberation of Palestine – established in November 1967 by the merger of the Heroes of Return (*Abtaal al-Oudeh*), the Palestinian Liberation Front, the Arab Nationalists (*al-Qumiyun al-Arab*), and Palestinian and Arab personalities – launched a campaign against Ahmad Shukeiry and his leadership. He was forced to submit his resignation as chairman of the PLO and Palestinian representative to the Arab League in December 1967. After his resignation a committee of four, headed by Yihye Hamoudeh, was appointed to serve as the transitional leadership of the PLO.[26]

During the period of Hamoudeh's leadership successful attempts were made to bring the *fedayeen* organizations closer to the PLO. Hamoudeh and the PLO leadership accepted the demands of Fatah and the Popular Front for changes in the composition of the Palestine National Council, which, starting with its fourth session, held in Cairo in July 1968, became a forum in which the seats were divided among the various organizations and their allies in the Palestinian people.[27]

The fifth session of the PNC, held in February 1969, produced significant changes in the PLO's independence of Arab rulers. The meeting approved changes in the Palestine Covenant to emphasize Palestinian distinctiveness "as part of the Arab nation". It also produced a significant personnel change when it chose Yasser Arafat, the spokesmen of Fatah, as chairman of the PLO executive committee – a position he still holds. This was the first step in the long-term process whereby Fatah and Arafat gained control of the policy, ideology, and structure of the PLO, and of the emphasis on the distinctiveness and independence of the PLO and the "Palestinian revolution" as understood by Fatah as the leading organization ever since. The PLO, led by Arafat, picked its way cautiously among the Arab regimes and managed to preserve a relatively independent position, despite the tug-of-war waged by Arab leaders, as a function of circumstances and Palestinian interests as understood by Arafat and his circle.[28]

The PLO: From Maximalism to Compromise

At the fourth session of the PNC, in July 1968, the Palestinian covenant was amended to emphasize Palestinian distinctiveness within the Arab nation. The changes were drafted and approved with the agreement of the *fedayeen* organizations and all those attending the PNC meeting. In general, the Covenant opted for maximalism and extreme language that stressed the fact that Palestine is "the homeland of the Palestinian people and an integral part of the greater Arab homeland"; that the territory of mandatory Palestine "is an indivisible territorial unit"; that the Palestinian people have "the legal right to their homeland"; and that Israel should be eliminated from the region. Judaism, according to the Covenant, "being a religion, is not an independent nationality, nor do the Jews constitute a single nation with an identity of [their] own; they are citizens of the states to which they belong".[29]

The uncompromising maximalism adopted by the PLO in the Covenant represented the consensus among Palestinians and was received sympathetically by the Arab world, then led by Nasser. Most Arabs believed that Israel was an obstacle in the way of possible Arab unity. The extensive literature about the conflict published in the Arab world in those days, official and unofficial, emphasized the main lines of the Covenant and the refusal to recognize Israel because it was, in the words of the Covenant, "a geographical base for world imperialism placed strategically in the midst of the Arab homeland to combat the hopes of the Arab nation for liberation, unity, and progress". The recurrent emphases of the fourth session of the PNC on the general principles of the Covenant, despite the results of the June 1967 war and the occupation of additional Arab territory by Israel and its defeat of the Arab armies, strengthened the PLO and its perception by other Arabs as representing the Palestinian people. It made a significant contribution to the increased prestige of the PLO in the world, and its recognition as the sole legitimate representative of the Palestinian people and as a revolutionary movement waging a just struggle for national liberation.

In parallel to the rising prestige of the PLO, a discussion began in the late 1960s, influenced by the outcome of the 1967 war, in various circles of the PLO and its supporters in the Arab world and elsewhere, about parts of the consensus expressed in the Covenant, and in particular the establishment of a Palestinian state and its attitude toward the Jews. The first glimmers of a change were the result of intentional pressure exerted by the PLO to break out into the wider world and expand its support and recognition as the representative of the Palestinian people by states and societies not necessarily Arab or Middle Eastern. This entailed a need to adopt positions that took account of the presence of Jews in Palestine. It placed the idea of "the establishment of a secular democratic Palestinian state after the liberation of Palestine from the Zionists" on the agenda of the Palestinians and PLO; the idea was first floated in May 1968 and adopted officially by the PNC at its eighth session, held in Cairo in March 1971.[30]

The concept of a secular state represented the first step toward recognition of the Jews and their right to equal treatment with the Palestinians. In particular the idea was based on the assumption that "after the liberation of Palestine from Zionist rule" the entity to be established in Palestine would be "an independent and democratic state whose citizens have equal rights, irrespective of their religious affiliation". In their attempts to market this idea, Fatah leaders emphasized the need to distinguish Judaism as a religion from Zionism "as a racist movement that is not appropriate to human identity"; in the future Palestinian state, civic equality for the Jews would be conditional on their renunciation of Zionism.[31] The Democratic Front for the Liberation of Palestine, headed by Naef Hawatmeh, went further than Fatah and recognized that "a Jewish people had been born" in Palestine that was distinct from the other Jews in the world and it would be necessary to take account of this identity in the future resolution of the conflict.[32] In practice, the Democratic Front came very close to the idea of a binational state in Palestine, but did not dare advance it as its preferred solution; instead, it continued to advocate a democratic state with "a special link to a united Arab socialist state".[33]

While the debate about the secular democratic state was going on, dramatic events were taking place, including the discord between Jordan and the PLO that culminated in Black September, 1971, and the expulsion of the *fedayeen* organizations from their bases in Jordan to the refugee camps in Lebanon. This was a significant development, because it relocated the *fedayeen* forces to areas without a Palestinian majority and removed them from the center of Palestinian population in the Israeli-occupied West Bank.

The animosity toward the Jordanian regime and the recognition within the Palestinian national movement of the difficulty of working a major change in Jordan – whether by overthrowing the regime or by getting the current regime to allow the *fedayeen* to return to their bases in Jordan – supplemented by the intensified political efforts after the October war in 1973, ignited a debate within the PLO about the best way forward. A school emerged that supported agreeing in principle to the establishment of a Palestinian entity in any area of the West Bank or Gaza Strip that Israel might return to Arab control. This school was initially spearheaded by Hawatmeh's Democratic Front; later Fatah adopted the same position, especially after the 1973 Arab summit meeting in Algiers, which recognized the PLO as the "sole representative of the Palestinian people". Fatah supported the idea of setting up a Palestinian entity in the West Bank and Gaza Strip on condition that this did not constitute a renunciation of the historic right to establish a Palestinian state in the entire territory of mandatory Palestine.[34]

In June 1974, the twelfth session of the PNC resolved on the official adoption of the phased plan, according to which "the Liberation Organization will employ all means, and first and foremost armed struggle, to liberate Palestinian territory and to establish the independent combatant national authority for the people over every part of Palestinian territory that is liberated".[35] This plan was the first step that explicitly recognized reality and the need to deal with it. As such it represented the beginning of a PLO retreat from its maximalist position with regard to the geographical scope of the future Palestinian state. For the first time the Palestinians explicitly accepted the establishment of an entity in only part of mandatory Palestine and not necessarily all of it. Although they did not yet speak of an independent Palestinian state alongside Israel, they had nevertheless moved in this direction; the actual reversal took place only after the Lebanon war and the expulsion of PLO forces from that country (1982).

In June 1982, PLO Chairman Arafat expressed support for a plan submitted by Egypt and France to the United Nations Security Council that called on the Palestinians and Israelis to agree to mutual recognition and the start of negotiations, with the participation of the PLO, based on Resolution 242 and a guarantee of the national rights of the Palestinian people. Subsequently the Palestinian news agency WAFA carried a report to the effect that the PLO recognized all United Nations resolutions about the Palestinian issue, including the 1947 partition resolution (Resolution 181).[36] These initial steps were backed by an accord worked out between Jordan and the PLO in February 1985, in which they agreed to field a joint delegation to future negotiations in the framework of an international conference, and that this delegation would negotiate on the basis of United Nations resolutions and the principle of "land for peace".[37] These developments encountered scathing criticism from the Palestinian rejectionists, supported by Syria, but were a significant milestone toward the acceptance of Israel's existence by the PLO mainstream. This sea change, influenced by the expulsion of the PLO from Lebanon after the 1982 war, gained momentum after the outbreak of the *Intifada* on the West Bank and Gaza Strip.

The popular struggle against the Israeli occupation – the *Intifada* – began in December 1987. The *Intifada* confronted the Palestinian national leadership – the PLO – with the immediate need to deal with a new form of struggle and options for resolving it. The *Intifada* forced the Palestinian leadership to focus on the demand for a Palestinian state on the West Bank and Gaza Strip alongside Israel. This entailed major changes in the emphases and major axes of the Palestinian national movement and its leadership and led to concrete steps to cope with these changes. The most significant expression of the PLO's change in its attitude *vis-à-vis* Israel and regional peace was at the nineteenth session of the PNC, held in Algiers in November 1988. This session, proclaimed to be the "*Intifada* session", approved the Palestinian declaration of independence unanimously; even the representatives of the rejectionist front supported the document.

The proclamation of independence included an explicit article but spoke of "UN General Assembly Resolution 181 (1947), which partitioned Palestine into two states, one Arab, one Jewish [and] provides those conditions of international legitimacy that ensure the right of the Palestinian Arab people to sovereignty and national independence."[38] This wording explicitly recognized the partition resolution and indirectly (but clearly) also Israel's right to exist. This orientation was clarified in the political manifesto issued by the PNC, according to which the PLO agreed "to participate in an international conference that would seek to achieve a comprehensive and lasting peace and would be convened on the basis of Security Council resolutions 242 and 338, supplemented by the right of the Palestinian people to self-determination". The manifesto demanded that "Israel withdraw from all Palestinian and Arab lands occupied in 1967, including Jerusalem."[39] This wording, adopted at the urging of the Arafat-led mainstream, represented a significant step toward clarifying the nature of Palestinian expectations from Israel and for peace. Along with Arafat's renunciation of terrorism, this led to a significant modification in the attitude of the United States toward the PLO and the Palestinians, and paved the way for the convening of the international conference in Madrid on October 18, 1991. At that conference the Palestinians formed a joint delegation with Jordan, albeit making plain the sole responsibility of the Palestinian delegates for negotiations about specifically Palestinian matters.

The head of the Palestinian delegation, selected by the PLO leadership in Tunis, was Haider Abd el-Shafi, one of the founders of the PLO in 1964 and a well-known personality in Gaza and among the Palestinians in general. In his opening address to the conference he presented the Palestinian position, reiterating the Palestinians' desire for peace with Israel based on Security Council resolutions and the Palestinians' right to self-determination, to be manifested in a state on the West Bank and Gaza Strip that would be confederated with Jordan.[40]

After the Madrid Conference, and on the basis of the discussions and agreements that preceded and followed it, the talks were continued in multilateral meetings that considered regional issues and in bilateral sessions at which Israel and each of the Arab delegations endeavored to make progress on specific issues. The bilateral talks with the Palestinians were held in Washington and continued intermittently from the Madrid Conference until the Oslo Accords were made known to the media and the negotiators in Washington. Six rounds of talks were held during this period without producing any significant progress. Even at the sixth round, held after the electoral victory of Yitzhak Rabin and the change of government in Israel, no change was evident in the Israeli position or willingness to move toward the Palestinians.[41]

The Oslo Accords and the Establishment of the Palestinian National Authority

The stalemate in the Washington talks, produced by the inflexibility of the two teams – the Israelis led by Elyakim Rubinstein and the Palestinians by Dr. Abd el-Shafi – stimulated both sides to look for other channels, secret or public, in order to arrive at concrete agreements. This became more urgent after Rabin took office, because during the election campaign he had promised to conclude an accord with the Palestinians within six to nine months.

On August 19, 1993, in Oslo, official representatives of Israel and the PLO initialed an agreement whose crux was the announcement of principles for achieving peace between Israel and the Palestinians. The agreement became a formal international commitment after the exchange of letters of mutual recognition on September 9 and the signing of the Declaration of Principles on September 13, on the White House lawn, with guarantees supplied by the United States and Russia. The Washington ceremony marked the end of six months of negotiations that had begun as talks between Israeli academics and PLO representatives aimed at investigating options for a peace agreement in light of the deadlocked negotiations in Washington. On the Israeli side the two chief negotiators were Dr. Ron Pundak of Tel Aviv University and Dr. Yair Hirschfeld of the University of Haifa, both of them close to the then deputy foreign minister, Yossi Beilin, and acting in partial coordination with him.[42] Beilin kept Foreign Minister Shimon Peres briefed on the contacts and of the flexibility displayed by the PLO representatives with regard to a future peace agreement with Israel, as opposed to the rigid positions presented by the Palestinian delegation in Washington. This flexibility signaled to Peres, and later to Prime Minister Rabin, that Arafat was interested in opening a secret direct channel of talks. They sent the director-general of the Foreign Ministry, Uri Savir, to meet with PLO representatives Ahmad Qreia (Abu Ala), Hassan Asfour, and Maher al-Kurd; later they added Yoel Singer, the legal advisor of the Foreign Ministry, to the team. These talks led to the Israeli recognition of the PLO and the signing of the agreement with it.[43]

The mutual recognition and Declaration of Principles opened the way to negotiations between Israel and the PLO, which in turn produced an interim agreement, signed in Cairo in May 1994, which established the Palestinian National Authority in the Gaza Strip and Jericho as the first step toward a comprehensive peace agreement based on United Nations Security Council Resolutions 242 and 383. The Palestinian Authority took shape in May–June 1994 and assumed concrete form with the arrival in Gaza of Arafat and his entourage from Tunis on July 1, 1994.

From the Israeli perspective the agreement with the PLO, including its recognition as the representative of the Palestinian people, was a significant breakthrough that ignited protests by the right-wing and religious opposition. For the government, the agreement was a practical manifestation of Rabin's campaign promise to make peace with the Palestinians, against the background of the *Intifada* on the West Bank and Gaza Strip and the appearance of the first signs of fatigue with the conflict among broad sectors of the Israeli public. The Israelis and their government had also taken note of the increased international insistence, especially by the United States, on the need for a solution in the Middle East, in the light of the radically new world balance of power after the collapse of the Soviet Union. One manifestation of this was the massive support offered by governments in Europe, North America, and elsewhere for a speedy resolution of the conflict between Israel and the Palestinians.

From the PLO's perspective, the agreement came at a very difficult junc-
ture. The Palestinians in the West Bank and Gaza Strip had begun to show
signs of being weary with the *Intifada*. The talks in Washington were not
producing any significant achievement in the field and to some extent
excluded the PLO leadership from the focus of the decision-making
process. The Communist bloc, which had consistently supported the
Palestinian position against Israel, had collapsed; and the Arab world was
in a state of turmoil after the Gulf War. Furthermore, the PLO and the
Palestinians in the territory had forfeited the support of the Gulf states
because of Arafat's support for Iraq during the Gulf War; the severe financial crisis that ensued forced the PLO to shut many of its missions around
the world. In the West Bank and Gaza Strip, a strong local leadership
began to emerge and showed an inclination to assert its independence of
the PLO leadership in the diaspora. Israeli settlement activity in the West
Bank and Gaza Strip, and collective punishment of the Palestinian civilian
population, continued unabated. The agreement with Israel was in fact a
necessary measure to rescue the PLO leadership from the abrupt termination of its historic role; it was an expression of its distress and desire to pay
almost any price to survive.

The political breakthrough was clearly the result of both external and
internal conditions related to the conflict. On the other hand, whereas
Israel still had other options, such as concluding an agreement with local
Palestinian leaders or with Syria about the Golan Heights or with Jordan
about the West Bank, the PLO was facing financial and organizational
collapse and really had no choice. This was obvious from the way in which
the negotiations were conducted. All the evidence available from the
memoirs and other books written to date about the Oslo negotiations indicate that the talks were directed by the Israelis, who prepared the draft
agreements, stipulated conditions, and decided on the core elements of the
Declaration of Principles, including the relegation of crucial questions such
as the future of Jerusalem, the future of the settlements, the future of the
refugees, borders, security arrangements, free passage, and many other
issues, to a later stage. In practice Israel obtained a cease-fire on the part
of the Palestinians without itself having to make any commitment about
the substance of the future agreement, while the Palestinians agreed to
almost all the Israeli conditions.[44]

The Palestinians who returned with Arafat from exile had made no
preparations for the move to the West Bank and Gaza Strip. The process
of setting up the Authority (described in general terms in the Interim
Agreement between Israel and PLO) was implemented in a disorganized
fashion and involved chiefly *ad hoc* decisions by Arafat, who did not
consult the professional echelons. The administrative arrangements that
had evolved in the PLO in the period before the establishment of the

Authority were reproduced partially and hastily in the West Bank and Gaza Strip. Mechanisms set up by the Israelis before and after the establishment of the Authority were inherited by it involuntarily. Still others were instituted on the spur of the moment, without sufficient forethought. The result of all this was chaos, duplication, and an utter lack of clarity as to spheres of responsibility and administration. This created a gap between the formal agreements and those actually implemented with regard to the type of regime practiced in the Authority. In sum, it led to many deviations from the principles of sound government. And it is this focus that is the main subject of the chapters that follow.

3

Democracy and Centralism in the Palestinian National Movement, 1967–1993

The story of the encounter between the Palestinians in general and their national movement (the PLO) in particular, on the one hand, and western democracy, on the other, is depicted in the scholarly literature, written chiefly by Palestinians themselves, as one of the most successful in the Third World and especially in the Arab world. The logic behind this view is that the unique Palestinian experience, reflected in the delayed establishment of a nation-state as a force that prevented the development of democracy in the Arab world, as well as the disaster that struck the Palestinians and dispersed them, generated a need for dialogue and consensus in pursuit of the liberation of the homeland and establishment of an independent state.[1] According to the literature, Palestinian democracy embodies a political pluralism expressed in the existence of rival parties and movements, the frequency of elections for various Palestinian bodies, an active civil society manifested in the existence and activity of voluntary organizations involved in a broad spectrum of areas, the Palestinians' enjoyment of basic freedoms (despite the occupation and life in foreign countries in the diaspora), and the ramified legal system in the West Bank and Gaza Strip (which dates back to the British Mandate and Egyptian control of Gaza, and Jordanian control of the West Bank).[2]

This picture of Palestinian democracy, which was disseminated chiefly during the period that preceded the establishment of the Palestinian National Authority (PNA), was nourished in part by a sympathetic and uncritical examination of the Palestinian experience with democracy. However, a close scrutiny of that Palestinian experience discloses a more complex and varied picture. In practice the democratic experience of the Palestinian national movement, a movement which began to recover from the trauma of 1948 and Palestinian expulsion only in the 1960s, is marked by a strong duality. In the institutions of the PLO, which began to function in the mid-1960s and received new stimulus after Yasser Arafat was elected chairman of the PLO Executive Committee in 1969, power gradually came to be concentrated in his hands. Arafat progressively took advantage of the difficulties associated with running a national liberation campaign to tighten his control of the PLO as a whole, including bodies and organiz-ations viewed as posing a threat to his dominant position within the organization. The first part of this chapter will be devoted to examining this phenomenon.

Since 1967, however, the Palestinian struggle has been concentrated in the attempt to establish an independent state in the West Bank and Gaza Strip under Israeli occupation (the West Bank, Gaza Strip, and eastern Jerusalem), and the inhabitants of these regions have become the core of the Palestinian national movement. Despite the harsh circumstances dictated by the occupation authorities, the institutions that evolved attest to a high level of political awareness and a desire for political and social pluralism. This will be the focus of the second part of the chapter.

Arafat's Control of PLO Institutions, 1968–1993

Since the 1960s, Yasser Arafat has dominated the leadership of the Fatah movement and of the PLO and its institutions. This control encompasses the political, financial, public relations, and organizational domains. During the last 40 years Arafat has been the only figure with the power to unite, make decisions, and lead – to the point that it can be said that the evolution of the Palestinian problem was in fact an expression of Arafat's mode of decision-making[3] and his life a direct result of the decisions he has taken in the name of his people. Arafat's Achilles' heel is also the principal source of his strength – his belief that he alone has the capacity to bring the aspirations of the Palestinian people to fruition.[4]

Over the decades Arafat has employed many means to influence various aspects of the Palestinian problem: in addition to his leadership qualities, he has appointed individuals loyal to himself to positions of power, in this way getting PLO institutions to take the decisions he favored.

Little has been written about the stages by which Arafat gained control of PLO institutions or about democracy in these institutions. The most reli-able testimony about Arafat's internal policy comes from persons who have worked with him or joined PLO institutions, only to quit at a later stage. Below I trace the stages and means by which Arafat extended his control over PLO institutions.

Control of the Armed Forces

Yasser Arafat was elected chairman of the PLO Executive Committee at the fifth session of the Palestine National Council (Cairo, February 1–4, 1969). A major change introduced then, and considered to be Arafat's personal victory,[5] was that, for the first time, the chairman of the Executive Committee was also named supreme commander of the forces of the revolution; in other words, Arafat himself ran the military wing of the PLO. It was also decided that the PLO's armed struggle would be overseen by representatives of the various Palestinian armed factions. Ever since, Arafat has served both as chairman of the PLO Executive Committee and as supreme commander of the forces of the revolution.

The Quota System

Arafat exploited the quota system of representation in PLO institutions to guarantee passage of the decisions he favored and the selection of his confidants to important posts. The Fatah movement has always had the largest quota, supplemented by so-called independents, who have generally been supporters of Fatah or have been supported by it, as well as the representatives of women's organizations, students, trade unions, professional associations, the representatives of exiles, and representation of the Occupied West Bank and Gaza Strip, and so on. In this way Arafat assures himself a majority that allows him to run PLO institutions, while staying within the formal ground rules of the organization.

One of the fundamental principles of PLO political activity is that there are "independents" associated with every faction, but most of them are identified with Fatah.[6] The quota system according to which positions and funds are distributed is the basis for the organizational structure of the PLO. This system produces frequent disagreements and quarrels.[7]

The quota system means that the true center of power is in another place – this system was instituted in order to guarantee the continued hegemony of the armed-struggle organizations within the PLO, as it existed in 1969. The system guaranteed these organizations most of the seats in the Palestine National Council and the central committee and representation on the Executive Committee. Accordingly, decision-making came to be controlled by the political groups; decisions were always made outside the legislative and executive organs of the PLO. Because these organs had no real power a vacuum was created at the top of the power structure – a vacuum that came to be filled by one man, a single individual who replaced the institution.[8]

During the period since the 1960s the Fatah movement has been able, at various levels, to restrict the struggle for "democratic reform" to a contest for the distribution of quotas; it describes this as action on behalf of "national unity" and as a reflection of the need to adopt policies that command a consensus. There is no doubt that, viewed objectively, the quota system paved the way for a gradual transfer of decision-making away from the national institutions (the Palestine National Council, the Central Committee, the Executive Committee, and its various commissions and affiliated organizations), because membership in these institutions came to be subject to the quota system, that is, to a particular form of arbitrary appointment. The quota system perpetuated the guardianship asserted by the various factions, and their leaders, over the Palestinian people and their right to elect representatives and hold them accountable. This system also encouraged the tendency to prefer the narrow advantages of these organ-izations over the broad national interest.[9]

Control of the Palestine National Council

Arafat gained control of the PNC by continually appointing new members to it: whereas in 1968 it had 100 members, today there are more than 500, from all over the world. This expansion has taken place gradually,[10] under the cover of guaranteeing participation by various sectors, such as trade unions and professional associations, students, women, authors, journal-ists, exiles, and residents of the Occupied West Bank and Gaza Strip. New members have been added at every session of the PNC. The eighth session of the PNC (Cairo, February 28–March 5, 1971) authorized the Executive Committee and chairman of the PNC to choose new delegates.[11] A similar resolution was passed by the 15th session (Damascus, April 11–19, 1981), which decided to add 30 to 40 members to the PNC, to be selected at a joint session of its presidium and the PLO Executive Committee.[12] Because Arafat controls both of these bodies, in practice he determined the identi-ties of the new members.

A number of leading figures objected to these arbitrary appointments. Bahjat Abu Ghariba resigned from the PLO Executive Committee at the ninth session of the PNC (Cairo, July 7–13, 1971) in protest. At the eleventh session (Cairo, January 6–12, 1973), it was decided that 50 percent of the new members of the PNC would be drawn from the popular organ-izations.[13] But these organizations are funded by Arafat himself and controlled by his close supporters.[14]

The system described above allowed the PLO leadership to make sure that "the PNC would be an empty forum in which strange and mysterious capers would take place, but not a forum that would allow the various social agents to put forward their demands and views, as an opposition to the executive branch. In practice, the role of the PNC is to provide formal legit-imacy without participating in any fashion whatsoever in the determination of Palestinian policy or monitoring the activity of the executive branch. The members of the PNC serve to rubber-stamp policies determined by others."[15]

Arafat's seizure of control of the PNC was assisted by the fact that the PNC was never elected and is in practice merely the constituent assembly of the future Palestinian entity. The leaderships of the various factions and the Executive Committee performed many of the functions intended for the PNC. What is more, the PNC was never meant to serve as a legislature and to draft laws. Its purpose was to set up a Palestinian national entity – and it has failed in this task.[16]

Control of the PLO Central Committee

Arafat reaped the benefits of the policy of setting up new leadership organs and splitting off new institutions from existing ones. Examples include the establishment of the PLO Central Committee in 1970 and of its Central Council in 1973. At the seventh session of the PNC (Cairo, May 30–June 4, 1970), the PLO Central Committee was established to assist the Executive Committee. In addition to the fact that the chairman of the Executive Committee – namely, Yasser Arafat – was made the head of the Central Committee, all its other members were his confidants. According to the resolution, they were the members of the Executive Committee, the speaker of the PNC, the commander of the Palestine Liberation Army, and three independent representatives.[17]

After the establishment of the Central Committee, the Executive Committee was stripped of some of its powers; in practice it was left with the task of implementing the decisions of the Central Committee. Because of protests against this constriction of the authority of the Executive Committee and against Arafat's control of management of affairs, the PNC decided, at its ninth session (Cairo, July 7–13, 1971), to abolish the Central Committee and restore the powers of the Executive Committee.[18]

This policy, which continues to the present, was reaffirmed in 1973, when the PNC, at its eleventh session (January 6–12, 1973), decided to set up the Central Council of the PLO as a liaison between the Executive Committee and the PNC.[19] Thanks to the independent representatives, representatives of popular organizations, the quota system, and the continual expansion in the size of the Central Council – from 32 members in 1973 to more than 100 today – Arafat gained control of it as well.[20] The dates and agendas of meetings of the Central Council are set by the Executive Committee,[21] that is, by Arafat.

Arafat guarantees that the various departments of the PLO do his bidding by appointing Fatah members and leaders, or "independents" close to him, to head them. This is the case with the following departments:

the secretariat, the political department, the military department (which Arafat appointed himself to head after his selection as head of the Executive Committee in 1968), the National Fund, the Departments for Occupied Homeland Affairs, the Department for Arab-National Relations, the Department for Refugee Affairs, the Department for Education and Higher Education, the Information and Culture Department, the Popular Organizations Department, the Department for Social Affairs, and the Department for Administration.[22]

Control of Financial Agencies (the National Fund)

Arafat controlled and still controls the PLO treasury, and that of Fatah as well. According to the rules of the Palestine National Fund, Arafat, by virtue of his position as chairman of the Executive Committee, must approve the transfer of large sums to various parties, which permits him to allocate funds and control supported groups. Arafat authorizes the monthly allocations to organizations and factions, the families of martyrs, the wounded and orphans, the political bureaus and propaganda offices, schools, hospitals, clinics, and cultural activities.[23]

Arafat exploits the vast sums contributed to the PLO in ways that his opponents consider to be illegitimate and unfair – for example, fostering splits in rival organizations by supporting oppositionist elements in them, and gaining control of newspapers, institutions, and miscellaneous forums. During the months that preceded the Oslo Accords in 1993 it was perceived that Palestinian leadership was concerned chiefly with money, and that excessive use was being made of it to influence internal Palestinian political activity.[24]

According to the bylaws of the PLO, the Palestinian National Fund is responsible for all its financial affairs and operations pursuant to the instructions of the Executive Committee. The activities of the Fund are overseen by a board of directors appointed by the Executive Committee; thus Arafat controls the activities of the National Fund through the Executive Committee.[25]

In 1969, Arafat decided to establish "Sammed" as an institution for economic production. Over the years this became a colossus overseeing dozens of productive enterprises and thousands of workers in Arab countries. Today its budget is enormous; Arafat is the source of its authority.[26] Even if Arafat himself leads an austere lifestyle, he does not repudiate the lavish habits of his aides. During recent decades Arafat has passed over in silence incidents of financial corruption involving his aides and even given them more money to fund their prodigality.[27]

Control via the Media

Arafat controls the electronic and print media. By financial means he has managed to extend his influence to many employees of Arab and foreign outlets. In many cases Arafat has placed journalists loyal to him with Arab periodicals in the Gulf states, Jordan, Egypt, and elsewhere. Radio Monte Carlo, which broadcasts from France, is very close to Arafat, follows his policy, and is subsidized by him; he also pays the salaries of some of its correspondents.[28] To this should be added the Voice of Palestine radio station, which broadcasts from Baghdad. The media in the Occupied West Bank and Gaza Strip generally display allegiance to Arafat; some receive direct financial support from him. With the exception of *al-Nahar*, which was pro-Jordanian before financial difficulties forced its closure, all of the following newspapers are financially and politically (by the selection of the editors) dependent directly on Arafat: *al-Oudeh, al-Bayader a-Siyasi, al-Adabi, al-Fajr, al-Fajr in English, al-Sha'ab*, and *al-Kateb*. The allegiance of *al-Quds* changed in accordance with the inclinations of its private owners, but Arafat managed to influence it and its coverage too, until it became the paper most supportive of Arafat and his policies.[29]

In the Occupied West Bank and Gaza Strip, Arafat paid special attention to propaganda and the widespread distribution of his picture. Indeed at a special gathering during the *Intifada* his supporters devoted most of the discussion to the waving of his pictures at demonstrations and not to consolidating the course of the *Intifada*.[30]

In 1972, three years after his election as chairman of the PLO, Arafat acted to take control of the media affiliated with all the Palestinian organizations by setting up the United Media Apparatus of the PLO. After Arafat decided to appoint Ahmad Abd el-Rahman, who was very close to him, as editor-in-chief of the official newspaper, *Falastin a-Thawra*, in place of Hana Meqbel, representatives of the other factions resigned from the editorial committee of that periodical. This turned it, to some extent, into the private domain of Fatah.[31]

The PLO Research Center was considered to be a success story, but following many squabbles between Arafat and the director of the center and several of its fellows, its cultural, intellectual, and information roles were curtailed. Dr. Anis Sayegh, the director of the center in the 1970s, relates that Arafat was in the habit of meddling in its activities, interfering in the appointment or dismissal of fellows in its journal, *Palestine Studies*, and even controlling the wording of its correspondence. Sayegh believes that Arafat wanted the center to be subordinate to his opinions and views, and to him personally.[32]

Sayegh also writes about attempts by Arafat to gain control of the *Palestinian Encyclopedia* published by *el-Alisqo* – the Arab Organization for Education, Culture, and Science – which is affiliated with the Arab League. He relates in great detail how Arafat intervened in various entries written for the encyclopedia; for example, his opposition to the entry about Iz ed-din al-Qassim, on the argument that he was Syrian and not Palestinian.[33]

Exclusivity in Decision-Making (the Executive Committee)

By the force of his personality, determination and strength, Arafat has been able to make decisions and run the affairs of the PLO on his own, to the point where he has been accused of lack of respect for the opinions of the Palestinian public, the organization, and even his closest colleagues, and failing to include them, if only for appearances' sake, in the responsibility for decision-making. Examples of this lack of respect can be seen in his reference to the members of the Palestinian delegation to the Madrid Conference as "political neophytes",[34] as well as his dismissal of the complaints of Feisal Husseini, Hanan Ashrawi, and Haidar Abd el-Shafi, the delegates to the Washington talks, about his treatment of them.[35]

Confirmation of Arafat's attitude can be seen in remarks by the head of the Palestinian delegation to the negotiations, Haidar Abd el-Shafi, who, referring to the problems faced by the delegation in Madrid, noted Arafat's stubborn insistence on making all decisions himself.[36] He adds that Arafat selected the members of the Palestinian negotiating team at the Madrid Conference without consulting him.[37]

The secret talks in Oslo were conducted far from the knowledge of the PLO leadership, the Executive Committee, and the negotiating team in Washington. After the Accord was announced, Arafat did not convene the PNC or the Central Council to ratify it. He called a session of the Executive Committee only in the wake of repeated pressure and demands, ten days after the meeting of the Fatah leadership, as if the Accord directly concerned Fatah and not the PLO.[38] Even those closest to Arafat, like Sakher Habash, a member of the Central Committee of Fatah, have spoken about the dangers of this one-man show. To prove his point, Habash noted that the Oslo Accords and its appendices were published in the Israeli media while members of the PLO Executive Committee and the Fatah Central Committee were the last to know about it.[39]

In 1994, Khaled al-Hassan, a member of the Central Committee of Fatah and an Arafat confidant for decades, wrote a book entitled *Lest the Leadership Become a Dictatorship*. Based on his experience, el-Hassan pointed out the problems in the leadership of the organization, which tended toward dictatorship and making decisions without consultations. Al-Hassan, who died in 1995, sought to make a final plea for a collective leadership in the Palestinian arena rather than a one-man dictatorship.[40]

Those in the know cite, as an example of Arafat's exclusive control of decision-making, his refusal to appoint himself a deputy in any of the organizations he heads: neither the chairman of the Executive Committee, nor the supreme commander of the forces of the revolution, nor the president of the state of Palestine, nor the head of the Palestinian National Authority, nor the chairman of the Central Committee of Fatah has a deputy. Arafat refused to name a deputy even after the need for this was made tangible in 1992 when his plane crashed in the Libyan desert and he was missing for a number of hours.[41]

Some Palestinian political thinkers believe that the hints that Arafat has scattered on a number of occasions about Abu Ala (Ahmad Qreia) or Abu Mazen (Mahmud Abbas) as potential successors were merely an attempt to embroil the two with each other and leave them in a weakened position and unable to challenge him.[42] In 1983, when Abu Musa and Abu Salah led a faction that seceded from Fatah, one of their declared justifications was protest against Arafat's one-man rule. In a statement they published they said: "Arafat has eliminated the role of the Central Committee and Revolutionary Council of the Fatah movement, while instituting one-man rule, in which, along with a handful of aides, he takes perilous and fateful decisions that harm the security of our cause and threaten the struggle of our people." One of the demands made by this group was that the movement be the commanding organization rather than the organization of the commander. Another example is Arafat's renunciation of terrorism on November 7, 1985. This statement was made of his own initiative and was not discussed by the Executive Committee until some two weeks after it had been made, even though by this date Arafat had become the decisive voice in the PLO and would evidently not have faced any significant opposition in the Executive Committee.[43]

Creating Divisions in Institutions and Factions

In pursuit of his ambition to consolidate his position within the PLO, Arafat benefited from the fissures, divisions, and schisms that frequently occurred in the Palestinian factions. Arafat also used this method to control the armed forces, for example by dispersing the thousands of fighters in different Arab countries in order to prevent them from taking any part in opposition to him.[44] Indeed Arafat is reported to have said: "I never put all my eggs in one basket."[45]

The schisms also contributed to the continued weakness of the Palestinian factions. The new groups asked Arafat for financial assistance, which helped him guarantee their loyalty to him. Some leaders believe that Arafat himself took a hand in fomenting these splits and encouraged senior members of some factions – such as the Popular Front, the Democratic

Front, the Arab Liberation Front, the Popular Struggle Front, the Islamic Jihad, and the Communist Party – to secede from their parent organizations and even gave them the necessary funding. Something similar has occurred recently with Hamas in the Gaza Strip.[46]

The Establishment of Alternative Institutions

Political leaders who worked alongside Arafat note a number of methods he employed in order to take control of Palestinian institutions, such as stripping them of their content and setting up alternative institutions. Arafat's intervention in their activities include: the appointment of his intimates to positions of power; the continual increase in the number of members of the organizations; the failure to convene to discuss fateful issues; the lavish distribution of funds to close associates; the dispersal of the armed forces in various Arab countries; and so on.

Here I shall focus on three key institutions in the military, financial, and intellectual domains: the Palestine Liberation Army, the Palestinian National Fund, and the PLO Research Center. With regard to the first of these Arafat, while scattering PLO fighters in camps in various Arab countries, maintained regular and irregular forces that competed within the PLO. These different forces made strenuous efforts to obtain Arafat's support.[47] The different armed forces were one of the reasons for the split that took place in Fatah in 1983; the statement published by the dissidents referred to the establishment of these groups as "a military and organizational coup" and added that their objective was to exclude from the military arm of Fatah all those capable of taking part in the struggle against the Americans.[48]

As for the money that should have been transferred to the Palestinian National Fund from the Arab world, a large percentage of it was transferred to Arafat's private accounts and other channels. Arafat sought to create confusion between PLO funds and those of Fatah, for whose treasury he is directly responsible. To this end he obtained control through an alternative fund, as became clear in 1993, when there were rumors of a PLO bankruptcy, while the Fatah treasury was still able to fund activities on a broad scale.[49]

In addition to Arafat's meddling in the activities of the Research Center, he also acted to weaken it by establishing an alternative institution – the Planning Center affiliated with the PLO. The competition between the two and struggle over spheres of cultural and intellectual responsibility would eventually weaken the activity of the two centers.[50]

Pluralism, Civil Society, and the Construction of Institutions among the Palestinians in the West Bank and Gaza Strip, 1967–1993

During the Israeli occupation of the West Bank and Gaza Strip, many Palestinian institutions were active in diverse fields, including politics, journalism, and community affairs. Despite the contradiction between the occupation on the one hand and the activity and influence of these institutions on the other, many of the institutions, whether they pre-dated the occupation or were established under it, continued their activity among the Palestinian population. Most of these institutions encountered difficulties. Under the occupation, Palestinian institutions had unique characteristics: while most dealt in activity that had a political emphasis; their historical and practical ties with the Palestinian national movement, including its parties and organizations, continued. As a result, professional and political coordination and cooperation emerged between the national institutions in the West Bank and Gaza Strip and the popular federations associated with the PLO. Some of the institutions – those founded before 1967 – were subject to judicial, financial, and administrative oversight by both the Israeli Civil Administration and the Jordanian government, while those established after 1967 were monitored by the Israeli Civil Administration only.[51]

The politicized nature of the Palestinian institutions in the Occupied West Bank and Gaza Strip created a duality: on the one hand, they sought to demonstrate their allegiance to the PLO, because of their need to give vent to their nationalism and to guarantee the continuation of the moral and economic support it provided them. On the other hand, they were subject to military regulation and endeavored to toe the fine line between their original objectives and Israeli military decrees. In this situation, philanthropic and nonprofit associations, the heads of the professional associations, newspaper editors and mayors, were subject to restrictions imposed by Israel, ranging from quarantine and curfew to deportation and arrest.[52] Some commentators believe that the intervention of the national factions prevented these institutions from serving their intended function; because the Palestinian institutions in the Occupied West Bank and Gaza Strip function as extensions of the various factions and conceal political goals behind their overt objectives, their original mission is de-emphasized.[53]

In the early 1960s, before the Israeli occupation, many Palestinian associations were formed in the West Bank and Gaza Strip, each with a number of branches. Among these were the General Federation of Palestine Workers, the General Federation of Students in Palestine, the General Federation of Palestinian Women, the Federation of Authors and Journalists, and associations of engineers, physicians, and other professionals. After 1967 these organizations relocated to Cairo, Beirut, and elsewhere. They did not return to operate openly in the Occupied West Bank and Gaza Strip. Because these institutions were established before the occupation and because they are no longer active in the West Bank and Gaza Strip, they will not be discussed here. Below I discuss the chief manifestations of pluralism, civic institutions, and the construction of institutions in general, under the Israeli occupation of the West Bank and Gaza Strip.

The Press

In the first years of the occupation, the Israeli authorities permitted a certain leeway in the publication of Palestinian newspapers and periodicals. The initial issue of *al-Quds*, the first newspaper published, appeared on November 8, 1968; it remains the paper with the largest circulation in the West Bank and Gaza Strip. Later, in 1972, *al-Sha'ab* and *al-Fajr* made their debuts. These three remain the leading periodicals in the West Bank and Gaza Strip. Many dailies and weeklies appeared during the 1970s and 1980s. Some were closed by internal decisions or at the order of the Israeli military authorities; others continue to be published. Table 3.1 provides some basic information about Palestinian journalism in the Occupied West Bank and Gaza Strip.

Initially opinions were divided as to why the Israelis allowed a modicum of press freedom. Some nationalist elements believed that the occupation authorities sought to keep political activity centered in the media, to facilitate control and to pave the way for the appearance of disagreements in print, thereby creating a favorable climate for a non-nationalist press loyal to the occupying power.[54]

Others believed that in the early 1970s the papers that circulated in the Occupied West Bank and Gaza Strip fell into three categories. The first was represented by *al-Quds*, an independent and profitable publication that at the time reflected the Jordanian viewpoint. The second category was that of publications subservient to the Israeli authorities and boycotted by the Palestinians, such as *al-Anba'*, *al-Yawm*, and *al-Mirsad*. The third category was represented by the Arab papers published in Israel proper, most of them on behalf of the Israeli Communist Party, including *al-Ittihad*, *al-Jedad*, and *al-Ghad*. In this situation the Palestinians realized the importance of taking advantage of the "freedom" allowed them by the Israeli authorities, despite the obstacles and censorship that impeded the newspapers and their editors.[55]

Most of the Palestinian newspapers and periodicals were affiliated with political parties or factions; for example, *al-Fajr* and *al-Sha'ab* tended to be pro-Fatah. In 1978, *al-Taly'a* began publication in East Jerusalem and served as the mouthpiece of the Communist Party. The Israeli authorities prevented its distribution in the other Palestinian urban centers. *Al-Mithaq* was founded in 1980 and *al-'Ahad* in 1981; the Israeli authorities shut down both of them, alleging that they expressed the opinions of the Popular Front for the Liberation of Palestine (PFLP). A similar pretext was used to shut down *Al-Shara'a*, founded in 1978 and closed in 1983. The same fate was met by *Al-Darb*, published in 1985 but closed for allegedly representing the views of the Democratic Front for the Liberation of Palestine (DFLP). The biweekly *al-Awdeh* (1982) and the daily *Al-Jadid*, published in 1979, were close to Fatah. *Al-Quds*, by contrast, originally pro-Jordanian, slowly moved toward the PLO mainstream. This spurred the founding of *al-Nahar* in 1983, which faithfully reflected the Jordanian line until its closure in 1997.[56]

Table 3.1   Newspapers published in the West Bank after 1967

Name	Editor-in-Chief	First Publication	Description and Frequency
al-Quds	Mahmud Abu al-Zuluf	Nov. 8, 1968	political daily
al-Fajr	Yusuf Nasri Nasser	April 7, 1972	political weekly
al-Fajr (English)	Paul Ajlouni	Unknown	political weekly
al-Sha'ab	Ali al-Khatib	July 23, 1972	political daily
Sawt al-Jamahir	Muhammad Abu Shalabya	1973	political weekly
Al-Turath wa-al Mojtama	Salim Tamari	April 1974	folklore periodical
al-Bayader	Jack Khazmo	March 1976	literary monthly
al-Bashir	Ibrahim Handal	Dec. 19, 1977	political weekly
al-Taly'a	Bashir al-Baragouti	Feb. 27, 1978	political weekly
al-Shira'a	Marwan al-'Asli	May 1, 1978	political weekly
al-Kateb	Assad al-Assad	November 1979	intellectual monthly
Umm al-Qura	Muhammad Nasser and Ma Mahmoud al-Garem	1980	political weekly
al-Mithaq	Mahmoud Ali al-Khatib	March 15, 1980	political weekly
al-Biyader a-Siyasi	Jack Khazmo	April 1, 1981	political biweekly
al-'Ahad	Ghassan Ali al-Khatib	Dec. 9, 1981	political biweekly
al-Wahda	Fuad Sa'ad	Feb. 20, 1982	political weekly
al-Marah	Yunis Hantoli	June 1982	political biweekly
al-Awdeh	Ibrahim Qara'in	October 1982	political biweekly

Despite the role played by the Palestinian partisan press in mobilizing public opinion, it failed in two spheres: first, it concentrated on the traditional factional lines more than it dealt with the needs of its readership, so that public support dwindled. Second, in the wake of the closures of papers by the Israeli authorities, the Palestinian factions frequently attempted to obtain new permits or to exploit the loophole in Israeli law that permits the publication of "one-time editions".[57] The Palestinian press under the occupation was not limited to newspapers and political periodicals. There were also journals dealing with culture, literature, society, women, economics, and religion, including *al-Fajr al-Adabi, al-Biyader al-Adabi, al-Hasad, al-Musrah, al-Burum, al-Maaref, Hoda al-Islam, al-auma'a, al-Muntada, al-Kitab, al-Turath we-al-Mojtama*, and others.[58]

The press in the West Bank was much more developed than that in the Gaza Strip. First, after the annexation of East Jerusalem the Palestinians took advantage of Israeli law and published most of these periodicals there. Second, the publication of newspapers in the Gaza Strip limped along for several reasons: Israeli censorship, their limited economic potential, the paucity of printing facilities, and competition with newspapers from Egypt. These limitations delayed the appearance of local newspapers in the Gaza Strip until 1975, when *al-Mawqef* began publication, followed by the weekly *al-Shuwruq* in 1978. A year later, in 1979, *Al-Asbua' al-Jadid* made its debut. All of these have ceased publication.[59]

The phenomenon of clandestine journalism in the Occupied West Bank and Gaza Strip during the 1970s merits attention. This refers to the periodicals put out by various Palestinian factions without indication of the names of the editorial staff or place of publication. These underground periodicals sought to mobilize their readers politically, to give them guidance in the methods of the struggle, and to recruit them against the occupation. These periodicals include *al-Watan, Falastin, al-Thawra Mustamera, al-Raya, Rayat al-Sha'ab*, and *al-Taqadum*.[60]

The newspapers and their workers were harassed by Israel; in addition to closure or a ban on their distribution, their journalists were deported, including Ali al-Khatib, editor of *al-Sha'ab*; Hassan Abd el-Jawad, a correspondent for several papers, who was deported in 1985; and Akram Haniya, who was the editor of *al-Sha'ab* before being deported in 1986. Many other journalists experienced imprisonment, house arrest, a ban on entering certain areas, and raids on and searches of newspaper offices by the Israeli army.[61] But the press itself bore some responsibility. Most of the papers did not publish serious investigative reports or profound analyses; their lack of interest in the daily problems of the residents of the West Bank and Gaza Strip and slipshod coverage of newsworthy events was evident. Another deficiency was their lack of a lively style and the fact that they were not distributed outside the main urban centers.[62]

Community Institutions

Various community institutions existed in the Palestinian West Bank and Gaza Strip under the occupation. They included thousands of residents who took part in various activities and periodically elected their boards. These institutions maintained a bond with the community by providing a variety of services. They are best discused in terms of three categories: public associations, women's organizations, and trade unions and professional associations.

Public Associations. These associations engage in diverse community activities. Most of them were founded before 1967. They had humanitarian and social objectives. Following the occupation, however, the nature of their mission changed from an emphasis on charitable assistance to social activities similar to those of the nationalist factions.[63]

Before 1967 there were hundreds of such philanthropic associations scattered throughout the West Bank and the Gaza Strip. In the West Bank in the 1970s there were three federations of public associations: that for the northern region, with 27 member groups, had its headquarters in Nablus; that for the central region had its headquarters in Jerusalem; and that for the southern region had its offices in Hebron. The first attempt to set up a federation of all philanthropic associations was made in 1988.[64]

The philanthropic associations have a historic tie with the Federation of Philanthropic Associations in Jordan. Their basis was familial and clan-based rather than political. Politicization began only after their link with Jordan was severed in 1988.[65] Because their activity focused on the elites and they adopted a very conservative line toward social welfare services, these associations represented the values and political leanings of the old ruling class. Consequently until 1988 they remained a major channel through which the Jordanian regime exerted its influence in the West Bank. They did not amass political power but simply continued to provide services to marginal sectors.[66]

These associations set up crèches, preschools, schools, hospitals, shelters for the handicapped and those with special needs, literacy centers, sewing workshops, orphanages, and so on. In the West Bank there were also cooperative associations that engaged in marketing, especially of agricultural produce. The best-known was the Association for Agricultural Marketing in Nablus, run by Tahsin Fares, a member of the Jordanian parliament. Also noteworthy are the Agricultural Cooperative Society, the Oil Press Cooperative Society, and the Nablus Strip Electricity Cooperative, founded in 1977. These cooperatives continued to be part of the Jordanian cooperation network until the late 1980s.[67]

During the occupation, and especially during the early 1980s, many charity committees were set up in Palestinian cities in the West Bank and subsequently spread to dozens and even hundreds of towns, villages, and refugee camps. At first these committees focused on the humanitarian, social, and charitable domains. Only later did they begin to develop economic projects, such as workshops and simple factories, in order to invest their profits on behalf of their charitable activities. These committees depended on contributions from the West Bank and Gaza Strip and more generous assistance from abroad, especially from the Gulf states. They did not engage in political activity and did not clash with the occupation authorities in the pre-*Intifada* period.

The early 1980s saw the emergence of new Palestinian institutions that were active in more professional areas, such as agriculture, health, education, and development – the various nongovernmental organizations (NGOs). The NGOs evolved as a response to the absence of a Palestinian political administration and the failure of the Israeli authorities to provide parallel services. They were also meant to meet the need for separating community activity from professional activity. Organizations of the political left, especially the Communist Party, were the main initiators of such institutions. These organizations provided assistance in agriculture, health care, human rights, and social development. To counter Palestinian backwardness and Israeli negligence, they developed new agricultural production methods, laid water networks, opened medical clinics, and monitored violations of human rights.

By the mid-1980s Palestinian political parties and factions established women's committees, agricultural committees, and health committees. They brought in professional teams to draft plans. PLO funds were available, and the committees also developed ties with foreign nongovernmental contributors. The Communist Party was the trailblazer in this area, followed by other organizations. Competition developed between the various organizations, for funding from the PLO, from European countries and from the United States.[68] These institutions increased political awareness and provided varied social services, but they also served as channels of recruitment for one faction or another. The factions, for their part, saw these activities and services as means to promote their political goals.[69]

Women's Organizations. Like other sectors of Palestinian society, Palestinian women have experienced many changes. Before and after 1967 women's organizations were established whose nature evolved over the years. In their early years the circumstances of their activities were similar to those of the philanthropic associations with regard to their focus on charitable activity, and to the later NGOs with regard to their humanitarian activity. By 1967 there were some 68 Palestinian women's organizations engaged in humanitarian activities.[70] They helped set up crèches, preschools, schools and literacy centers, and engaged in vigorous activity to preserve and strengthen the Palestinian folk heritage. They trained tens of thousands of women and girls in various trades and handicrafts, so as to provide them with a suitable source of income. They also organized small productive enterprises, such as sewing workshops, beauty salons, and fitness centers, in addition to providing financial assistance to needy families and outstanding students.[71] Prominent in this domain was the Association for Family Welfare Services, founded in el-Bireh in 1970, and still now at the height of its activity. Also worthy of mention is the Women's League (the Women's League hospital), founded in Nablus in the 1970s, which continues to provide unique services.

The status of Palestinian women improved in the first years of the occupation, for two reasons. First, the Israeli military government did not incorporate the Muslim and Christian religious courts, as it had the authority to do, and accordingly the legal status of women was not influenced by military decrees but remained subject to amendments to Jordanian law. Second, women were given the right to vote in municipal elections, in accordance with military decree No. 627, published in 1976, which abrogated the clause in the Jordanian municipalities law that denied suffrage to women.[72] The women's organizations experienced an important turning point in the late 1970s, after which they were subject to significant political influence. In addition, new women's organizations were established that were affiliated with the Palestinian factions and participated directly in political activity, propaganda campaigns, and confrontations with the occupation. The result was that these organizations were no longer engaged exclusively in charitable endeavors. Evidence of the change is the large number of Palestinian women who were imprisoned by the Israelis – 3,000 in 1979. The women's slogan was: "social liberation hand in hand with political liberation".[73]

In 1978, the various factions, whose views were very close to national unity at that time, spearheaded the efforts to merge the women's organizations into a single umbrella organization, the Federation of Work Committees for Women. This body registered as a member of the General Federation of Arab Women, whose headquarters are in Cairo. However, because of the significant role played by the factions, women's organizations began to emerge that were not part of the Federation, each affiliated with a different faction. During the 1980s a number of women's federations were established, similar in their operating methods, but with prominent differences in other spheres and with fierce competition among them.[74] The largest of these groups was the Federation of Women's Committees for Social Work, founded in 1982, which represented and was funded by Fatah. Its membership comprised about 15,000 women, drawn from the various "West Bank and Gaza Strip committees", of which there were 165 at the end of the 1980s. These committees composed the General Conference, which had its own elected institutions.[75]

In 1982, the Popular Front for the Liberation of Palestine started its own federation, the Federation of Palestinian Women's Committees. It encompassed 116 branches in the West Bank and Gaza Strip, three cooperative associations, and about 45 preschools. In the late 1980s the Democratic Front for the Liberation of Palestine set up the Federation of Women's Committees for Cooperative Labor, while the Communist Party set up the Federation of Committees of the Struggle for the Palestinian Woman. The activity of the latter two, however, was limited. In 1981, the Federation of Palestinian Working Women Committees was founded; it focused on working women and their rights, and sought to establish an umbrella organization in the form of a labor union for Palestinian working women. This group also established 17 cooperative associations for women in the West Bank and five in the Gaza Strip. In addition, it developed extensive overseas contacts and organized trips for working women and children to various countries, including France, Greece, and Austria.[76]

Trade Unions and Professional Associations. Palestinian society became familiar with trade unions at a relatively early date, in the 1920s, in the form of two Communist organizations. After the Israeli occupation in 1967 the Palestinian labor movement tried to reorganize itself, but its efforts ran up against Israeli policy that repressed the labor movement and even deported some of its leaders. With the growth of the Palestinian working class and its accumulated experience, however, the labor movement managed to rehabilitate itself.[77]

In 1969, the General Federation in the West Bank definitively seceded from the General Federation of Labor Unions in Jordan. Spearheaded by the Communists, a new organization, the General Federation of Palestinian Labor Unions, was set up in 1973. At first this federation was not particularly successful, perhaps because of the meddling in its work by the Palestinian factions, which led to a bitter split in 1981. After the schism there were four different organizations, each of which called itself the General Federation and each of which was affiliated with a different faction – Fatah, the PFLP, the DFLP, and the Communist Party. Since 1981, there have in practice been no elections and the labor federations have lost all semblance of democracy.[78]

The General Federation of Labor Unions in the West Bank did not represent the workers in the Gaza Strip, who had their own federation that operated under Egyptian law. Most of the labor unions in the West Bank itself, except for those established during the period of Jordanian control, were illegal. The various Islamic organizations did not set up labor unions until after the outbreak of the *Intifada*.[79] In the early 1980s there were about a hundred labor unions in the Occupied West Bank and Gaza Strip, with more than 40,000 members. By the end of the decade the official number of labor unions in the West Bank alone stood at 161, although about 90 percent of them existed only on paper. During that period there were about 390,000 Palestinian workers, of whom about one-third were employed in Israel proper and the rest in the West Bank and Gaza Strip. Only about 20 percent of them were members of a union.[80]

The labor unions' involvement in the workers' struggle was marginal and limited; what is more, the Palestinian unions were powerless to protect the Palestinians who worked in Israel. In the West Bank and Gaza Strip the unions occasionally resorted to methods of protest, such as sanctions or brief strikes, but generally in an unplanned or disorganized fashion.[81]

Palestinian working women were added to the board of the General Federation of Workers in 1979,[82] but their destiny was that of the schism of 1981. In that year, the Federation of Palestinian Working Women's Committees, already mentioned above, was founded. In sum, there was no great progress in the status of women as a result of political developments and changes in the labor unions.

Professional associations covers the associations of physicians, engineers, attorneys, accountants, and others. Those in the Gaza Strip are totally separate from those in the West Bank. Associations began to develop in the early 1980s, when their number and activity began to swell. In the wake of this significant growth, and after the PLO exodus from Lebanon in 1982, all factions began to take an interest and paid attention to community and institutional activity in the West Bank and Gaza Strip.[83]

Professional associations, like other social and civic institutions, were subject to the dictates of the national and political agenda, as well as to the requirements of loyalty to one faction or another, in their work and activity. Because of the background, quality and culture of their members, however, these groups were more committed to preserving a democratic culture than were the Palestinian social and civic organizations. Accordingly democratic elections and a periodic turnover in their governing bodies were important to them.[84]

The Palestinian professional associations provided a reservoir of educated and hard-working people who constituted an important part of the political elite of Palestinian society. The Palestinian factions frequently drew their leadership from these associations. In addition to the role of these associations in protecting their members' interests, they also made a substantial contribution to the struggle against the Israeli authorities. Of all the Palestinian civic organizations, the professional groups played their role best and were least influenced by internal political disputes.[85]

Some of these professional organizations maintained a form of affiliation with their Jordanian counterparts and saw themselves as their branches: examples included the associations of engineers, farmers, physicians, dentists, veterinarians, and attorneys. These ties persisted even after the official severance of the Palestinian–Jordanian link in 1988. There are a number of possible reasons for this: they could take advantage of the economic advantages that the Palestinian professional associations had achieved, such as pensions and social security; the professional associations in Jordan, controlled by Islamic and nationalist trends, did not recognize the decision to dissolve the connection between the East and West Banks; and the fear of a takeover by one or other Palestinian function of the professional association's funding, which would provide them in turn with actual control.[86]

Public Institutions

Under this rubric we may include a number of institutions, of which the most important are the universities, the municipalities, and the chambers of commerce.

The Universities. During the 1970s, the Israeli authorities allowed some of the colleges and institutes in the Occupied West Bank and Gaza Strip to develop into universities. They also permitted the establishment of new universities, controlled by boards of trustees to oversee their affairs and finances. By 1979 there were six universities in the Occupied West Bank and Gaza Strip: the Islamic University in Gaza, and five in the West Bank – in Bir Zeit, al-Najah, Bethlehem, Hebron, and the outskirts of Jerusalem (which included separate faculties for the sciences, humanities, nursing, and theology).

Before the first university was established, thousands of students went abroad to study every year, most of them to Amman, Damascus, Beirut, Cairo, and Soviet bloc countries. Their stay abroad provided the students with an opportunity to become acquainted with Palestinian organizations, train with weapons, and join the ranks of the Palestinian revolution. Thus Israel's objective in permitting the founding of Palestinian universities was to prevent thousands of Palestinian students from joining the ranks of the resistance. At the same time, however, they provided an excellent opportunity for the thousands of needy students who could not afford to go abroad to study. During the 1980s the number of university students exceeded 10,000, in addition to thousands of alumni of previous years.[87]

The universities were the scene of ramified activity by student groups staging confrontations with the Israeli military forces. These groups were affiliated with the Palestinian organizations and factions active in the Occupied West Bank and Gaza Strip.[88] Among these groupings we may number the Fatah Student Movement, the Islamic Bloc (originally affiliated with the Islamic Movement and later with Hamas), the Student Labor Front (PFLP), the Student Unity Bloc (DFLP), the Student Federation Bloc (Communists), and finally *al-Jama'a al-Islamiya* (Islamic Jihad) founded in the late 1980s. The Palestinian student movement was so strongly politicized that its political coloration overshadowed its student-oriented activities. And this frequently had negative effects on students' academic performance. Even student services such as tuition, art exhibitions, conferences, educational activities, and recruitment were political in nature.[89]

On the campuses themselves, however, the student organizations reflected the changing ties among political parties and organizations. Sometimes the political competition reached the level of violent clashes, leading to the closure of some universities because of fights among students, and not necessarily with the occupation forces.[90]

The Palestinian universities had student unions, whose officers were elected periodically. The elections provided opportunities for fierce competition among blocs of students, which generally pitted two groups: Fatah and the Islamic bloc. In the University of Gaza the situation was somewhat different, because there the Islamic bloc was in control from the very beginning. At Bethlehem University, by contrast, the Islamic bloc never managed to gain control of the student union. In the 1970s and 1980s, the various nationalist blocs that supported the PLO sometimes formed alliances. The Islamic bloc, by contrast, never concluded pacts with other groups, because of political and ideological disagreements. Only after the *Intifada* and the Oslo Accords did the Islamic bloc and leftist groups forge successful alliances at Bir Zeit and al-Najah universities, as a result of their joint opposition to the peace process.

Palestinian student movements played an important role in the national struggle against the Israeli occupation. They did this through political recruitment and organization in regular frameworks, and the organization of direct confrontations, demonstrations, and clashes. This led to repeated closures and military roadblocks on an almost daily basis. Many student leaders were arrested or deported. Bir Zeit University was the most politicized of all the universities and was consequently subjected agressive Israeli harassment.[91]

The universities faced other forms of Israeli restrictions, such as: the refusal to grant building permits, detentions by the intelligence services, the delay or banning of the import of books, the prevention of the construction of athletic fields, restrictions on receiving funds from abroad, the creation of a deep gulf between the universities and society through a ban on social activities, and the deportation of lecturers who lacked residence permits. The Israeli restrictive measures reached their zenith in military order No. 854, which appointed a military commander for universities. The commander was responsible for providing certificates to lecturers, a certificate that gave the army permission to enter the campuses and monitor the universities.[92]

The Municipalities. After the Israeli occupation in 1967, military order

No. 80 extended the terms of the incumbent mayors and required munici-pal councils to continue in office, even in the absence of a quorum.[93] The Israeli authorities agreed to the holding of municipal council elections in early 1972 under Jordanian law, as long as the elections carried no politi-cal connotations. Turnout was high – about 80 percent of eligible voters, which meant males only, since Jordanian law did not extend the suffrage to women. The winners, younger and with a new nationalist orientation, replaced the traditional figures who had long controlled the municipalities. Nevertheless, the municipalities did not play a prominent role. The PLO was opposed to the 1972 municipal elections, arguing that they were intended to put an end to the Palestinian problem; but it had changed its mind by the time of the 1976 elections.[94]

In 1976, women were allowed to vote; the national institutions, including the PLO, also decided to participate. This time the turnout was about 72 percent of all eligible voters. The outcome was a 70 percent majority for PLO supporters in most cities of the West Bank. Among the prominent figures elected mayors were Bassam Shaka in Nablus, Ibrahim al-Khalil in el-Bireh, Karim Khalef in Ramallah, Fahd Qawasme in Hebron, and Muhammad Milhem in Halhoul – all of them well-known nationalists who expressed their full support for the PLO and vigorous opposition to Israeli policy.[95] In 1980, the Israeli authorities began dissolving municipal councils and deporting some of their leading figures, including Fahd Qawasme and Muhammad Milhem. Some of the mayors were targeted and severely injured by a group of Jewish right-wing activists, known as the "Jewish underground". The end of an important chapter in the annals of nationalist activity in the Occupied West Bank and Gaza Strip and the start of a new stage came with the establishment of the Civil Administration. This was accompanied by the creation of a vacuum on the Palestinian side and the loss of the support of the organizational and pol-itical leadership.[96]

In the 1980s, after Israeli officers had been placed in direct control of the cities and municipalities, many municipal officials resigned. This led to a substantial deterioration in services. The municipalities were deprived of budgets and lost the authority to issue building permits to their residents. As a result, in the mid-1980s some Palestinians agreed to accept an Israeli appointment to serve as mayors of their cities.[97] The most prominent example was Thafer al-Masri, appointed mayor of Nablus in November 1985, with the agreement of Israel, Jordan, and the Fatah. Al-Masri's assassination on March 2, 1986, put an end to the policy of appointed mayors.

The situation in the Gaza Strip differed from that in the West Bank. Elections had not been held there since 1946, during the British Mandate. There were four municipal councils, established according to the mandatory Municipalities Ordinance of 1934. Local government had a clan or tribal basis, unlike the political character it had in the West Bank.[98] The municipal councils elected in 1976 were strictly political in nature. During these subsequent years a number of important events affected the municipalities, but because of their political nature and the status of their leadership, we will defer discussion of them to consideration of the topic of political organization, below.

Palestinian cities suffered greatly under the occupation. Their relations with the Israeli military authorities and the Civil Administration were tense. Ultimately these tensions affected the services required by residents. The operation of the municipalities was restricted by the requirement that every new project (water, electricity, health, education, roads) receive the prior approval of the Israeli military authorities. The budgets of the Palestinian municipalities required an Israeli counter-signature. Even the levying of local taxes or modification of existing taxes required such approval. The flow of funds from abroad to the Palestinian municipalities and other Palestinian organizations troubled the Israeli authorities, who suspended many projects submitted for approval by municipalities because of the involvement of foreign Arabs, mainly the Jordanian Bank for Urban and Rural Development, which provided loans and grants to West Bank municipalities between 1967 and 1978.[99]

Chambers of Commerce. Over the last 30 years, dozens of Palestinian chambers of commerce have been set up. Nine of them are in the major towns of the West Bank – Nablus, Jenin, Tulkarm, Qalqiliya, Jericho, Ramallah, Jerusalem, Bethlehem, and Hebron. The tenth, in the Gaza Strip, has four branches – in Rafah, Khan Yunis, Jabalya, and Dir al-Balah. In 1988, after Jordan renounced its claim to the West Bank, a new federation of these chambers of commerce was created. Its offices were in Jerusalem and its director was the head of the Arab Chamber of Commerce in that city.[100]

In 1974, despite PLO opposition, partial elections were held for some of the chambers of commerce – those in Nablus, Jenin, Qalqiliya, and Jericho.[101] Elections were held again in 1991 and 1992. The Civil Administration had the right to intervene in Chamber of Commerce elections, unlike the situation in elections for other professional groups, where prior Civil Administration approval of elections and candidates was required.[102] Given the absence of any official Palestinian agency during the occupation, the chambers of commerce issued the various certificates required by Jordanian government ministries as well as certificates for products intended for export to Jordan. These bodies operated according to the Jordanian Chambers of Commerce and Industry regulations.

Between July 1967 and September 1988, that is, before the establishment of the Federation of Chambers of Commerce, all ten chambers made efforts to coordinate their activities in an umbrella organization called the Joint Coordinating Committee. These attempts were unsuccessful for a number of reasons, including Israeli actions, economic factors, and administrative ineptitude.[103]

During the occupation the chambers of commerce faced a number of problems. They did not have close relations with the general public, were not political enough, and did not attract public interest on a par with other Palestinian organizations. The chambers suffered from the fact that merchants did not want to belong to them, while those who did join were not particularly active. In addition, the members of the chambers of commerce complained about the limited services extended to them. The discontent was exacerbated by the fact that their officers continued to hold office for protracted periods without new elections.[104]

Political Institutions

The focus in this section is on the Palestinian political situation under the occupation: the political organization and the political leadership.

Political Organization. Following the Israeli occupation in 1967, there were attempts to set up centers of opposition in which groups and individuals could resist the new military regime. The National Guidance Committee was a quasi-underground group in Jerusalem, with representatives from the Communist Party, the Arab nationalist movement, and the head of the Higher Muslim Council, dignitaries, and *waqf* functionaries, who continued to be subordinated to the Jordanian Ministry of the Waqf. Committees were established under the aegis of the National Guidance Committee, whose members tended to be conservatives. Its political platform called for the return of the West Bank to Jordan and implementation of Security Council Resolution 242. The Israeli authorities, for their part, adopted a policy of harassment, arrests, and finally deportation of committee members. The deportation of its chairman, Sheikh Abd el-Hamid al-Sa'ah, and of the head of the Higher Muslim Council put an end to the committee's activity.[105]

The Palestinian National Front was officially launched in late 1973. Although its basis was the Communist Party, it also incorporated representatives of Fatah, the DFLP, several independent figures and mayors, as well as representatives of the trade unions, professional associations, and women's organizations. The PFLP opted to stay out of this grouping. This was the first time since the Israeli occupation of the West Bank and Gaza Strip that the Palestinians assembled a political leadership they viewed as representing the prevailing currents in the Occupied West Bank and Gaza Strip.[106]

The platform of the National Front focused on resistance to the occupation, and on the struggle to liberate the country and restore national rights; defense of the land against expropriation and Judaization; vigorous opposition to steps toward economic annexation, destruction of the national institutions, and the eradication of Arab culture and heritage; protection of those imprisoned by the Israelis; and assistance to community organizations.[107]

Initially the National Front and PLO maintained cordial relations, manifested in coordination, mutual consultation, and meetings in Damascus and Beirut. The National Front declared its commitment to the central status of the PLO, but relations soon deteriorated in the shadow of mutual recriminations. The Front, for example, accused the PLO of aspiring to take control of it and charged that while Israel was staging its own assault on the Front, by means of arrests and deportations, the PLO was helping Israel by attempting to corrode the Front from within. The results of this internal struggle paralyzed the Front; by 1976 it was no longer active.[108]

During its short life the National Front raised two issues: first, it sparked an internal political debate in the West Bank and Gaza Strip and within the PLO about the establishment of an independent Palestinian state in the West Bank and Gaza Strip occupied in 1967. This meant support for a two-state solution long supported by the Communists. In addition, the Front initiated a tradition of overt political activity, taking advantage of the small leeway permitted by the occupation authorities, and especially political activity in Jerusalem, because it paid no attention to the jurisdiction of Israeli law applied by the military authorities.[109]

The Fatah leadership believed that the failure of the National Front would guarantee the establishment of a more flexible movement in the Occupied West Bank and Gaza Strip. The results in the 1972 municipal elections, however, did support the PLO but were closer to the Palestinian left than to Fatah.

In the late 1970s, the mayors constituted the political leadership within the Occupied West Bank and Gaza Strip. Most prominent among them were Bassam Shaka, Karim Khalef, Ibrahim Tawil, Fahd Qawasme, and Mohammad Milhem, already mentioned above. Menahem Milson, head of the Civil Administration in the late 1970s, acknowledged that the mayors turned the municipalities into political power centers. In this way they changed from being a factor that controlled only the street into the main organized political leadership. The mayors became the paramount symbols of Palestinian steadfastness in the eyes of the Palestinians themselves. They set up a sort of political coalition and collective leadership. This showed its strength when 21 mayors submitted their resignation to protest the decision to deport Bassam Shaka, the mayor of Nablus, forcing the Israelis to revoke the decision. This solidarity was also manifested when 24 municipalities declared a strike as their contribution to a general boycott of the Civil Administration. The Civil Administration did indeed fail later.[110]

After the Camp David agreement between Egypt and Israel in 1979, the Palestinians in the Occupied West Bank and Gaza Strip began working to set up a new organizational structure. In October 1978, a conference was convened in Jerusalem with the participation of representatives of the municipalities, the labor unions and professional associations, and the national institutions. Despite a request for a delay by the PLO leadership, the conference published a manifesto that condemned the idea of autonomy and the Camp David Accords. Later the second National Guidance Committee was established; unlike the National Front, it focused on overt activity. This committee was composed of figures from the West Bank and Gaza Strip, including mayors, representatives of unions and professional organizations, universities, and women's and student organizations. It operated successfully and was banned on March 11, 1982, and the nationalist mayors were dismissed.[111] On both occasions when the residents of the Occupied West Bank and Gaza Strip saw fit to establish a political and organizational framework (the National Front and the National Guidance Committee), they found themselves taking positions that sometimes ran counter to those of the PLO. In both bodies, the Communists and left had a more prominent presence than Fatah did. Both the Committee and the Front were viewed as legitimate, although not formally elected, because they were seen as the fruit of political partnership with a broad basis and as expressing a certain measure of democracy.[112]

In the 1980s, however, the situation changed radically because the PLO, after having been forced out of Beirut in 1982 – and especially Fatah – began to transfer the center of the struggle to the Occupied West Bank and Gaza Strip. The process was promoted by the abundant funds channeled to this purpose and the recruitment of leaders and personnel from various sectors, especially the universities. This led to the start of the Fatah domination of the "Palestinian street" and a decline in the strength of the Communist left, especially in light of the rise of the Islamists.

Before the outbreak of the *Intifada*, in December 1987, Fatah was active through the public institutions, universities, women's organizations, research institutes, and newspapers. The Islamic organizations were concentrated in the universities, mosques, philanthropic associations, and charitable committees. The Palestinian left organized activity in NGOs, women's organizations, and universities. After the *Intifada* became more severe, in early 1988, and after the establishment of Hamas, the Palestinian constellation entered a new phase that had a significant influence on the institutions of civil society. This stage continued until 1993, when the peace process began.

The Political Leadership[113]

In the 1970s and 1980s, there emerged a Palestinian leadership that represented three trends: the nationalists, the pro-Jordanian element, and the
Islamicists. The *national leadership* team consists of three groups: institutional leaders, public figures, and independents.

The power and legitimacy of the *institutional leaders* derive from four
main sources. First of all, their organizational affiliation and relations with
the faction leaderships outside the West Bank and Gaza Strip make them
the chief liaison between the West Bank and Gaza Strip and abroad. All
decisions, directives, and proclamations pass through this group. Second,
they hold a very strong card – their history of militant resistance to the
occupation, manifested by the fact that its members were subject to detention, house arrest, and so on. Third, they occupy the apex of the pyramid
of the organizations of various factions, an advantage that permits them to
recruit personnel and supporters in all the cities, villages, and refugee
camps in the West Bank and Gaza Strip. Fourth, they enjoy continuity,
because they are the only group within the national leadership that has
mechanisms to renew itself without having to change its ideology.

The *institutional leadership* also has its weak points. These include, first
of all, the eagle eye of the Israeli authorities and repeated arrests, which
impact on its operation. Second, contacts with groups abroad limit its political mobility and cause it to reflect the views of the various factions with
which it sometimes does not agree, rather than expressing an independent
opinion. Third, its ties with the factions force it to coordinate its positions
so that it can present a united front acceptable to the PLO.

By *public figures* I mean individuals drawn from the traditional leadership and new faces that support the PLO. Two factors contributed to the
appearance of these figures. Internally, the iron-fist policy of the Likud
government liquidated the infrastructure that publicly supported the PLO.
Externally, the PLO's departure from Lebanon in 1982 sparked off a
debate about a peaceful resolution instead of the military option advocated
by the PLO.

After it left Lebanon in 1982, the PLO began looking for its "dignitaries"
in the traditional leadership within the Occupied West Bank and Gaza
Strip. To this we should add the transfer of the Palestinian center of gravity
after 1982 to the Occupied West Bank and Gaza Strip, a transfer accompanied by the return of the rivalry between the PLO and Jordan.

Nevertheless, because of the PLO's fear of changes in the position of the
indigenous leadership and of the "dignitaries", and of the possibility that
they would impose their own interests in the future, the organization began
to encourage the entry of new faces, whose loyalty to the organization was
guaranteed. But the newcomers lacked the qualities and experience of the

traditional leaders, and the necessary elements required to wage the struggle which the organizational leadership possessed.

The public figures had several main advantages, including their ties with the PLO mainstream, a pragmatic political platform, and moderate views. In addition, the fact that they were actually present in the West Bank and Gaza Strip provided them with an important role in the political process when it began. Finally, their ability to address the West in its own language and concepts opened the doors of foreign missions and the media to them. Their weak point was the rivalries among them and the attacks on them by more radical factions.

The *independents* are figures with prominent standing in society, such as physicians, engineers, attorneys, university lecturers, and successful businessmen. They support the PLO as the sole legitimate representative of the Palestinian people, but are not affiliated, at least publicly, with any faction. This is the source of both their strength and their weakness. It is a source of strength because of their ability to analyze facts and events with an independent mindset and from a comprehensive perspective, remote from factionalism, and their distance from the internal struggles among the various factions. At the same time, their independence weakens them and limits their influence by leaving them outside the practical political arena, which is fueled by the connections among the various factions.

The *pro-Jordanian leadership* was not very popular in Palestinian society. It derived its power from temporary circumstances and the force of personality rather than positions. The source of power and influence of this group was the Jordanian government, which authorized them to serve as intermediaries between itself and the inhabitants of the West Bank and Gaza Strip, to satisfy people's needs from Jordanian government ministries. They enjoyed a privileged social and economic background as members of large and wealthy families, and were treated leniently by the Israeli authorities. They were also propped up by the ties that bound Jordan with the Occupied West Bank and Gaza Strip, especially the West Bank, in the form of social and demographic relations, civil servant salaries, and so on.

The *Islamic leadership* began to be active in the 1980s. The growth of its influence was gradual but accelerated after the outbreak of the *Intifada*. Its rising influence stems from a number of causes, the most important of which is the solid organizational infrastructure of the religious political stream, based on charitable institutions in the West Bank, and the general religious revival sweeping the area. On the other hand, this group had weaknesses that undercut it in the Palestinian street, including its point of departure *vis-à-vis* the Palestinian problem, which it views as a religious or pan-Arab problem. In addition, it lacked charismatic figures with a public presence. Finally, its rigidity with regard to private morals and marriage law did not increase its popularity.

To sum up, two parallel processes of democratization have taken place in the Palestinian national movement and what has been its main target group since 1967, the Palestinians of the West Bank and Gaza Strip. These two processes are the basic foundation of the Palestinian "Partial Democracy" regime that emerged in the West Bank and Gaza Strip after the creation of the Palestinian National Authority (PNA) in 1994. On the one hand, Arafat tightened his control of the military, political, economic, social, and cultural organs of the PLO – an experience he brought with him when he returned to Palestine to build the state of Palestine, as we shall see in later chapters. On the other hand, the national, political, social, economic, and cultural institutions that emerged among the Palestinians in the West Bank and Gaza Strip were characterized by an advanced process of pluralism and acceptance of the rules of democratic decision-making, which today constitutes the main hope for the appearance of a democratic regime in the Palestine of tomorrow.

4

The Formal Structure of Powers in the Palestinian National Authority

A basic foundation in regulating the functions of the powers in a state which preserves basic rules of democracy is the separation of the legislature, the executive, and the judiciary. This chapter provides a concise survey of the structure of these powers and their existing functions on the formal level as they appear in the peace agreements signed between the PLO and Israel, and in the various laws and decrees promulgated by the PNA. In describing the functioning of the various authorities, as described by media reports and testimonies of political activists interested in the subject, the aim is to elucidate the rules of the functioning of the PNA on the formal level since its establishment in 1994.

I shall not deal in this chapter with the extent of preservation of the principle of a separation of powers in the Palestine National Authority, but will postpone that argument till chapter 7, which will show that the formal political structure of the PNA and the existence of the three powers (legislative, executive and judicial) is only one segment of the political regime of the PNA, and constitutes the positive element of the Palestinian "partial democracy".

The first features of the structure and character of the various authorities in the PNA were drawn up in the interim agreement between Israel and the PLO. The agreement included a theoretical arrangement of the subject of each authority and the relations among them – rules that were changed between one agreement and another in accordance with circumstances and developments. A detailed description of the authorities and their functions on the formal level also appears in the draft for the Basic Law (the constitution) of the PNA, a draft that was approved in second and third readings by the legislative council and placed on the table of the government and the PNA Chairman for approval and subsequent referral for additional deliberation by the legislative council. The legislative council worked out internal statutes, which serve as a set of guidelines for its work. These statutes encompass a detailed analysis, on the formal level, of the rules of activity of the legislative power and its relations with the other powers.

All the aforementioned sources will serve in presenting a concise picture of the rules of separation of powers within the PNA. In the original version of the principles of the peace agreements between the PLO and Israel in Washington on September 13, 1993, there is a general reference to the setting up of an "Autonomy Authority" in the form of an "elected council of the Palestinian people in the West Bank and the Gaza Strip". The election of the council would take place in "general, direct and free political elections". In the original declaration and the other interim agreements there is nothing about the "Gaza–Jericho First" agreement or an interim agreement.

The "Council" is mentioned in very general terms as a formula paralleled by the formula "the Palestinian Authority", but this did not reflect a clear separation between the powers of the government or between the election of the Authority Chairman and the members of his cabinet and the election of a legislative authority.[1] But there was a reference to the transfer of responsibilities from Israel to the Palestinians and to the fact that these powers would be transferred to the temporary authority, which would then transfer them to the council following the election of the latter.[2] However, in Chapter 7 of the Declaration of Principles it was stated that the interim agreement to be signed in the future between the parties would include "a detailed account of the structure of the Council, the number of its members, the transfer of authorities and responsibilities from the Israeli Military Administration and the Civil Administration to the Council". In the same passage, it stated that "the interim agreement will also define and lay down the executive authority and the legislative authority of the Council and the Palestinian independent legal authorities". In fact, in the Declaration of Principles there was talk of a joint council that would be composed of two government powers – an executive one and a legislative one.

During the period between the signing of the Declaration of Principles in September 1993 and the signing of the Interim Agreement in September 1995, the "Gaza–Jericho First" agreement was signed as an agreement regulating the transfer of government jurisdictions in Gaza and Jericho to the Palestinian side as a first step in transferring the entire control over the West Bank and the Gaza Strip (which were recognized in the Declaration of Principles as one territorial unit) to the Palestinians. This agreement included separate parts on the structure of the Palestinian Authority. According to the fourth passage of that Agreement, "the Palestinian Authority will be composed of one body numbering 24 members and will be responsible for carrying out the overall legislative and executive jurisdictions in accordance with the agreement . . . and will be responsible for carrying out the judicial jurisdictions". In fact, the agreement placed all jurisdictions under the responsibility of one joint authority.

The sixth paragraph of the "Gaza–Jericho First" agreement, on the subject of "jurisdictions and responsibilities of the Palestinian Authority", states that "the carrying out of the terms of this Agreement means that the responsibilities of the Palestinian Authority are: it will have legislative and executive jurisdiction, it will manage judicial matters by means of an independent judicial authority, it will have the jurisdiction to design policy and to observe it and to set up institutions, authorities and government administrations . . . " In the minutes[3] it is also mentioned that the spheres of responsibilities of the PNA will be transferred to it from the "Israeli military government" by means of a joint committee.

The Interim Agreement signed between the PLO and Israel in Washington in September 1995, in accordance with the Declaration of Principles, contained a detailed enumeration of the structure of the Authority, its jurisdictions and its various ramifications. These rules were later anchored in the "basic law" (constitution) for the Authority and in various laws and regulations published by various bodies, such as the Chairman of the PLO, who, according to these agreements, also became Acting President of the PNA; and also in regulations of the legislative council and the executive authority, which were set up in accordance with the Agreement.

The Legislative Council

In accordance with the Declaration of Principles, the "Gaza–Jericho First" agreement and the Interim Agreement, it was concluded that the Palestinians under the rule of the PNA would elect a legislative council, which was to have jurisdiction to promulgate laws and regulations and to supervise the activities of the executive council. The elections to the "Palestinian Council" and the developments in the structure of the authority in general led to meaningful changes in the character, the functioning, and the structure of the council, which had meanwhile been declared to be a legislative council or a "parliament". It shouldered a task equivalent to a legislative authority in a normal state, as reflected by the internal statutes of the council and by various publications on its behalf or on behalf of research-related or media-related organizations and bodies.

The following section discusses various aspects associated with the legislative council, including the structure of the PNA, its functions, its procedures of work as well as an evaluation of its activity.

Structure of the Legislative Council

The structure of the council refers to its different aspects and its hierarchy.

(a) *The plenum* means the entire number of council members who are members of the rank-and-file and who convene for their first meeting at the start of the second week after elections have been held, by invitation of the Chairman of the PNA. The council comprises 88 members who represent 16 election districts.[4] These elected members, in accordance with the statutes, submit at the first session after the elections their "oath of allegiance", whose content is: "I swear by the great God to be loyal to the homeland and to preserve the rights and interests of the people and the nation and to respect the constitution and to fully fulfill my obligations, and God be my witness of all the aforesaid by me." On being elected, the members become representatives of all the voters, not only those of their own election district. Membership of the council can be discontinued in three cases: *decease, resignation,* or *following a decision of the council.* A resignation is accepted following the submission of a letter of resignation by the council member. If the member desirous of resigning has not reconsidered this step, the resignation must be resubmitted to the council two weeks after having been submitted or during the first meeting to be convened after the letter of resignation was submitted. Resignation must be approved by the legislative council.[5] The internal statutes of the legislative council do not propose a certain threshold of consent or rejection to a petition to resign submitted to the council.

The third means of terminating the office of a member of the council is in the wake of a decision by the council by secret ballot, and with the approval of two-thirds of the council members, to terminate the membership of one of their peers, on the grounds of a verdict of a special Palestinian court convicting one of the members of having committed a crime, or a transgression involving dishonorable conduct.[6] On the strength of the verdict of the court of law, a proposal in writing is to be submitted to the chairman, signed by ten members, to discontinue the membership of the person involved. The chairman is to inform the member that a proposal to abolish his membership has been submitted and the chairman is to put the matter on the agenda of the coming council meeting.[7] The council for its part is requested, at its first meeting after submission of the petition to abolish the candidacy of one of its members, and after having given the respective member the chance to defend himself in front of the other members, to refer the proposal for discontinuing that member's membership to the legal committee, which is part of the legislative council (for the committees of the council, see below), at its first session, provided of course that the contents of the petition for the abolition of membership of the member concerned is approved.[8]

The legal committee is requested to consider the proposal of abolishing the membership and has to prepare a conclusive report with regard either to continuing membership or to the additional steps necessary for the abolition of that membership.[9] Where the petition to abolish membership is approved, the council must defer discussion on the decision to another meeting than the one at which the report was made, if the member concerned has requested this.

When the council holds a special meeting relying on the report of the legal committee, the discussion must be held in the presence of the member concerned, who is given a chance to state his case, but he will be requested to leave the meeting when a vote is taken.[10] Voting is conducted by secret ballot and its outcome has to be approved by a two-thirds majority of council members.[11]

By virtue of being members of the council, council members are granted across-the-board immunity which protects them against being charged or interrogated by a court of law. This accords them relative freedom of speech. The council member may not be searched, in his home, his car or his place of work, throughout his period of office. This immunity is valid throughout the term of his membership of the council and also during the period subsequent to his membership of the council; nor can a member of the council renounce such immunity without the approval and consent of the legislative council.[12]

Abolishing the immunity of a member of the council is possible in the case of a crime confirmed by witnesses, in the wake of whose testimonies procedures to have the immunity abolished can be opened. The petition to abolish the immunity has to be submitted in writing to the chairman of the council on behalf of the president of the supreme court. The petition is to be accompanied by a memorandum detailing the sort of crime committed, the place where it occurred, the time, and the evidence warranting legal action. The chairman of the council shall on his part refer the petition for the cancellation of the immunity to the legal committee and inform the council accordingly. The legal committee shall discuss the petition in the presence of the member concerned, should he so wish, and shall then submit a report to the council. Should its recommendation to cancel the immunity of the member concerned be positive, the council will hold a discussion and arrive at a decision by a two-thirds majority with regard to abolishing the immunity.[13]

(b) *The presidency of the council.* The presidency of the council includes the chairman of the council, his two deputies, and a secretary. These are elected by secret ballot during the first meeting after the elections, and each year they are elected anew at the start of the new year of activity. The first session after the elections is conducted by the oldest council member and the first thing to be enacted at that session, after the opening address of the

PNA Chairman, is the procedure of electing the council presidency, who immediately after being elected take upon themselves the tasks of conducting the house. Ministers or the PNA Chairman are barred from the presidency of the council as an expression, in theory and practice, of the separation of powers. If a member of the presidency discontinues his membership for any reason whatsoever, the council elects a replacement for him.

The members of the presidency are responsible for running the administrative and financial affairs of the house and they also care for its daily management. The chairman of the council is the person representing it, is its spokesman, and is responsible for the security and order within it. He inaugurates and closes each meeting, and conducts the discussions, granting the right of speech to the council members, or withdrawing it under various circumstances such as irrelevance to the subject matter, exceeding the allotted time, etc. In the case of the chairman being absent, the meeting is to be conducted by one of the deputies and if these too are absent, the meetings and administrative affairs of the council are to be entrusted to the oldest member of the council present on that day.[14]

(c) *The committees of the council.* The Interim Agreement between the PLO and Israel signed in Washington on September 28, 1995, included a clause saying that the elected council would be able to set up small committees from among its members so as to facilitate the carrying out of the council's work.[15] The council, which wanted from the start to resemble the parliaments of independent states, took pains to set up permanent sub-committees and later set up committees for particular purposes, such as the special committee for the examination of the report of the PNA Chairman about corruption and the squandering of public money in the PNA. The committees deal with the promotion of three central subjects: (1) The subject of legislation – the committees prepare proposed bills and adjust them for the second reading; they also work out bills for consideration by the plenary session and deal with follow-ups of existing laws and regulations with a view to suggesting required modifications. (2) The subject of control – the committees deal with current control and supervision of the activities of the executive. (3) The subject of follow-up programs – that is, activities and agreements conducted by the executive authority; this includes reports to the plenary session so that the latter is able to conduct current deliberations based on the committees' findings.[16]

There are eleven permanent committees of the council:

1 *The Jerusalem Committee* deals with the promotion of the status of Jerusalem as the prospective capital of the anticipated Palestinian state. *Inter alia*, this committee conducts deliberations with the participation of public figures from Jerusalem so as to propose operative steps serving the

Committee's purpose. Such steps may be within the sphere of issues that are currently prominent in the area: in the negotiations with Israel as regards the future of Jerusalem, as well as with regard to public relations activities throughout the world centering on the status and future of Jerusalem.[17]

2 *The Committee on Land and Settlements* deals with means and ways to stop the transfer of land from Palestinians to Israelis, and with Israeli measures in the sphere of settlement in the West Bank and the Gaza Strip. Specifically, this committee deals with the preparation of proposals, resolutions and laws within the sphere of its responsibilities, and their submission to the plenary session. The committee also deliberates activities of the *Waqf* and the land reserves in general, and follows up the measures taken by the PNA with regard to land and settlements, including the submission of proposals to the Council of Ministers on these issues.[18]

3. *The Committee on Palestinian Refugee Affairs abroad* (including emigrants and displaced persons) deals with deliberations on Palestinian refugees with special emphasis on alleviating their suffering, or bringing forward solutions to special problems. The Committee also deals with the measures of the PNA concerning the refugees and their future, such as making agreements and conducting negotiations on the subject with Israel and the Arab world.[19]

4 *The Political Committee* deals with the follow-up of the activities of the executive authority in the political sphere. These activities include: negotiations with Israel, and inter-Arab and international relations. The committee is requested to prepare reports on these subjects and to submit them to the plenary session for deliberation and decision.[20]

5 *The Legal Committee* (constitution, law and justice, and council affairs) deals with the preparation of proposed laws to be submitted to the legislative council by the Council of Ministers or by one of the members of the legislative council, so as to determine whether the proposal should be submitted for a second reading at the plenum. This committee deals with all spheres of legal matters which the council is confronted with, such as the abrogation of the immunity of a council member, the status and the independence of the judicial authority, public memoranda submitted to the council, and the like.[21]

6 *The Budget Committee* deals with controlling the PNA in the areas of expenditure and revenue, including office expenses, the squandering of public funds, imposing customs duties and taxes, and banking and finances in general. It also deals with the preparation of the budget proposal submitted to the council by the Council of Ministers, for approval by the plenary.

7 *The Economic Committee* (industry and trade, investments, housing, food, tourism, and planning) deals with the control of developments in

economics and trade, including internal developments within the Palestinian economy, employment in Israel, trade, purchases and sales from and to Israel, and from and to foreign countries. The committee is responsible for conducting deliberations on a whole range of economic aspects of the PNA and for submitting reports to the plenary for deliberation and decision-making.[22]

8 *The Committee for Interior Affairs* (interior, security, and local government) deals with following up developments in the government and its credentials. It is concerned with the activities of the security agencies of the PNA, and with agreements or cooperation with foreign countries, including Israel, in the area of security or local government.[23]

9 *The Educational and Social Committee* supervises the activities of the PNA in a broad range of areas associated with the life of all Palestinian citizens, or of specific sectors among them. The committee deals with developments associated with education, school instruction, culture, public relations, religious affairs, archeology, welfare, health, work and employment, prisons, victims of war and terrorism, war veterans, children, youth and women, and with all the internal and external measures taken by the PNA in these realms.[24]

10 *The Committee for Natural Resources and Energy* deals with the supervision of all the activities of the PNA in the spheres of general development. Specifically, it deals with the promotion of: water supplies, agriculture, rural life, ecology, energy, livestock and fish. It utilizes resources and supervises their application, and prepares detailed reports to the plenary for consideration and decision-making.[25]

11 *The Committee for Public Control, Human Rights and General Freedoms* deals with current control of the activities carried out by the PNA in the realms of administration, human rights and citizenship. The committee is requested to prepare detailed reports, including the summoning of various persons to give evidence, and to submit the materials obtained to the plenary for consideration and for decision-taking.[26]

The council took care to mention in its internal statutes that "the number of members of a permanent committee will be at least five and not more than nine". The council is entitled to set up additional committees for *ad hoc* or permanent requirements, and for defined aims.[27]

The election of members of the committees takes place at the first session of the council. Every member is entitled to propose his or her candidacy to the committee in which he or she thinks they are most suitable to serve. The office of the chairmanship (the "presidium") of the council assembles the applications and makes the arrangement in consultation with their submitters and in mutual agreement with them, provided that no council member serves on more than three committees. Thereafter, the chairman presents the final composition of members to the council for approval.[28] In accordance with the internal statutes, a member is not permitted to serve simultaneously both as a minister and as a member of the office of the presidium of the council or as a member of a committee.[29] With regard to changes in the composition of the committees, decisions are subject to a decision of the council presidium at the beginning of the regular session each year.[30]

Every committee elects a chairman and a secretary. In the absence of either, or both, of these, the committee elects someone to act temporarily on their behalf;[31] the current work of the committee is conducted jointly between its chairman and the secretary, who is responsible for convening the members by invitation of the chairman of the council and in coordination with the chairman of the committee, or at the request of most of the latter's members. The invitation to convene the committee must be delivered at least twenty-four hours prior to the date and time of its convening and the members of the committee have to be notified of the agenda of the meeting.[32] Deliberations of the committees are in closed sessions, unless the members of the committee decide otherwise; the meetings are legal only in the presence of a (majority) quorum. Decisions are taken by absolute majority vote of those present. If there is a tie, the chairman casts the deciding vote.[33] The committees are entitled to ask the council chairman for information and clarification associated with subjects submitted for its consideration by any minister or senior member in the institutions of the PNA, and even to ask for their presence during the deliberation.[34] At every meeting of the committee, minutes are taken which include a list of members present and absent, a summary of the discussion, and the text of the resolutions. The minutes are signed by the committee chairman and by the official taking down the minutes.[35]

Every committee is obliged to submit a report on any subject referred to it, within a period laid down by the council. Should the committee be unable to keep to the timetable, the council chairman will ask the committee chairman for an explanation for the delay and will stipulate the time required for the completion of the report. The council chairman will present the matter to the council so as to get the latter's comment on the subject. The council is entitled to include the subject in its agenda, in which case the report is then submitted to the council chairman for inclusion. The report is printed and distributed among the members at least twenty-four hours prior to the time of the meeting at which it will be discussed. The report shall include the position taken by the committee on the subject referred to it, the background of the subject, and other views about it. The report shall also include the text of the proposals and their clarifications. The committee chairman then submits the report to the council. In the committee chairman's absence, the chairman of the council will ask the secretary of the committee or one of the committee members present to submit the report. The committees are entitled to ask the council chairman, via the secretary of the committee, to return any report that is being dealt with by it so as to complete the discussion on it, even after the council has begun looking into it, provided the council agrees to the request.[36]

At the beginning of every session of the legislative council, the chairman will inform the Council of Ministers of the bills and laws about which deliberations have not yet been concluded. If the Council of Ministers does not ask to look into them, they will be considered as non-existent. If the Council of Ministers asks to look into them, the bills and proposals will be referred to the appropriate committee.[37]

Functions of the Legislative Authority

The legislative council acts on a formal level as a parliament. It is identical, as far as its functions are concerned, to other parliaments in western democratic countries. It controls the actions of the other authorities and actions of legislation, etc. There follows a survey of the subjects the legislative council has dealt with since its foundation, through election, in January 1996.

(a) *Votes of confidence or no-confidence in the government.* The legislative council takes measures whose purpose is continuous control of the operations of the other authorities and particularly of the executive. It is entitled to summon to a discussion, or require clarification from, any minister of the Council of Ministers or any official employed in a government ministry; these individuals are legally obliged to appear before it. The council is in charge of holding votes of confidence in the Council of Ministers as a whole, or in one or more of its members; these ministers cannot begin to carry out their duties without having obtained a vote of confidence on the part of the legislative council by a regular majority.[38] The legislative council can, at the request of ten of its members, consider and approve a no-confidence resolution in the Council of Ministers or on the part of several of its members.[39] The president must then submit alternative candidates at the meeting of the legislative council following the meeting at which the no-confidence vote was taken.

(b) *Current control of operations by government authorities.* The legislative council supervises the current operations of government ministries by means of "interpellations". A member of the council is entitled to submit queries to the ministers and ask that they reply, on matters in which the questioner is interested, so as to confirm events that have come to the questioner's knowledge, or inform him or her as to what steps have been taken or will be taken on any given subject. The question or the request for a reply must be clear and lucid, and is restricted to the subject of the query, without any commentary.[40] Every council member is entitled to ask the minister concerned to peruse announcements or relevant documents connected to the query submitted to the council. The application for such a perusal must be submitted in writing to the council chairman,[41] who will pass it on to the minister concerned and will include it in the agenda of the next meeting to be held at least one week after the minister has received the query. The council will devote the first 30 minutes of its deliberations to queries unless the council decides differently.[42]

A minister will reply to queries brought before him which are included in the agenda. The minister is entitled to ask to defer the reply to the query to another meeting; the council will determine whether to allow this. In case of urgency, the minister is entitled to reply to the query at the first meeting after the query has been submitted, even if it was not included on the agenda. The minister will inform the chairman accordingly and the matter will be recorded in the minutes of the meeting.[43]

A council member who has submitted a query is entitled to ask for clarification from the minister and to react to his reply at once.[44] The reply to the query will be submitted, in writing, to the council chairman, who will determine a date for its reading, which will be brought for discussion as soon as possible. The time will be determined after the minister's reply has been noted. The discussion must not be extended for more than 10 days.[45]

After the minister has given his reply, the members are allowed to take part in the discussion. Thereafter, if the submitter of the query has not been convinced by the reply, he or she is allowed to explain why. The submitter and other members are entitled to deny confidence in the ministers, or in an individual minister.[46] The submitter of the query is entitled to withdraw it and to take it off the agenda. In such a case, the query will not be discussed unless five council members or more make a request. In accordance with the statutes, "queries are to get preferential treatment ahead of any other subjects on the agenda".[47]

In addition to queries of council members it is also possible to direct queries orally to ministers present during the discussions of the legislative council and to receive replies accordingly.[48]

(c) *Approval of the budget.* The PNA budget must be submitted for approval by the legislative council four months prior to the beginning of the financial year for which the budget proposal is earmarked. The Council of Ministers of the PNA will submit the annual budget proposal to the legislative council. The council will in turn convey the Budget Bill to the Budgetary and Financial Committee for examination and detailed comment. The committee will then submit its recommendations to the council within one month at the latest from the day on which the Budget Bill has been transferred to it. The council will hold a special meeting to discuss the budget in light of the report of the committee and its recommendations. The Budget Bill will be approved, or returned to the Council of Ministers with the comments of the legislative council, in which case the Council of Ministers will make the necessary amendments and return the Bill to the legislative council for approval.[49]

(d) *Legislation.* The legislative council is responsible for drafting and promulgating laws, which can be submitted either as government-initiated bills by the Council of Ministers or a minister representing that council, or as private bills of a group of members of the legislative council. The Council of Ministers is entitled to submit bills for legislation in the legislative council. These laws can be submitted to the Council of Ministers by ministers, in accordance with their responsibility,[50] or by the PNA Chairman. The Council of Ministers will transfer the bills to the council chairman together with a submission of the reasons why the matter is to be brought before the legislative council. In addition, a member or a group of members is entitled to promulgate a new law, or to amend or abolish an existing law. The Council of Ministers is entitled to request the return of a bill it has submitted, before a vote on it is taken. The secretary of the council will send a copy of any bill which is to be presented to the council to every member, together with written explanations for its submission, three days prior to the time set for presenting the bill to the council. Every proposal will be conveyed together with written clarifications and basic principles, to the appropriate committee for comments. The council is entitled to read the proposal after its transfer to the committee, or to decide that the proposal and its elucidations will be printed and distributed among the members.[51] Following approval of the bill at first reading, the council chairman refers it to the appropriate committee which will be asked to consider the proposal and all its sections, and to approve it and return it to the council plenum.

Following approval by the committee, the discussion of bills takes place in two separate readings. At the second reading, discussion is restricted to a vote on the amendments proposed, and the sections and paragraphs amended. Thereafter, a final vote is taken, which includes the approval of the bill. A third reading takes place at the behest of the Council of Ministers or of five council members;[52] discussion at this stage will begin with the presentation of the general principles of the proposal. The council is entitled to decide to read the report of the committee before the start of the discussion.[53]

Should the council not reach a decision, the bill will be rejected. If the council does reach a consensus on the bill, the discussion on the various sections or paragraphs will begin, one by one, after the council members have read the elucidations accompanying the respective sections and paragraphs. Voting will take place on every section separately and thereafter on the bill as a whole. Bills are approved by an absolute majority of council members. Once a law has been approved by the legislative council, it will be referred to the Chairman of the PNA for approval and will thereafter be published as required.[54]

(e) *Current discussions on national subjects.* The council regularly holds current discussions on subjects that are of concern to the Palestinian people in general and to those under the rule of the PNA in particular. *Inter alia*, discussions are held on strategic matters associated with the peace process, on the resolution of the Palestinian problem and its ramifications, including relations with Israel, as well as on daily subjects associated with the lives of Palestinians in exile, in the West Bank, and in the Gaza Strip. The council from time to time hosts foreign personalities who visit the Palestinian Authority. On occasions the council sends a special delegation to foreign countries or international congresses so as to explain the situation in the Palestinian Authority in general and the activities of the council in particular.[55] The decisions of the legislative council on subjects of general discussion on political, social and economic themes are not binding, but they constitute a position representing the council, which in turn represents all the Palestinians in the West Bank and the Gaza Strip. In this respect the legislative council constitutes a unique forum in the West Bank and the Gaza Strip for deliberations on the positions of all the Palestinians under the administration of the PNA.

The Rules of the Legislative Council

The plenary session of the legislative council is convened by invitation of the PNA Chairman. In its regular annual conventions, the year is divided into two sessions – each of which lasts for four months. The first session begins in the first week of February, the second session in the first week of September. In addition, the council is convened for special sessions by invitation of its chairman, or following a request on the part of the Council of Ministers or of one-quarter of the members of the council. Unless the council chairman has convened such a gathering, the gathering will be held at the place and time requested by the council members or the Council of Ministers.[56]

The sessions of the council will be open to the public at large unless the council's chairman decides otherwise. The meeting convenes two days a week, on Wednesdays and Thursdays, unless the council has decided differently.[57] The council will decide if the current discussion should be in open or closed session: the decision will be taken after submissions from two of those supporting and two of those rejecting the closure to the public have been heard.[58] When the council convenes *in camera*, all those who had been permitted to enter the plenary hall and the balconies are asked to leave the premises. Nobody except members of the council are present at the meeting, except with the council's approval. None of the council officials are present during *in camera* deliberations, unless the council chairman has permitted them to be present.[59] At the end of a discussion in closed session the chairman will obtain the council's consent to terminate the *in camera* part, and the session will again be open to the public.[60] The secretary will take down the minutes of closed sessions, which are kept in the General Secretariat of the council. Only members are allowed to peruse them. By majority decision, the council is entitled to publish them, in full or in part.[61]

A convention of the council is considered as valid in the presence of more than half the number of its members. Decisions are taken by absolute majority of the members present, except for those cases in which a special majority is required. At the time of convening, if the required quorum has not been attained the chairman shall defer the opening of the meeting by half an hour. If by then the required quorum is still not attained, the chairman shall defer the meeting for another date, which must not be later than one week from that day.[62]

The council chairman will inform its members of the agenda at least two days before the council convenes. A subject not appearing on the agenda shall not be discussed, except by request of the PNA Chairman, the council chairman, or by request in writing submitted by at least 10 council members. The council will decide on this after hearing for five minutes an explanation by one of the submitters of the request and by one of its rejecters, and by absolute majority vote of the members present, except for extraordinary cases, as detailed in the statutes[63] (for example, in cases in which the council is host to a member of the Council of Ministers or other senior public figure who has come to deliver an address to the council, which convened for this purpose, without the subject having been included in the agenda).[64]

With the consent of the council, the council chairman may announce a break in the meeting or its termination, and also the day and time of the next meeting. The chairman of the council is entitled to convene the council before the date fixed if this is justified by external events, or at the behest of the Council of Ministers.[65]

At every meeting, detailed minutes are to be taken with regard to all matters with which the meeting deals, of all the subjects that were brought up, of all the discussions held, and all the decisions taken.[66] After confirmation of the minutes, the chairman and the secretary sign them. The minutes are kept in the archives of the council and are published as a special publication of the council.[67] The secretary of the council distributes the council's decisions and the minutes of the previous meeting among members twenty-four hours prior to the opening of each meeting. These decisions and the minutes will be considered as official so long as no reservations have been registered with regard to them.[68]

The statutes concerning speeches during meetings point out that nobody will be allowed to address a meeting unless he or she has asked beforehand for the right and until permission has been given to this effect by the chairman. The chairman will not withhold the possibility of addressing the meeting for any reason not justified by the internal statutes. In the case of differences of opinion, the council will hold a vote and will reach a decision without discussion.[69] The secretary of the council is responsible for organizing the applications to address the meeting, by chronological order of submission. An application for the right to speak on a subject that has been transferred to one of the committees will not be accepted except if that committee has submitted a report on the matter.[70]

The chairman will give the right of speech in accordance with the order that has been determined. In the case of controversy, the right of speech will be given first to supporters of the proposal, then to anyone wishing to introduce an amendment, and finally to any individual voicing objections. Each of those requesting the right to speak is entitled to renounce his or her turn in favor of a peer, who will address the meeting instead.[71]

A member shall not speak more than twice on the same subject, once in the course of the general discussion and once when proposals, programs and resolutions are brought up.[72] The council chairman is entitled to allow ministers to address the meeting each time they ask to do so if the subject of the discussion is associated with the spheres of activity of their ministries.[73] However, in special cases, mentioned in the statutes hereafter, it is permissible to address a council meeting: (a) to draw attention to the need to abide by sections of the Constitution and of the internal statutes, (b) to ask for a deferment, (c) to correct a fact brought up in the course of the discussion, (d) to comment on a statement which is detrimental to the person who asked to be granted the right to speak, and (e) to defer dealing with the subject under consideration until a resolution has been reached with regard to another subject. All these petitions have priority over the original subject. They oblige a cessation of deliberations until the council has decided on the matter. In these cases, no right of speech will be granted until the person speaking has finished his or her address, except for a petition to draw attention to the relevant sections of the Constitution and the internal statutes or to correct a fact which has been included in the argument.[74]

As regards presentation, the statutes point out that a council member who addresses the members "will not repeat his words or the words of his peer and will not digress from the subject under discussion". The right to draw attention to such a matter is given to the chairman only. The chairman is also entitled to draw the attention of the speaker to the fact that a view has been clearly articulated and that there is no need to speak any further.[75]

From the point of view of the contents of a member's speech, general restrictions have been mentioned, the main feature of which is: "A speaker shall not avail himself of expressions which are not appropriate and he shall not do anything that can be construed as a violation of the statutes."[76] The chairman is entitled to call by name a speaking member who has violated this section, and he can draw attention to the need to respect the statutes. If the need arises, the chairman is entitled to prevent the speaking council member from continuing to speak. If the member objects to the decision, the chairman will accept the view of the council, which will reach a decision without discussion.[77] The speech should not be interrupted while it is ongoing and no remarks should be directed at the speaker. The right to draw attention to the speaking member, at any time during an address, to the need to respect the internal statutes, is exclusively reserved to the chairman.[78]

The council has the right to punish a member who violates the statutes or does not comply with a decision of the council prohibiting an address to the council, in one of the following ways: (a) preventing the speaker from speaking until the end of the meeting, (b) evicting the speaker from the plenary hall and prohibiting that individual from taking part in deliberations on other subjects on the agenda, and (c) prohibiting the speaker from participating in the work of the council during a period not exceeding two weeks. The council will reach a decision on this matter in the course of the meeting itself and after the member or the member's representative has voiced a view.[79] The chairman is entitled to take action against a member who does not comply with a decision of the council requiring the member to act in accordance with the rules.[80]

If order has broken down and the chairman is unable to restore it, he will announce a break in the session. If order is not restored, he will discontinue the meeting for at least half an hour. If the disturbance continues after the session has been reconvened, the chairman will defer it and will announce the date of the next meeting.[81] The council is entitled to accelerate the deliberations on any subjects which its members are confronted with or to determine an earlier date for them, and it can even decide on an earlier date for special cases such as a vote of confidence, a vote of no-confidence, and with respect to voicing reprimands and criticisms with regard to the executive authority or one of the ministers, without a discussion.[82] In cases defined as urgent, the council and its committees will discuss these subjects as a matter of priority, and the sections dealing with the times of deliberations will not be applicable to them. The council is entitled to decide to consider any subject during the very meeting itself. In such a case, the committee concerned will submit its report to the council immediately, in writing or orally.[83]

If the subject which has been defined as urgent is a bill, the council will refer it to the committee concerned, to establish whether it is justified in discussing the matter and to examine the subject. The committee will submit a report and only thereafter will the subject be presented to the council. The council will express its view as to whether there is a need to consider the bill. The council is entitled to decide whether to consider bills without first referring them to committees.[84]

Discussion in the council may come to an end after at least two supporters of the subject and two of its objectors have voiced their views; discussion ends either following a proposal of the chairman if in his view the subject has been adequately considered, or on the strength of a motion by at least five council members, providing the minister concerned has been allowed to address the council immediately after the last speaker.[85]

A proposal to terminate the discussion will not be allowed, except after one of the supporters and one of the opponents have been granted the right of speech for at least five minutes. Priority will be granted to whosoever originally asked to speak on the subject. Thereafter, the council will decide whether to terminate or to continue the discussion. If it is decided to terminate the discussion, a vote is taken on the original subject.[86] After the discussion has been terminated and prior to a decision having been arrived at, the right of speech cannot be requested except to define the structure of the question in regard to which a vote is being held.[87]

After termination of the discussion the chairman of the council requests that the subject discussed is put to a vote.[88] If the subject for discussion contains several matters, every council member has the right to ask the council chairman to split the discussion accordingly. A decision will be reached for every and each matter separately.[89] The decisions of the council are obtained by an absolute majority of the votes of the members present. Before the vote is taken, it has to be ascertained whether there is the legal quorum required for an orderly vote on the subject under discussion. If the voting concerns a basic law of the regime, a named vote must be taken. Otherwise, voting is exercised by lifting the hand, by members getting to their feet, or by secret ballot, the method being chosen by majority decision.[90] Thereafter, voting will take place.

In case of a tie, there is one repeat vote only. If there is a tie again, the side with whom the chairman voted[91] will decide the issue. A member who abstains is entitled to clarify the reasons for his abstention after the vote has been taken and before its results have been published.[92]

Those abstaining are neither supporters nor opponents of the motion. Should the number of members who voted be smaller than what is required in order to reach a decision, the subject under consideration will be deferred to another meeting. At the next meeting, a decision will be reached by an absolute majority of those participating in the vote *de facto*, even if their number is smaller than is required for a majority as a result of abstentions.[93]

The chairman will then announce the result. A subject on which a vote has been taken may no longer be discussed, except for those cases mentioned in the statutes.[94]

The Legislative Council in Action

The Palestinian Legislative Council was elected on January 20, 1996, and held its first meeting on March 7, 1996. In the course of more than 30 months that elapsed between then and the end of 1998, the council held 68 regular meetings and eight extraordinary meetings, which were held in the course of three sessions. During that period the council attained a number of achievements within the framework of the declared aims of any parliament, but at the same time it failed in other operations and many of its decisions were not a success. The activities of the council from the day of its election up to the end of 1998 can be divided into seven different spheres.

First, *laws*. Up till the end of 1998, 46 laws were brought to the council for consideration and of these, 30 were proposed to the council by the Government; there was one law, a basic law, which was referred to the council by the minister of justice; and then there were eight laws referred to the council by the different committees and by seven council members. The council approved some of these laws, and others are still under consideration. Deliberations with regard to certain laws were postponed and other bills were not accepted at all.

Second, *decisions*. The legislative council has published a great many decisions on political, economic, social and various administrative issues. Up to the end of November 1998, the council published 344 decisions or resolutions, most of which bore the mark of recommendations to the executive authority and many of which were not binding because they were not approved as laws. This fact detrimentally affected the link between the legislative and the executive authority. In addition, dozens of other decisions were no more than manifestations of opinions of a political character and many others dealt with the readings of laws and the reports of the committees.

Third, *general budget*. The general budget of the Palestinian National Authority has been submitted to the legislative council twice: a budget for 1997 and a budget for 1998. In addition to these two cases, the budget was delayed for some months.

Fourth, *votes of confidence in the Government*. The legislative council has passed a vote of confidence in two governments presented to it by President Yasser Arafat: for the first time on June 27, 1996, after deliberations on the basic lines[95] of the Government, which were presented to it by the President. Fifty members voted in favor of granting confidence in the Government and 24 voted against. The rest abstained or absented themselves. On the second occasion, on August 8, 1998, 55 members voted confidence in the Government and 28 voted against. Three members abstained and one absented himself.

Fifth, *criticism and posing queries.* The legislative council took a number of measures to promote methods for control and criticism and for submitting queries, i.e., setting up commissions of inquiry, posing queries to ministers, interrogating and accepting complaints from citizens. All of this was in addition to the task of the Control Committee of the Committee for Control and Human Rights, to investigate findings in matters concerning general freedoms and human rights – both on the strength of an initiative by the committee.

As to commissions of inquiry, by means of investigating some of its members the council succeeded in disclosing a number of cases of corruption in the Palestinian Authority. The most important case was the affair of the spoiled flour, which was uncovered in Nablus in March 1997. In addition, the committee examined many cases of corruption which had been discovered and had come to the knowledge of the public at large, the most important of which was mentioned in a report by the authority for public control.

Sixth, *parliamentary links and foreign relations.* In the course of the first four years of the PLC establishment, the council has maintained successful parliamentary and foreign relations, which have found their expression in the council's receiving parliamentary delegations and political leaders from many countries, and dispatching parliamentary delegations for visits to parliaments abroad. The aims of these links were twofold: to learn from the parliamentary experience of other countries, and to obtain support for Palestinian positions.

And seventh, *institutional construction.* From the point of view of institutional construction, the legislative council succeeded in stabilizing its internal structure and could register a number of achievements in spheres associated with the council itself – such as the internal statutes of the council, which were approved. The various sections of the internal statutes lay down the composition of the committees, the order of speeches and the manner of voting, the taking of minutes, membership issues, deliberations on the submission of bills, and matters pertaining to the immunity of the members of the council. At the beginning of each session, the permanent committees of the council are elected and their spheres of responsibility defined. A number of departments have also been set up which serve the activities of the council, namely: the Legal Department, the Public Relations Department, the Administrative Department, the Library Department, the Department for Parliamentary Research, the Department for Matters of the Council, the Department for Financial Affairs, the Department for Public Relations, the Technical Department, and the

Computer Department. Regional offices for members of the council have been opened all over the West Bank and the Gaza Strip – a step which is intended to improve the connection between the public and the members of the council; there are 16 of these regional offices. A special Guard unit (the "Council Police") has been set up, whose task is to safeguard the security of the council and its members and to ensure the orderly functioning of the council and of its meetings. The members of the Guard are dressed in special uniforms, which they received when the unit was established.

The Executive Authority

The Declaration of Principles signed between the PLO and the Israeli government on September 13, 1993, included a General Agreement for the setting up of "the Council", "which will be elected by the Palestinian people in the West Bank and the Gaza Strip". Section 7 of that Agreement mentions that the Interim Agreement will include a clear definition of the legislative authority and the executive authority of the council, the implication being that the council would have precisely defined legislative and executive tasks and authority. The Interim Agreement included a special reference to a council that would have tasks of legislature and execution, and the executive authority was understood to be a system fully subordinate to the council. The Agreement contained a special section which defined the character and the composition of "the executive authority of the Council", which would conduct the affairs of the Palestinians "on behalf of" the council. Its members were to be from among the elected members of the council, and the Chairman of the Executive Authority, elected parallel to elections to the council, would have the right to appoint to the executive authority 20 percent of members who were not members of the council.

After the initial design following the elections of January 1996 the executive authority described itself as constituting a government composed in principle of two main legal bodies, the President and the Council of Ministers, in addition to the various government ministries.

The President

The President of the PNA is the highest governmental authority together with the Council of Ministers, whom he appoints and heads. They constitute the executive authority of the PNA. According to the Interim Agreement between Israel and the PLO, the President "will be elected directly by the Palestinian constituency".[96] It was also provided for in the Agreement that "the head of the Authority is a member of the executive authority of the PNA". The same rules of election, swearing-in and functions of the President were repeated in greater detail in the Basic Law of the PNA approved at the third reading by the legislative council, without the approval of Arafat.[97]

In that same law it was noted again that "the President of the PNA is elected in general and direct elections by the Palestinian people, in accordance with the Law for Palestinian Elections".[98] There were also regulations for the beginning and termination of the tenure of the President, so for instance it was stated that after the elections "the President will be sworn in, will give the oath of allegiance to the Legislative Council, in the presence of the Chairman of the National Council and the President of the High Court" in accordance with the formula "In the name of Allah, I hereby undertake to be loyal to the homeland and its sacred values, to the nation and to its national heritage. I undertake to respect the constitutional rule and its laws and to care for the interest of the Palestinian people and give it my full concern, and God be my witness."[99] It was also determined that the duration of the tenure of the President of the National Authority would be an interim phase. Afterwards the President will be elected by law. The additional rules for the termination of the President's work are in accordance with the Basic Law of the Authority No. 1. The Office of the President of the National Authority will become vacant in one of the following cases: "(a) Death. (b) Resignation submitted to the Palestinian legislative council and accepted by a two-thirds majority of its members. (c) Loss of legal competence, in reliance on a decision of the high court for the Constitution and by consent of the Legislative Council by a two-thirds majority of its members." In each of the cases mentioned above it was laid down by law that "the Chairman of the Palestinian Legislative Council accepts upon himself the functions of the chairmanship of the PNA temporarily and for a period not exceeding two years. In the course of this period, there will be free and direct elections for the election of a new president in accordance with the Palestinian Election Law."[100]

In addition to what is laid down in the agreements and the law – that the President serves as the head of the executive authority, including the Council of Ministers – a number of functions for the President have been specifically laid down in the Basic Law, which states that "the President of the National Authority is the supreme commander of the Palestinian forces".[101] It has also been laid down that "the President of the National Authority will appoint representatives of the National Authority in states, international organizations and in overseas bodies and will decide as to the termination of their term of duty. The President will receive letters of accreditation of the representatives of these bodies in the Palestinian National Authority."[102] It was also noted that the President is entitled to submit bills for the approval of the legislative council, to publish regulations, and to take measures required for the execution of the laws. It has also been laid down that it is in the competence (and the obligation) of the President to publish approved laws "within thirty days from the date on which they have been conveyed to him after having been approved by the Palestinian legislative council".[103] In addition, it is within the jurisdiction of the President in accordance with the Basic Law "to grant personal pardon from punishment or to reduce punishment".[104]

As well as all the functions and powers bestowed upon the President, the Basic Law also bestows on him unlimited jurisdictions for "publishing decisions which have the validity of a law" in "case of need that cannot be delayed and at times in which the legislative council does not assemble",[105] even though it is also noted in the law that these decisions must be presented to the legislative council at the first meeting following the publication of these decisions. All these functions show the very substantial powers that are vested in the President of the PNA.

The Council of Ministers

The Council of Ministers consists of the members of the government who are responsible for various portfolios: together with the President they constitute the Government; each of them is responsible for one or more specific areas and is called a "minister". Although the Interim Agreement stipulated that at least 80 percent of the ministers should be among the elected members of the legislative council, the Basic Law of the Authority did not mention this condition even though it did state that "every member in the Council of Ministers shall be an elected member in the Legislative Council, but the President is entitled as an exception to appoint ministers who are not members of the Legislative Council". There is no clear stipulation about the number of ministers whom the President may appoint. Every minister is obliged, by law, to swear an oath of allegiance before the President, before starting to deal with the affairs of his ministry.

The legislative council is a body directly subordinate to the President which helps him to manage the affairs of the state; each minister is responsible for the conduct of the ministry which has been entrusted to that individual. It is possible for a minister to be responsible for more than one ministry, in accordance with what is written in the letter of appointment and subject to the approval of the legislative council, except for ministers "without portfolio", who have to be appointed by the President.

In general, the legislative council as a joint body is responsible for the drawing up and defining of general lines of policy of the Authority and of each ministry separately; for the execution of the policy of the Authority in accordance with the decisions of the government or of other lawful bodies such as the legislative council and the judicial authority; for the preparation of budget proposals and their submission to the legislative council; for the preparation of government-sponsored bills and their submission for the approval of the legislative council; for the execution of laws and a close follow-up of their correct enforcement by issuing regulations, the purpose of which is to be of assistance in implementing the laws and overseeing the implementation of policies by each ministry or any other government authority; and for deliberations on the policy of the Authority and its implementation.[106]

Every minister in the Government will be responsible for proposing specific lines of policy for the ministry under his or her jurisdiction; for the follow-up of the implementation of the policy of the ministry; for responsibility for conducting the current affairs of the ministry and for issuing regulations that assist the implementation of the budget earmarked for the ministry; for specific bills pertaining to the ministry *vis-à-vis* the Government; for delegating executive powers to the director-general of the ministry or the heads of departments in the ministry; and for submitting a detailed report on the activities of the ministry to the Government and to the legislative council or to one of its committees, for deliberation and approval.[107]

The Ministries of the Government

Government ministries function as arms of the executive authority, and are responsible for carrying out government policy. There are 22 government ministries responsible for defined spheres of activity.

1 *The Ministry for Local Government Affairs.* Under the existing political conditions of the Palestinians in the West Bank and the Gaza Strip, this is an important ministry, since it is responsible for a great many spheres concerning the daily life of the population. The minister is responsible for instituting a regional legislative council in every area with a Palestinian population where there are 1,000 inhabitants or more. The minister is also responsible for narrowing the gap between the Palestinian village and the Palestinian town by: initiating and developing infrastructures in rural areas; supplying financial support for essential projects required by the population; giving priority to the development of water supplies and road construction, constructing sewage lines and waste disposal, and developing infrastructure in municipalities; promoting the qualifications of the manpower employed by municipalities; founding a union of local authorities for the exchange of information and expertise; and having responsibility for the structural planning of Palestinian towns and villages, including names and street numbers in Palestinian towns. Top priority is given to projects involving water, refuse collection and the internal roads of the Palestinian villages and towns.

2 *The Ministry of Labor.* The ministry's responsibilities cover labor and professional training. It deals with organizing labor contacts with a view to ensuring stability and raising productivity as well as reducing unemployment; coordinating joint efforts with other ministries and authorities to promote a coordinated labor policy, including rules of supervision; supplying professional and vocational training, and raising standards in line with the requirements of development schemes; organizing the affairs of foreign laborers and supervising their working conditions; assisting in the setting up of a general institution and legislation for social insurance that will achieve social security for employees; regulating legislative proposals pertaining to working and environmental conditions; supplying means of work security and locating opportunities of employment for Palestinian manpower; investigating, collecting and preparing the statistical data pertaining to wage policy and laying down minimum wage rates; establishing the legal, organizational and constitutional criteria for defining relations at work, in particular individual and group-related relations; overseeing research; initiating training with a view to improving the economic and social situation of workers, the registration of labor organizations and employers' organizations and their societies, and supervision of their activities; caring for the work environment, work safety, and prevention of injuries and diseases relating to employment; and the publication of instructions and laws relating to work safety.

3 *The Ministry of Culture.* The ministry is responsible for the development and management of affairs to do with culture and the arts under the auspices of the National Authority. It deals with the setting up of a college for music and theater, and a national library and cinemas; setting up new cultural centers; supervising the professional studies of arts center staff; developing Palestinian folklore, arts and popular professions; supporting general libraries and promoting the publication of books and printed materials (magazines) of a cultural character; participating in theater and arts festivals, and in meetings (symposia), in order to strengthen the links between the ministry and the Palestinian people, particularly writers and artists; strengthening cultural activity within the Authority; promoting cultural and artistic activity; and preparing legislation with regard to the many different levels of cultural activity of Palestinian society.

4 *The Ministry of Transport.* The ministry has accepted responsibility for the preparation, design and implementation of projects such as the construction of main roads and streets within villages; and for maintaining roads in a usable state. The ministry is responsible for examining the materials in use in the construction projects, and assuring their compatibility with requirements of the Standard Institute for Building Construction. The ministry also carries out theoretical and practical research into projects, based on accepted engineering practices. The

ministry recognizes its obligations in the training of contractors; it also prepares plans for training engineers and students of other technologies, thereby promoting their scientific and practical standards. The ministry is responsible for establishing direct and indirect road routes, and railroads between the Gaza Strip and the West Bank; for the construction of a coastal road for the development of tourism in the Gaza Strip; for the improvement of the main road connecting the north of the West Bank with the south; and for the improvement of the network of local roads in the West Bank and the Gaza Strip.[108]

5 *The Ministry of Communications and Postal Services.* The ministry is responsible for the development of the existing telephone exchanges and for constructing new ones; setting up new cable networks; expanding and developing existing networks; and expanding and setting up new telephone networks at locations were there are no telephone lines in Palestinian towns and villages.[109]

6 *The Ministry of Social Affairs.* The ministry is responsible for implementing the policy of the PNA in the spheres of social affairs for all age groups, and more specifically for dealing with citizens of all ages; for raising the standard of social services and assisting poverty-stricken groups of the population; for supervising the activities of welfare societies and of local and international social institutions, and laying down procedures and instructions for organizing the progress of work and its development; for developing social services by means of societies and authorities, and local development councils, and caring for the requirements of Palestinian society by means of administrative centers throughout all districts; for promoting the even-handed development of the various social services by raising the standards of all groups in need; for coordinating between the work plan of the Ministry for Social Affairs and the institutions of the PLO; and for establishing training for ministry staff and issuing regulations in social affairs matters.[110]

7 *The Ministry of Health.* The ministry deals with the development, planning and implementation of projects in all areas relating to health. It is responsible for: rebuilding and expanding existing hospitals; renewing and replacing equipment; the setting up of health centers for village services; promoting first aid and setting up centers for this purpose; founding specialist laboratories and the establishment of a central laboratory in Ramallah and a branch in the city of Gaza; caring for health in schools; caring for the development of services for various age groups; promoting the welfare of the family and developing clinics and centers; promoting health education and training, and educating staff to achieve the necessary qualifications; issuing guidelines for preventive medicine and its development; promoting environmental health; conducting scientific research and planning information procedures; developing the expanding

health services for the armed forces; unifying and developing active branches which belong to the Palestinian Red Cross; and supervising hospitals and outpatient clinics.[111]

8 *The Ministry of Housing.* The ministry is responsible for affairs relating to housing and residence. It is responsible for the application of modern methods for utilizing state-owned land and its distribution in a just manner for housing projects; encouraging citizens to purchase apartments by arranging mortgages; promoting legislation to vouchsafe investment in housing projects; encouraging friendly societies and public cooperative societies; ameliorating the conditions of life in the refugee camps; and organizing regions that have built up spontaneously by providing them with the necessary infrastructures.[112]

9 *The Ministry of Justice.* The ministry carries out all the legal operations of the PNA. This ministry has set up a legal authority in the West Bank and the Gaza Strip which includes a supreme legal council. It standardizes laws; has set up a special legal committee for the study of projects that are submitted to the ministry, and will prepare projects under a uniform law that will be valid in the West Bank and the Gaza Strip; it will deepen the legal knowledge required by staff at the various law courts, and act for the organizational regulation of the legal profession by setting up a society of attorneys and giving the right to each and every Palestinian attorney to be a member in that society.[113]

10 *The Ministry of the Interior.* Arafat has reserved for himself the responsibility of this ministry. The most important aims that the minister of the interior intends to achieve are: preserving public security; issuing documents connected with civilian concerns such as passports and identity cards, etc.; carrying out the supervision of security at border crossings; appointing governors; and dividing up the responsibility between the various official bodies in the PNA.[114]

11 *The Ministry of Youth and Sport.* The ministry is in charge of the development of sports for Palestinians, and also cares for the current concerns of youth. The ministry regards as its task "to re-integrate the Palestinian youth into society; to foster the potential of Palestinian youth and strengthen the feelings of belonging and of nationalism among young people, as well as developing independence and a feeling of partnership, and increasing the understanding of democracy and social justice; to lay down and to prepare laws dedicated to a reorganization and reconstruction of the institutions for youngsters and sport, so as to ensure the functioning and the activity of young people in this sector; to set up the required infrastructure for furthering the sporting activities of youth by establishing youth centers and youth clubs, and by strengthening the function of clubs and centers, and of non-governmental youth institutions and societies; to work for the integration of young girls into society by

promoting their participation in all sport, social and cultural activities; to pay particular attention to the needs of disabled persons by means of plans aimed at their integration and preparation for participating in all social and sporting activities; to strengthen contact and solidarity with the Palestinian youth in the lands of exile, by taking them into consideration in all sports plans, so as to strengthen their feeling of national belonging; to strengthen the friendship and partnership between Palestinian youth and youth in other Arab countries and in the whole world; and to benefit from the proficiency of sportsmen and sportswomen, in addition to participating in festivals and regional and international competitions."[115]

12 *The Ministry of Industry.* The ministry is responsible for industrialization and industry under the PNA. It is responsible for preparing development plans, and the supervision and implementation of these plans; for designing the medium- and long-range policy of industrial development; for encouraging industrial investment; strengthening industrial cooperation with Arab countries and the world at large, and with Arab and regional organizations specializing in these spheres; and for issuing industrial certificates for new projects and for attending to their development. The ministry follows up problems in all spheres of the industrial sector and tries to find solutions where possible. It collects and analyzes industrial statistics, prepares standard measures for all sorts of merchandise and materials, and supervises their application; it issues a symbol of quality and an accompanying certificate, and participates in establishing industrial security statutes within institutions; it trains and selects administrative and technical staff for the branches under the supervision of the ministry, and establishes and develops industrial zones as well as encouraging investments in these zones.

13 *The Ministry of Economy and Trade.* The ministry is responsible for the execution of the policy of the PNA in the spheres of external and internal commerce and economic development. With regard to Israel, the ministry is responsible for protecting Palestinian rights in the spheres of economics and trade as laid down in the agreement of the Declaration of Principles and the Israeli–Palestinian economic agreement (the Paris Agreement), as well as for negotiating appropriate amendments to achieve a transfer of jurisdictions in this sphere from the Israeli side to the Palestinian side and to establish a network of Palestinian customs inspections. The ministry makes an effort to arrange free trade with Egypt and Jordan in addition to establishing links with the countries of the Arab Gulf so as to learn about, and benefit from, opportunities for establishing economic and trade contacts with these countries. In the international context the ministry tries to reach economic agreements that will advance the Palestinian economy. On an internal Palestinian level, the ministry is responsible for supporting the private sector and the establishment of

essential institutions; for activities to correct the negative trade balance of the PNA by developing a fund for national productivity; and by acting with a view to attaining the required laws for alleviating the situation of Palestinian merchants and supporting commercial activities in line with international law, as it is applied to the PNA by the International Trade Organization.[116]

14 *The Ministry of Muslim Consecrations and Religious Affairs.* The ministry is responsible for religious affairs and for the property belonging to religious bodies within the area of the Palestinian Authority. The ministry deals with the establishment of new fund holdings belonging to Muslim consecrations in many places in the West Bank and Gaza; it deals with the maintenance of the land and property interests of the Muslim Consecration and their utilization; it controls all the land and the property of the Muslim Consecration and registers them in the official gazette; and it sets up housing units and establishes public facilities on lands belonging to the Muslim Consecration. The ministry carries out large investment projects on such land, including improving mosques and burial places, and renovating buildings. The ministry supports societies and institutions for the study of the Qur'an in all regions, it organizes summer camps and has set up Islamic cultural centers and encouraged scientific research. It also organizes the season of the "Al-Haj" (pilgrimage to Mecca).[117]

15 *The Ministry of Tourism and Archeology.* The ministry is responsible for the structure of the official tourist establishment. The ministry reappraises existing laws and legislation within its remit. Among its tasks is to encourage the acceptance of the principle of tourism planning, which incorporates the elements of continuous development. The ministry seeks an active partnership in all regional and international organizations; encourages investments in tourism, especially in providing accommodation for tourists and building hotels; it is preparing and developing an infrastructure for Bethlehem, and provides services in various tourist ports; it endeavors to market external and internal tourism; and works to improve transportation and the freedom of passage between the various Palestinian districts.[118]

16 *The Ministry of Works.* The ministry is responsible for the design, implementation and maintenance of all development projects, including projects of the national armed forces if required; it supervises stone quarries and mines associated with building materials, since they are national assets; it carries out excavations of roads and the construction of bridges, and develops existing roads by maintaining and expanding them. It has prepared future plans for solving sewage and sanitary problems in Palestinian towns and villages. It has carried out an investigation about the percentage of rainfall and the movements of water in brooks and the possi-

bility of utilizing brooks for agriculture, or for storing the water in underground aquifers so as to increase the water reserves.

17 *The Ministry of Planning and International Cooperation.* The ministry is responsible for the development and supervising of foreign relations of the PNA and for preparing the long-term plans of the works of the Authority. Mr. Khalil Najem (the deputy director-general of the ministry) has declared: "The aims of the Ministry are to work for implementing infrastructure plans such as a network of roads, networks of pipes for drinking water, and projects of the air and sea ports. We also supervise areas connected to the welfare of women and work for defending women's rights, and to improve their conditions of life by means of economic and social development and by effectively utilizing natural resources."[119]

18 *The Ministry of Education and Study.* The ministry is responsible on behalf of the Authority for the development and strengthening of the systems, institutions and organizations in charge of education and study. It is in charge of raising the level of studies in colleges of higher education; for renovating and maintaining existing school buildings and constructing new ones; for renewing administrative systems through the use of computer programs; for improving study opportunity in Palestinian villages; and following policies that will increase the number of teachers in relation to the number of pupils, so as to improve performance and to raise the level of studies. The ministry has joint plans with the Ministry of Works with the aim of raising the level of technological and vocational education, and of increasing the number of pupils.[120]

19 *The Ministry of Finance.* In a special interview with *El-Melad* (The Birth) journal, Deputy Minister Dr. 'Atef 'Alawne[121] summed up the tasks and operation of the Ministry of Finance: "The Ministry of Finance has two primary aims: the supervision of the management of public funds represented in the budget of the PNA and its expenses; and to put in place a financial policy that will safeguard the implementation of Palestinian economic aims, and to adjust financial policy so that there should be no budgetary deficit."[122]

20 *The Ministry of Agriculture.* The ministry is responsible for agriculture, and for all matters concerning land and soil under PNA jurisdiction. In an interview for *El-Melad*, Deputy Minister 'Ata Abu Qersh[123] pointed out that the responsibilities of his ministry are as follows: "Setting up grants for agricultural machinery for the maintenance of agricultural equipment and its use in practical ways; supervising the border crossings and bridges for checking imports and exports of agricultural produce; supervising the water wells (*al-Jawffiyeh*) that had been dug spontaneously, and afterwards laying down a procedure for the digging of new wells."

21 *The Ministry for Citizen Affairs.* Officially, this ministry transfers the powers of the civilian rule from the Israeli authority to the Palestinian

Authority and works to resolve the daily problems that citizens encounter (for example border crossings), by supervising cooperation with the Israeli administration on entry and exit to areas of Palestinian control and the transfer of essential goods within them.[124]

22 *The Ministry of Information.* The ministry is in charge of information matters of the Authority on the international stage, with regard to Israel and the Palestinian areas. In an interview, the director-general of the ministry Mr. El-Mutawakkel Taha stated: "The Ministry of Information has, within the short time it has been active, succeeded in establishing stable principles for creating a strong media infrastructure to complete the tasks of attaining national independence and of achieving the establishment of the national state with Jerusalem as its capital."[125]

The Judicial Authority

In contrast to the legislative and the executive authority, which were established along with rules for their functioning which had been determined within the framework of peace agreements signed between Israel and the PLO, the judicial authority (which means the system of law courts and the office of state attorney) described in accordance with the Gaza–Jericho agreement and the Interim Agreement is under the jurisdiction of the PNA as part of the government structure that was set up in the wake of the agreements. It is a system that was established already many years ago and which continued to function during the rule of Jordan in the West Bank and Egypt in the Gaza Strip. In principle, the judicial authority also functioned under the Israeli occupation as part of the Israeli system of rule over the Palestinians. The Declaration of Principles and the Interim Agreement contained clauses which mention the need for an "independent judicial authority as part of the Palestinian National Authority".

Jordanian rule in the areas of the West Bank after 1948 was strengthened after the announcement of the unification between the two banks of the Jordan river on April 24, 1950, when the West Bank became an integral part of the Hashemite Kingdom of Jordan. In the wake of this announcement, the authorities started to embark on a number of changes, both legal and constitutional, so as to give clear expression to this unification. In 1952, the new constitution of the Kingdom of Jordan was approved; it referred to the two banks of the Jordan river. The law for "establishing a civilian system of justice" was also approved. In accordance with this law, the judicial authority in the Kingdom of Jordan was regulated; an announcement was made that the highest court would be the *El-Tamyeez* Court and that it would be at the head of a judicial hierarchy in the Kingdom. In accordance with the announcement of the constitution a law of "judicial independence" was promulgated in 1955. This law bestowed immunity to judges and employees of the state attorney's office and justified the announcement of the establishment of an independent judicial system which would be entitled to try members of the executive authority or of the legislative authority in cases in which this should prove necessary.

In accordance with the Jordanian constitution dating back to 1952, the judicial system encompasses three types of law courts: (a) Civilian law courts, which were law courts that could be divided into nine magistrates' courts; law courts for all the towns of the West Bank; three initial law courts which deal with matters digressing from the jurisdiction of a magistrate's court; law courts in the entire West Bank, in Jerusalem, Hebron and Nablus; a court of appeal which deals with examining appeals reaching the magistrates' courts or the initial courts and whose location is in Jerusalem; and the high court (*El-Tamyeez*), which is located in Amman and deals with appeals reaching it from the court of appeals or with matters pertaining to the constitution. In addition, and in accordance with the law for the setting up of law courts dating back to 1952, the institution of the state attorney was established. It consists of the chairman, his assistants, and representatives the state attorneys assign to the courts. (b) Religious courts are sub-classified into eight Shari'a courts, dealing with matters of the personal status of Muslims; and five courts for non-Muslim communities. (c) Unique courts which deal with unique subjects, the most important of which is the court for matters of land and soil, and the court for income tax.[126]

In the Gaza Strip, the Egyptians, unlike the Jordanians, preserved the structure of the judicial system that had been set up by the British as the rulers of mandatory Palestine. The law courts were sub-classified into three categories: (a) Civilian law courts, which were sub-classified into four magistrates' courts; courts for all the towns of the Gaza Strip; a court which dealt with subjects that digressed from the jurisdiction of the magistrates' courts (located in Gaza); a court for extensive claims, which dealt with major trespasses that might be punished by death; and a high court which dealt with appeals from the magistrates' courts, the central court or the court for extensive claims (also located in Gaza). (b) Religious courts, sub-classified into Shari'a courts dealing with matters concerning Muslims and a court for affairs of the Christian community. (c) Unique courts dealing with unique subjects.[127]

After the Israeli occupation in 1967, Israel created, as a governing force, military courts which dealt mainly with questions and cases of resistance on the part of Palestinians against Israeli rule. In accordance with a special military decree, the high court in the West Bank (which was located in Amman) was abolished and its jurisdictions were transferred to the court of appeals; the various unique courts were also abrogated. The Israeli military government took over all the jurisdictions of the various authorities and intervened in the jurisdictions of the civilian courts; the military government also changed procedures and judicial and legal rules by publishing more than 1,400 decrees on various subjects and setting up a large number of committees which focused on dealing with many issues concerning the lives of Palestinians under the occupation, such as property, land registration, the transfer of goods, subjects associated with natural resources, etc. Th Israeli military authorities thereby also severely restricted the spheres of responsibilities of civilian courts which had been left over under the Israeli administration.[128]

In the wake of the signing of the Declaration of Principles and the Interim Agreement, and of setting up the Authority, the military law courts created by Israel restricted their jurisdiction to areas which still continued to be under direct Israeli rule; the courts of law from the Jordanian period in the West Bank, and the Egyptian period in the Gaza Strip (except for the high court in the West Bank and the unique courts, which were abolished by Israel), continued to function as a judicial authority under the PNA. The main changes were seen in the fact that the various law courts were transferred from Jerusalem, which had been annexed to Israel, to areas of the West Bank, and that the law court for appeals established itself in Ramallah. The agreements included a specific reference to the judicial authority as a part of the political authority that functioned independently. In an interim summary it was pointed out in the chapter which introduces "the legal matters", that "the council, within the framework of its jurisdiction, will have legislative, executive and judicial responsibilities as mentioned in the agreement".[129] According to the first chapter, which describes the main points of the establishment of the council, there was talk about the council having executive functions, including "the authority to make appointments, to submit claims or to judge";[130] it was also pointed out that "in accordance with the rules of this agreement, the council will within the framework of its jurisdiction have a system of independent judicial powers, consisting of law courts and of a Palestinian judicial institution".[131] The Palestinian Authority established, from the beginning, a court for state security and military law courts.

In accordance with the Basic Law of the Palestinian Authority (the constitution), there is a clear emphasis on the independence of the judicial authority. The law states that "the independent judicial authority includes law courts of various categories and degrees. The law will lay down the manner of their establishment and the spheres of their responsibility. Their verdicts will be given in accordance with the law. The verdicts will be published and will be carried out on behalf of the Palestinian Arab nation." It was also stated in the Basic Law that "the judges are independent. There is no authority over them except the authority of the law, no authority is entitled to interfere with a judicial process or with issues of justice." With regard to the categories of the law courts, the Basic Law referred partly to this subject, mentioning, with regard to civilian courts, that "a high court for the constitution will be set up. And these are the matters with which it will deal: (a) The legitimacy of the laws, the regulations, the procedures and the like. (b) Giving interpretations to the text of the basic law and its sections. (c) Ruling in cases of a conflict of interests between judicial and administrative factors by living up to its judicial responsibility." It was also pointed out that "temporarily, the high court will deal with all the functions imposed on administrative law courts and on the high court for the constitution". With regard to the Shari'a courts, it is mentioned in the Basic Law that "matters of the Shari'a – the Islamic religious codex – and matters of personal status will be dealt with in Shari'a courts and religious courts, in accordance with the law".[132]

In the Basic Law it is declared that "military courts will be set up by special laws. These courts have no jurisdiction and no sphere of responsibility outside the framework of military matters." It was also mentioned in the Basic Law that "under the law, it will be permitted to establish law courts for matters of administration so as to deal with administrative conflicts and disciplinary claims . . . the other spheres of its responsibilities and the procedures of their work will be laid down by law"; the Basic Law also states that "the Attorney-General will be appointed by a decision of the President of the Palestinian National Council and in reliance on a recommendation of the highest council for matters of justice, with the approval of the Palestinian Legislative Council. The Attorney-General will deal with public claims on behalf of the Palestinian Arab nation, and his spheres of responsibilities and his obligations will be laid down by law . . . the law will regulate the manner of setting up the office of the Attorney-General and its spheres of responsibility. The conditions for appointing members of the general state attorney's office and their transfer, their discharge and their interrogation will be laid down by law."[133]

The proposed law for the judicial authority (still under consideration, February 2001) defines specifically the connection between the judicial authority and other authorities, its jurisdictions, its functions, its structure, its budget, the manner of appointing judges, etc. The same law states that "the judicial authority is independent, manages its own budget, and all its income and expenditure will be included under one paragraph of registration in the State budget";[134] the law as laid down from the point of view of the structure of the judicial system, comprises: "a court for the constitution, a high court; of courts of appeal, and of courts of the first instance as well as magistrates' courts."[135]

According to the proposed bill, the jurisdictions of the law courts will include acts of judgment in general, which will be carried out under the Authority. That is to say, "the law courts will decide on all sorts of conflicts and crimes"; the law courts will also have the jurisdiction of the judicial system to discuss or to abrogate any law, regulation of the law, or directive, which is not in conformity with the constitution, "if one of the litigating parties submits a claim with regard to the illegality of any regulation in the law or in any decree, and if the law court believes that there is a basis for its stance, the date to deal with the claim will be deferred and a new date will be fixed within three months for the purpose of re-submitting a claim to the court of the constitution . . . In any case in which courts of law think that a certain regulation in the law or a certain paragraph of any decree are not compatible with the constitution, the law courts are entitled to defer dealing with the claim at their discretion and to transfer the constitutional issue to the court (for the constitution), provided the decision contains a clarification about the instruction and aspects of the contradiction in relation to the defined constitutional text . . . Decisions of the court concerning illegality of the law in general or parts of it, oblige all the authorities of the State and the public . . . It has been ruled that if a law is unconstitutional the law ceases to be applicable, from the day after a decision has been taken. If such a verdict has been given with regard to a criminal section, the sentences that were published on the strength of that law will be null and void."[136]

The high court used to sit in the city of Jerusalem; the city of Gaza is its temporary seat at this time (February 2001). It will be composed of "the president, one deputy or more and a number of judges as required. Its benches will be laid down as required in accordance with the law and at the head of each bench there will be a president of the law court, his deputy or the oldest member. It is possible to compose a number of benches as required, each one having to be made up of five judges. In the high court, a professional office for professional rules and professional research will be set up. The office will be composed of a director and of a number of members from among the judges of the high court, as required."[137] The president of the high court will enjoy identical conditions to those of the head of the executive authority and the head of the legislative authority, from the point of view of salary, increments and pension.[138]

The court of law for the constitution has the same composition as the high court or a part of it. Under the law, "the general assembly of the high court will set up a body of seven or nine of its judges, according to circumstances, who will exclusively deal with the following subjects:

1   Judicial control of the legality of laws, regulations or procedures etc.;
2   Voicing commentaries to the instructions of the Basic Law and the various legislation;

3   Deciding on conflicts over the spheres of responsibility between judicial factors and authoritative administrative factors;
4   Dealing with dossiers or issues that were transferred to it by one of the benches of the high court."

The court of law for the constitution arrives at its decisions with a majority vote "so long as there is no aberration from the principle that this court itself has laid down in the past. In order to establish that there was such an aberration, there is need for a majority of five of its members if the court making the deliberation was composed of seven judges, or a majority of seven of its members, if it deliberated composed of nine judges."[139]

There will be three courts of appeal sitting in Jerusalem, Ramallah and Gaza. In each court, there will be a number of benches, each of which will have three judges, as required, and at the head of each bench there will be a judge of appeal, or in case of need, the oldest of its members will be its head. Its verdicts will be accepted by the three members.[140] The president of the court of appeal will enjoy the same conditions as those of a minister from the point of view of salary, increments and pension.[141]

In each area of jurisdiction of a court of the first instance, one or more magistrate's courts will be set up, which will be manned by one judge. The decision with regard to the seat and the region of jurisdiction of this court will be published by the Minister of Justice. In case of need, the magistrate's courts are entitled to hold their meetings at any location included in the area of their jurisdiction and this by decision of the president of the court.[142]

The general prosecution, which is part of the judicial authority, will be composed, in accordance with the law, of a Prosecutor-General, a deputy Prosecutor-General (or sometimes more than one), of the heads of the prosecution, of first-grade representatives of the prosecution, and of assistants of the prosecution.[143] From the point of view of jurisdiction and its function, the law states that "the general prosecution acts in accordance with jurisdictions that were vested in it by law and it alone has the right to submit criminal charge sheets (charge sheets of general justice) and to deal with them, so long as the law does not determine otherwise".[144] The functions of the general prosecution in the courts will be carried out by the Prosecutor-General or one of the other members of the general prosecution. The assistants of the general prosecution will carry out the assignments imposed on them, under the supervision and responsibility of members of the prosecution responsible for their instruction. It will not be permissible for any one whose grade is lower than that of the "head of the prosecution" to represent the general prosecution in the high court.[145] The officials of the judicial system are subordinate to the general prosecution as far as the implementation of their duties is concerned.[146] The law also states that it is the responsibility of the general prosecution to supervise the prisons and other locations in which criminal verdicts and detention orders are carried out.[147] The Prosecutor-General enjoys identical conditions to those of a minister, from the point of view of salary, increments and pension.[148]

To sum up, this chapter has explained the basic components of the Palestinian formal regime. The three powers (executive, legislative, and judicial), in addition to the elections procedure that will be explained in chapter 5, constitute the positive elements of the Palestinian partial democracy. This side of the Palestinian political regime draws its legitimacy from two sources. First, from the democratic and plural political life among Palestinians in the West Bank and Gaza Strip before the establishment of the PNA. Second, from the peace agreement between Israel and the PLO in which it was agreed that the Palestinian regime will establish executive, legislative and judicial powers, and keep them separate. However, to the detriment of the potential for a true democracy in the Palestinian entity, a proper separation of powers has not yet been achieved in practice. And this will be the focus of discussions in chapters 6 and 7.

5

The First Palestinian General Elections

On January 20, 1996, general elections were held within the West Bank and Gaza Strip of the Palestinian Authority – the first national elections in the history of the Palestinian people. In 1972 and 1976 elections had been conducted in a limited number of cities on the West Bank, with Israel's consent, as a goodwill gesture. These elections became an important step toward the building of the Palestinian national movement when some of the mayors elected then immediately declared their loyalty to the PLO. Thus, those municipal elections were one more step in the politicization of the Palestinians in the West Bank and Gaza Strip which had been occupied by Israel in 1967. The development of political pluralism and the estab-lishment of popular movements[1] contributed to preparing the ground for the *Intifada*, the subsequent peace agreements, and the general elections which were held in January 1996.

From the time of the announcement of the agreement between the repre-sentatives of Israel and the PLO to conduct elections in the West Bank and Gaza Strip, as part of the peace agreements,[2] the Palestinians themselves, the political international community and political scientists were occupied in a debate over two central questions: to what degree would these elections be a significant step in the process of emancipating the Palestinians in the West Bank and the Gaza Strip from Israeli domination, and establishing an autonomous Palestinian national entity; and to what degree would these steps be the beginning of the building of a democratic nation rather than an Arab totalitarian state?

This chapter analyzes various aspects of the elections, in an attempt to find preliminary answers to the above two questions. The election system, the election campaign, and the results will be examined in terms of demo-cratic theory in order to learn about possible political developments in Palestine in the future.

Students, scientists, politicians, and observers have debated the elections' contribution to the Palestinian people's emancipation from the occupation and to the establishment of an independent state. Two opposing viewpoints have emerged – in keeping with the views of the PLO, on the one hand, and of the Palestinian opposition, on the other. The negotiators for the Arab side (that is, representatives of the PLO and persons close to it) considered the elections an important step toward winning legitimacy so that they could conduct negotiations with Israel on the permanent settlement from a position of political strength. They believed that a strong election result would give greater force to their demands for Israel's evacuation of all the West Bank and the Gaza Strip and the establishment of an independent state. They perceived elections as an important step toward building the Palestinian state.[3]

The Palestinian opposition in the West Bank, the Gaza Strip and the Palestinian diaspora viewed the elections as one more step in the implementation of the Oslo Accords, to which they were opposed. They argued that these agreements did not promise the Palestinians what they were seeking – namely independence and the establishment of a state alongside Israel. They believed that the elections gave the Palestinian entity its final shape, with the elected institutions possessing sovereignty only over areas evacuated by Israel *up to the time of the elections*, and the concentrations of the Palestinian population, without any authority over the other areas in the West Bank and Strip, which would actually remain under Israeli control.[4]

The debate over the elections' effect and contribution to the process of democratization was largely parallel to the earlier debate. Those supporting the elections thought their effects would be decisive in the formation of a democratic regime and a pluralistic political system in the West Bank and Strip. Those opposing or holding reservations concerning the peace process looked on the elections as a sold game, manipulated by Israel on the one hand and the institutionalized Palestinian leadership on the other. They saw the elections as serving the purposes of a narrow oligarchy in the PLO leadership, who would continue to dominate because of the manipulations they employed to decide the elections in their favor. The elections' effect would thus be limited to providing legitimacy for this group, who would establish a regime of force, prepared to employ improper methods in order to maintain its domination.

Political scientists who have examined election processes, and the connections between them in legitimizing a regime and democratic institutions, have distinguished between elections that are part of a continuing process, as in traditional democracies like Britain, the United States, and elsewhere, and founding elections conducted at the beginning of a new era, like those held in 1990–1 in the former Communist countries as part of a transition to a new, democratic era, in which governments would be elected

every few years for specifically limited terms.[5] The latter type of elections
are conducted under transitional conditions and are not based on any
previous democratic tradition or regime. By definition, they are a stage in
the formation of a system and an important step toward the establishment
of a democratic political regime. But such elections are insufficient to determine the degree of democratic commitment of the system and those in
charge of it; two consecutive democratic elections, at least, are required,
including fair competition between contending forces and programs, to
permit any trustworthy generalizations about their democracy.[6]
Preliminary elections cannot be described as "free", because there can be
free elections only in conditions of a free regime and legitimate government
accepted by all the citizens. They can, however, lead to a democratic regime
and the formation of a system that will make it possible for opposition
forces to organize and bring about future changes in the regime.[7]

The Legitimacy of the Elections

The holding of elections in the West Bank and Gaza Strip, occupied by
Israel in June 1967, was an issue raised at various stages of the negotiations
between Israel, as the ruling power, and the Palestinians, represented by
either the PLO or local elements. The question of elections was placed on
the agenda at the Madrid negotiations, as well as during the negotiations
leading to the Oslo agreements and after their conclusion.[8] The elections
were considered to serve the Palestinians' local interests and help
Palestinian–Israeli relations, as well as the international aspects of the
agreement. Almost all the parties involved in the process and in the search
for compromise between Israel and the Palestinians favored holding elections.

Most Palestinians supported elections as a preparation for the transition
period.[9] Elections were considered the most fitting manner of choosing the
participants in the negotiations with Israel, and a means toward consolidating a democratic system different from the regimes in surrounding Arab
countries. It was also important for the Palestinian leadership to reveal a
strong commitment to the democratic process. They did not want to be seen
as holding on to the reins of power as the natural continuation of Arafat's
leadership move to the West Bank and Gaza Strip, but rather to offer a new
beginning based on the direct and democratic choice of the Palestinians
dwelling in the West Bank and the Gaza Strip. It was also important for
the leadership to win legitimacy for its measures in the course of the peace
process, by proposing itself as responsible for the process and winning the
trust of the Palestinian population.[10]

Israel, too (or at least those in Israel supporting the peace process), as well as the United States, Russia, and the countries of the European Union who were patrons of the peace process and those Arab countries that supported it, also had an interest in providing wide public approval of the peace process and the agreements between Israel and the PLO. The elections were seen as a Palestinian referendum ratifying the peace agreements and institutionalizing the ties with Israel. The elections would also enhance the status of the leadership with whom Israel was negotiating. Moreover, it was important for Israel to give some permanent status to the geographical areas concerned in the negotiations. Holding the elections only within those areas would delineate the boundaries of the future agreement and contribute to separating those "within" from those "without"; it would also separate the past aspirations of the Palestinian struggle for the liberation of all Palestine, including the territory upon which Israel had been established, from the present and the future, so that the boundaries of the Palestinian struggle would be limited to the West Bank and the Gaza Strip. Israel was also interested in the formation of an elected parliament, as an alternative to the Palestinian National Council, which would be controlled directly by the Palestinian leadership conducting the negotiations with Israel. The Israeli perception was that this format would assist in promoting the peace process. Such a body would act as a counterweight to the PNC, where the Palestinian opposition was relatively strong and could, under certain circumstances, torpedo the process.[11]

The legitimacy of the general elections in the West Bank and the Gaza Strip derives from the Agreement on Principles concluded in Oslo between Israel and the PLO and signed at the White House in the presence of the American President, Bill Clinton. Paragraph 3 of the Agreement, dealing with the elections, defined three guiding principles:

1   In order to enable the Palestinian people in the West Bank and the Gaza Strip to govern themselves in keeping with democratic principles, general, direct and free political elections will be held for the Council, under agreed-upon international supervision; the Palestinian police will care for public order.

2   The Parties will reach an agreement upon the definite form of the elections and its conditions . . . in order to hold the elections within a period which shall not be more than nine months after the Agreement on Principles goes into effect.

3   These elections will be an important preparatory step toward the attainment of the legitimate rights of the Palestinian people and its just demands.[12]

According to these paragraphs – which were ratified once again in the

Interim Palestinian–Israeli Agreement Concerning the West Bank and the Gaza Strip, signed also in the White House in September 1995, two years after the Agreement on Principles – it is clear that the elections depend on Israeli–Palestinian agreement; the legal authority for the elections, as for the Palestinian regime in general, is the peace treaty. This matter aroused a great deal of opposition among the Palestinians, especially among the opposition, who considered it a direct breach of Palestinian sovereignty and of one of the outstanding signs of independence.[13]

The agreement was formulated in keeping with the basic principles of democratic elections in their liberal, western form, guaranteeing free, direct and general elections with the aim of electing legitimate Palestinian representation with whom Israel would conduct the negotiations. A maximum period within which the elections would be held was also set, to dissipate fears on the Palestinian side that Israel might seek to draw out the timetable over a long period of time. The agreement also declared that the elections were not the end of the process but testimony of the beginning of a new era, in which the Palestinian people would be able to "fulfill its legitimate rights".

The issue of Palestinian inhabitants of Jerusalem voting in the election came on the agenda and found its solution by mutual agreement. The appendix to the Agreement on Principles and the text of the interim agreement mention that "Palestinians dwelling in Jerusalem will be able to participate in the elections according to the rules laid down in this agreement and in accordance with the special appendix." It was also decreed that the rules and orders concerning the elections would be agreed on by the parties. This was indeed implemented in the interim agreement, which was concluded about four months before the elections were held in 1996.

The Election System

The rules of the elections formed an integral part of the Israeli–Palestinian agreement. The declaration of principles contained a general approach to the system of the Palestinian elections, to the effect that "general, direct and free political elections to the Council" would be held in the West Bank and Gaza Strip, but without any specific mention of the election of the President of the Council. This agreement, in addition to separating the election of the Chairman of the Authority and the election of the members of the Council, contained full details of the rules according to which the elections were to be held. It also specifically mentioned the "law for the election of the Chairman of the executive Authority and the members of the Palestinian Council".[14] It was specified that this law would be formulated by the two parties, Israeli and Palestinian, who would abide by their decisions. The election law was ratified by the Authority Council and its Chairman, Yasser Arafat, in December 1995. The law contained an expanded version of the election rules as agreed upon in the Interim Agreement, including the appendices, which dealt with the subject of international observers and their status. The election rules, identical in content to the agreement and the election law, are presented below.

According to the interim agreement and the election law, elections for the Chairman of the Executive Authority and of the council would be held simultaneously, using separate ballots. The official date of the election would be announced by the Chairman of the Palestinian Authority in a formal order that would include official appointment of the members of the election supervisory committee and of the appeals committee. The dates for beginning to prepare the voters' roll and for presenting the candidates for elections would also be announced. The representatives elected would be responsible for governing "the regime in the interim period".

For the purpose of electing the Chairman of the Authority, all the territory of the West Bank (including Jerusalem) and the Gaza Strip would be considered one election district. For the purpose of electing the Council, the West Bank and the Gaza Strip were divided into 16 election districts. It was decided that each district would be allotted a number of representatives in proportion to the number of inhabitants with voting rights in the district (see table 5.1). Participation in the elections would be open to all Palestinians who had reached the age of 18 on election day, who were living in their election district, and whose names were on the voters' rolls. The exception would be citizens who had been deprived of their right to vote by court order or had been imprisoned for a crime or for public order offences.

Candidacy for membership in the council was open to every Palestinian who was 30 years of age or older on election day, and who complied with the other conditions applicable to voters. The candidate's name had to appear on the voters' rolls and candidates must have permanent residence in the district in which they were presenting their candidacy for membership in the council. The candidates' names could be tendered to the central or regional elections committee by an officially recognized party authority. Every party tendered a list of candidates in its name, their number not to exceed the number of seats allotted to the specific district. Independent candidates had to provide a list of at least 500 supporters from the specific election district, with their signatures. A person could not be a candidate in two districts or be a candidate for both the position of Chairman of the Executive Authority and membership in the council. Public functionaries, including ministers and civil servants, and employees in public institutions, including police officers and members of the security divisions, desiring to present their candidacy, must tender their resignation at least ten days before the last date to register their candidacy.

Table 5.1 Election districts and number of seats in the Council

District	Seats in Council	No. of voters	No. of voters per seat
1 Bethlehem	4	55,134	13,780
2 Hebron	10	133,084	13,300
3 Jenin	6	82,314	13,719
4 Jericho	1	12,906	12,906
5 Jerusalem	7	80,051	11,430
6 Nablus	8	111,651	13,950
7 Kalkilyia	2	27,278	13,639
8 Ramallah	7	79,108	11,300
9 Salfit	1	18,996	18,996
10 Toubas	1	15,914	15,914
11 Tulkarem	4	56,319	14,070
12 Northern Gaza	7	61,123	8,730
13 Gaza city	12	122,724	10,277
14 Dir Al-Balah	5	56,015	11,203
15 Khan Yunis	8	71,629	8,950
16 Rafah	5	44,034	8,800
Total	88		

Candidacy for the position of Chairman of the Executive Authority (the president) was open to any Palestinian who had the right to vote and was at least 35 years of age on election day. Every official and recognized party authority, or any citizen desiring to be an independent candidate, on presenting a list of 5,000 sponsors of the candidacy, with signatures, would be entitled to present the candidacy for the position of Chairman.

According to the election law, the Chairman of the Authority would be elected in national elections, with voters voting directly for the candidates. The candidate obtaining the largest number of votes would be declared the victor. In the special case of an equal number of supporters for the two leading candidates, the elections committee would cast lots between them in order to decide the winner. Should there be only one candidate for the position of Chairman, he would be declared the winner if the number of ballots supporting him was larger than the number of invalid slips and white slips testifying to abstention from voting.

Election of the members of the council would be through regional elections, with the voters voting personally and directly for the candidates who had presented candidacies in their district. Even in cases where the candidate was presented by a party list or a joint *ad hoc* list formed for the elections, the voter would indicate the candidate preferred by him or her among all those presented in the list. Every voter would have the right to vote for a number of candidates equal to the number of seats allotted the district, and he or she would be permitted to support candidates from different lists. The winning candidates would be those receiving the largest number of votes in the polls. In the event of equality between two candidates, the elections committee would cast lots publicly to decide the victor.

According to the election law, in the council elections six seats were reserved for Christians – five in Jerusalem, two in Bethlehem, one in Ramallah, and one in the city of Gaza. One seat was also reserved for the Samaritans in Nablus. In addition, Christians and Samaritans retained the right to enter the contest for the other seats in the districts in which they were dwelling. This feature added an important communal aspect to the electoral system and provided a basis for the distribution of power among the various groups within Palestinian society. This phenomenon was noted by Arend Lijphart as a dimension adopted by consensus by a number of countries – for example, Belgium and India currently, and Lebanon prior to 1975.[15]

The course and orderliness of the elections was supervised by the national elections committee and the regional committees subordinate to it, and also by polling committees in all those places where polls are situated. These would be aided by international and local election supervisors. The national committee would certify the results of the elections and publish them. According to the Interim Agreement and the election law, the national elections committee would be appointed "by a special order of the President of the Palestinian Authority, who would consult for this purpose with the other members of the National Authority". The committee would include among its members jurists, academics and lawyers known for their professional standing.

The Election Campaign

The term "election campaign" encompasses all the logistical considerations involved in preparing for elections, including: voters, candidates, election propaganda, polls, and international observers.

The voters

The Election Committee announced the opening of voter registration about two months before the elections and concluded the operation about a month before them. The number of voters whose names were published as eligible to participate totaled 1,028,280.

The registration of voters was conducted by officials appointed by the election committee for this task. Generally the registration officials were members of the educational system, who collected the registration forms by going from house to house. Except for Jerusalem, no special delays or problems were encountered. In Jerusalem, officials encountered some problems which held up the registration, mostly because of the opposition of some of the Palestinians, citizens of East Jerusalem, to registering, for fear of losing their Israeli identification cards and the benefits entailed, such as national insurance, unemployment insurance, etc. In some cases there were reports of violent opposition of some Jerusalemites to the registrars, and this demanded particular intervention on the part of Palestinian public leaders in the city.[16] The different estimations noted an especially large gap in Jerusalem between those eligible to vote according to the criteria of the election law and the Interim Agreement, and those prepared to be registered in voting rolls. In any case, Jerusalemites with Israeli citizenship, and not only non-Israelis with blue identification cards, were not eligible to participate in the voting. The former were required to waive their Israeli citizenship in order to participate.[17]

The candidates

Registration of candidates for Chairman of the Authority and membership of the council began on 19 December, 1995, a month before the elections. Official registration concluded at the end of December, but registration was opened for additional candidates in four districts – Jerusalem, Hebron, Khan Yunis, and the city of Gaza, by special order on Arafat's instructions. This measure aroused strong debate over its legality; some considered it an infringement of the rules of the election law, others thought the step necessary because of circumstances on the ground.[18]

On election day it was discovered that there were two contenders for the position of Chairman: Yasser Arafat, as the representative of Fatah, and Samiha Khalil, an independent candidate. Khalil, an inhabitant of Al-Bira, had been active in the Palestinian women's movement during the occupation period. The 88 council seats were sought by 725 contestants, that is, 8.7 contestants for every seat, a very large number from all points of view. This was caused mainly by the personal election system, which made it possible for any person able to collect a minimum number of signatures and a small amount of money to present a candidacy. The phenomenon testified to the deep divisions characterizing Palestinian Arab society in the West Bank and the Gaza Strip. These divisions can be found in all the election districts, as can be seen in table 5.2.

Table 5.2   Number of candidates compared to seats in each district

District	Seats in Council	Candidates	Candidates per seat
1 Bethlehem	4	30	7.5
2 Hebron	10	72	7.2
3 Jenin	6	36	9.0
4 Jericho	1	6	6.0
5 Jerusalem	7	52	7.4
6 Nablus	8	55	6.8
7 Kalkilyia	2	12	6.0
8 Ramallah	7	46	6.6
9 Salfit	1	11	11.0
10 Toubas	1	12	12.0
11 Tulkarem	4	38	9.5
12 Northern Gaza	7	67	9.6
13 Gaza city	12	92	7.7
14 Dir Al-Balah	5	50	10.0
15 Khan Yunis	8	66	8.2
16 Rafah	5	27	5.4
Total	88	672	*Average* 7.6

Although the elections were personal, the system permitted movements, parties, and also individuals to organize and present joint lists from which the voter could choose the candidates he or she preferred; that is, a voter could vote for candidates from different lists. On the voting form the candidates appeared in alphabetical order and not according to the lists to which they belonged. The 672 candidates included 559 independent candidates, who offered themselves on the basis of their previous activities or personal wealth, or as belonging to one of the larger clans in the specific district. In total 166 candidates were represented on election lists, 36 of them being new lists that had been established as the elections approached, and 130 representing pre-existing movements and parties. The distribution is shown in table 5.3.

Publicity

According to the election law, the term "publicity" encompasses "all the legal activities conducted by the party institutions and the candidates to explain their programs to the voting public". The law bars the Palestinian Authority from being involved in election publicity or trying to convince persons to vote for any specific candidate; but it assigns to the Authority the right and obligation to publish declarations stressing the importance of participating in the voting. The rule was openly broken, since even during the period of the election campaign, candidates for election continued to serve as ministers in the Palestinian Authority and thus enjoyed a clear advantage over the other candidates. There was also very strong newspaper coverage for members of Fatah and the Authority, and their associates, including Arafat himself, who during the course of the campaign enjoyed wide coverage in the press.[19]

Table 5.3 Distribution of candidates representing organizations and political parties

Movement	Number
Fatah	76
Peoples Party (former Communists)	25
Arab Liberation Front (temporary command)	8
Fidah Party (split from Democratic Front)	10
Al-Aksa Regiments (split from the Islamic Jihad)	4
Arab Liberation Front	4
Islamic Struggle Front	2
Palestinian Ba'th Party	1
Popular Struggle Front (new list)	11
National Movement for Change (new list)	2
Democratic National League (new list)	4
Progressive National List (new list)	5
The List of the Future (new list)	4
Freedom and Independence List (new list)	4
The National League (new list)	3
Free Meeting List (new list)	3

According to the law, election campaigning could begin only 22 days before the elections and had to come to an end 24 hours before election day. On the last day before the elections and on election day itself campaigning was totally banned. This rule, too, was blatantly ignored; the election publicity began with placards, stickers, signs and newspaper ads well before the end of December and continued into election day when that day's papers carried notices in the names of the candidates mentioning their candidacy and districts, and also conveying greetings for the beginning of the Muslim fast of Ramadan.[20] The election law had made the local election committees responsible for determining the sites where campaigning could be conducted by the putting up of posters or distribution of leaflets. The law also decided on the allotment of free time for the candidates to present themselves via electronic media. This rule also was broken: candidates distributed leaflets and hung their signs almost everywhere possible, while unequal amounts of time were allotted to the candidates on the radio.

In general, there was widespread use of the media, especially of the daily press, to transmit messages. According to a survey published on election day, election publicity took up about one-quarter of press space; the ads every day filled 23 of the total 92 pages of the daily papers. The survey also revealed, however, that only about half of the candidates, 359, used press publicity. These were generally the party candidates, candidates who could not rely on the votes of a specific sector or clan, or candidates who appealed to the general population and were financially in a position to pay the high costs of newspaper advertising. On the other hand, the survey revealed that most of the candidates had visited notables from the clans and the religious communities in order to win their "blessing" – a well-known traditional tool. This was all the more popular because the election district system gave great weight to local and traditional factors.[21] In summary, the candidates employed both traditional and modern tools in order to advance their cause and win support.

Election Centers and Polls: Each district had a number of voting centers in accordance with the number of voters in the district and the region's geographic conditions. In total, there were on election day 1,696 election centers, distributed as follows: Jerusalem – 165, Jericho – 22, Bethlehem – 88, Jenin – 145, Hebron – 230, Ramallah – 162, Salfit – 34, Toubas – 25, Tulkarem – 99, Kalkilyia – 54, Nablus – 175, Northern Gaza – 82, Gaza city – 183, Khan Yunis – 106, Rafah – 55.

Every voting center had two polling booths, in keeping with the election law, red boxes for the election of the Chairman, white boxes for the election of council members. The voting slips and envelopes matched – red slips for the chairman, white slips for council members. All the slips were of the same size and format. Officials of the elections committee were stationed in the polls, receiving the voters, crossing out their names and directing them to the ballot box behind a curtain. After they had voted, the citizens received back from the officials the voting certificate they had been issued by the central election committee.

International observers: According to the interim agreement "the elections would be open to international supervision, which would be carried out according to accepted world principles". The international observers were stationed throughout the West Bank and the Gaza Strip to watch over the elections. These observers formed the central body supervising the course of the elections, including the registration of voters, the campaign publicity, the work of the voting centers, the vote count at the district and country-wide levels, and publication of the results.

About 500 international supervisors from throughout the world arrived, representing countries, organizations, research institutions, voluntary organizations, etc. The supervisors were divided into about 150 smaller teams on election day and stationed in all the voting centers; their presence was noticeable because of the special uniforms they wore. On election day a number of international observers reported some local trouble, and in Jerusalem they intervened to dilute the Israeli security presence. The observers published their impressions concerning the course of the elections in a special report, about two months later.

Factors shaping electoral behavior: Many factors intertwined and contributed to shaping the Palestinians' electoral behavior in the West Bank and the Strip. Three groups of factors had a decisive influence; other factors were of course involved, but they were significantly less influential. The first factor is the complex of Palestinian–Israeli relations: the residues of the past linked to the occupation and the results of the peace treaty, and the Israeli attitude toward the Palestinian Authority on the one hand, and to the Palestinian opposition, on the other. A decisive role was played here by considerations for or against the peace agreement on the part of contestants and voters alike. Among the contestants there were some whom Israel had permitted to return to the West Bank and Gaza Strip; on the other hand, there were Palestinian leaders whose return Israel had prevented and who could not therefore be candidates. According to the results of a special survey conducted by the Institute for Palestinian Research and Studies on election day,[22] which surveyed the position of 3,200 Palestinian voters in 148 voting centers as a representative sample of all the voters, it appears that the trait most preferred among those elected by the voters was the candidate's participation in the struggle against the Israeli occupation. Of those participating, 27.4 percent in the sample said that it was this characteristic that decided their choice (see table 5.4). In addition, 30.9 percent said that the most essential and important question the elected council would have to deal with was the conclusion of the negotiations with Israel.

A second factor was the relationship among the various groups within the Palestinian people, such as the relationships between the West Bank and the Gaza Strip, between the Palestinians in the West Bank and the Gaza Strip and those in other areas, and between the Palestinian leadership and institutions in the West Bank and Strip and those outside them. Here an important role was played by considerations of the status of the candidates for the new council as compared with the status of the Palestinian National Council, and the view of the Authority as an Israeli creation and calls for its boycott by some of the Palestinian leaders of the opposition front situated in Damascus. The debate over the bonds between the various sections of the Palestinian people and their representation in the elected council influenced Palestinian voters and was prominent in the election campaign publicity.

Table 5.4 Factors that were most important in voting for a candidate

1 Religious character	24.1%
2 Belonging to a prominent family	3.4%
3 High moral character	17.0%
4 Participation in the struggle	27.4%
5 Service in region/district	16.3%
6 Educational level	11.7%

The third factor shaping the elections was the social, political, and economic relationships within the Palestinian population dwelling in the West Bank and the Gaza Strip as these relationships were reflected in the candidates. These were the factors of city versus village or refugee camp, the candidates' personal wealth, membership of a clan and its size, communal and religious affiliations, the relationships between the various political trends and party affiliations, the age of the contestants and of the voters, the candidates' past, etc. According to a survey conducted on election day, a large proportion of the voters stressed personal factors as decisive: degree of religiosity – 24.1%, high moral character – 17%, education – 11.7%, and belonging to prominent family – 3.4% (see table 5.4). Some participants (17.6%) voted for a candidate from their own clan. A large proportion mentioned their concern with domestic issues the elected council would be called upon to deal with; 28.5% cited the solution of economic problems; 17.9% the need to reinforce democracy and freedom of opinion; and 22.7% security and internal order. Empirically, it is impossible to measure the exact relative importance of each factor, but it can be argued with near certainty that all the factors mentioned by voters played a role in shaping the decisions of the Palestinians in the West Bank and Gaza Strip on election day.

The Election Results

A distinctive feature of the election results was the proportion of the total electorate that participated, as opposed to abstaining, as well as the distribution of votes. The extent of participation, 76.7 percent (see table 5.5), is high in comparison with western democracies (in the United States and the European countries, participation is generally between 50 and 60 percent), but it is slightly lower than in Israel (78 percent in the last elections). It is also lower than in Arab countries that hold elections, and especially in comparison with first elections in other countries in the world.[23]

Table 5.5 Participation in voting in the elections

District	Number of registered voters	Number of actual voters	Proportion of participation (%)
1 Bethlehem	55,134	41,465	75.21
2 Hebron	133,084	88,364	66.4
3. Jenin	82,314	60,919	75.32
4 Jericho	12,906	10,685	77.86
5 Jerusalem	80,051	32,316	40.37
6 Nablus	111,651	87,005	76.76
7 Kalkilyia	27,278	19,724	70.94
8 Ramallah	79,108	56,429	71.33
9 Salfit	18,996	15,274	79.45
10 Toubas	15,914	13,166	81.42
11 Tulkarem	56,310	44,802	78.23
12 Northern Gaza	61,123	53,567	87.63
13 Gaza city	122,724	108,759	88.62
14 Dir Al-Balah	56,015	45,156	80.61
15 Khan Yunis	71,629	63,649	88.85
16 Rafah	44,034	38,824	88.16
Total	1,028,271	780,104	76.7

Comparing the West Bank and the Gaza Strip, the proportion of participants in the district was much higher than that in the West Bank: 86.77 percent of registered voters in Gaza as compared with 73.5 percent in the West Bank. This was because of the Palestinian Authority's direct control over the entire Gaza Strip, as opposed to its limited control over the West Bank. Two districts notable for their high proportion of abstentions were the Jerusalem District, where only 40.37 percent voted, and Hebron, 66.4 percent. During the election period these two districts were under direct Israeli rule, a situation that limited political activity and election campaigning, and decreased the motivation to participate in elections that were viewed as an expression of the liberation process, which these two districts were not party to.

The 24.14 percent rate of abstention can be explained, in addition to the factor of Israeli rule, by a variety of reasons, some of them routine factors such as illness, travel, work or other personal matters, as well as by reasons of principle and ideology, such as ideological or tactical opposition to the elections by the opposition fronts, especially the Popular Front and the Democratic Front, which announced their boycott of the elections, and the vaguer, less clearly stated position of Hamas, which boycotted the elections but did not adopt an unequivocal position on the matter. The opposition derived, of course, from general opposition to the Oslo Accords, which were the source of the elections' legitimacy.

After counting the votes, and deducting the invalid ballots, it appeared that the leading candidate, Yasser Arafat, had won a sweeping victory of 87.1 percent, with Samiha Khalil receiving only 12.9 percent. The result was foreseeable. The distribution of valid votes for council membership was also not very surprising. Although there were 55 independent candidates (contending on a personal basis, they received about 60 percent of the votes), they won only 35 seats in the council, that is, 39.8 percent. This was due to their lack of organization and the large dispersion of votes among the clan candidates. Most of the independent candidates were Fatah members who had not been included in the organization's list; some were candidates of districts or clans.

The Fatah candidates running in the organization's name received only 30 percent of the votes in the balloting, but 51 council seats – comprising 58 percent of the organization's 76 candidates. Only 25 Fatah candidates were defeated and did not enter the council. This impressive achievement may be ascribed to the methods of directing the votes, organization in the districts, and the care taken not to disperse votes among various Fatah candidates.

The candidates of the other organizations (see table 5.3) received 10 percent of the total vote, but only two candidates were elected to the council: one for the Fidah Party in Ramallah, and the other for the Democratic National League in Gaza. The distribution of votes among 55 candidates, the regional majority system, Fatah's control of the elections and the clan tendencies, were all instrumental in the other candidates' failure; with just two elected members, they constitute only 2.2 percent of the council. Added to these are the seven independent members who are associated with the Islamic trend (about 7.9 percent). From all the lists, five women were elected to the council (5.7 percent), 7 Christians (7.9 percent), and a single Samaritan, from Nablus.

To sum up, the elections conducted in the West Bank and Gaza Strip of the Palestinian Authority on 20 January, 1996 were a part of the peace agreements and form an important step in the liberation of the Palestinians in the West Bank and the Gaza Strip from Israeli rule, which has existed since June 1967. These first elections were "founding elections", and that is how they must be judged. They do not allow any conclusions to be drawn about the nature of the voting system or the ability of the Palestinian entity to develop into a democratic or dictatorial system, according to circumstances that will prevail in the future. These matters will depend primarily on the commitment of the various political forces and their leaders to the democratic process, and on the political pressures exerted on them in the future.

The Palestinian elections, as they were conducted, hold components of a "partial democracy", which could under conditions of political stability turn into integral components of a democratic system. At the same time, however, there were components at work in these elections that could serve opposite processes and lead to the development of a Palestinian dictatorship.

The measures taken in preparation for the elections, the complex voting and registration methods adopted, the Palestinian Authority and its head's intervention in the electoral procedures, and the fact that the election committee was appointed by Arafat himself – all these have added to skepticism concerning the elections' contribution toward the establishment of a real democracy.

Despite all the difficulties involved in the election system and process, it is fair to conclude that these elections were an important element in the "partially democratic" Palestinian regime. The elections, in addition to the three powers (executive, legislative, and judicial) that were discussed in chapter 4, constitute the positive substance of the Palestinian "partial democracy". The other face of this regime will be discussed in chapter 6.

6

The Centralization of Power and Political Conduct in the PNA

This chapter presents and analyzes the actual power and decision-making structures in the Palestinian National Authority (PNA), that is, the power structure that functions in parallel with the formal structure presented in chapters 4 and 5, which is supposed to provide for the democratic conduct and operation of the regime. I shall examine the non-formal structure of the Authority as a government and source of power that leaves the formal structure and systems with only symbolic meaning or at most overshadowed by an undemocratic apparatus similar to the systems in states considered by the literature to be dictatorial, of the sort that developed after independence in many countries of the Middle East, Africa, Asia, and Latin America.

In parallel to the formal system that is supposed to reflect the ostensibly democratic political behavior and structures of the PNA, the presidency, which is also part of the formal structure, has endeavored – ever since the establishment of the Authority after the withdrawal of Israeli forces from Gaza and Jericho and following the subsequent enlargement of the territory under its control – to concentrate power in ways that relegate the formal structure described previously to a secondary role, existing in the shadow of a regime that amasses power and controls Palestinian institutions and general population by means of various techniques that fall into three categories: concentration of power, surveillance (intimidation), and largesse that purchases quiet and supporters (bribery).

Centralization of Power

The Palestinian political system operates by virtue of the centralization of power in the presidency and its head, Yasser Arafat. All decisions, both external and internal, are made exclusively by Arafat, who, according to the testimony of those close to him, invests many hours in the "how" of consolidating all decision-making, even negligible matters. Political, economic, and security issues are fully subject to Arafat's direct authority and supervision, and these constitute the main manifestations of the centralization of political power in his hands.

Political Power

The process of the concentration of political power in the Palestinian liberation movement – Fatah and the PLO – began long before the signing of the peace agreement with Israel and the establishment of the PNA. Already in the 1950s and 1960s Arafat was recognized as the head of Fatah; he was chairman of the PLO in 1968 after the Arab defeat in the 1967 war and the occupation of the West Bank and Gaza Strip by Israel. During the ensuing years Arafat employed various methods to amass power and to become almost unchallenged in the PLO. He held political and diplomatic posts in the Fatah movement and in the PLO as the umbrella organization of all the Palestinian organizations. By virtue of his control of the Fatah and PLO treasuries, no sum, small or large, could be disbursed without his consent, not even to the leaders of rival factions in the PLO such as the PFLP and DFLP. Arafat also became the supreme commander of the Palestinian armed forces, neutralizing other commanders and subordinating them totally to himself.

Arafat carried on with the powers and positions he held before Oslo to the post-Oslo period and the founding of the Authority; he even added a long list of new titles and positions that consolidated his power. The *Ra'is* (Arafat) is the source of all political power and the only person authorized to make political decisions about both external and internal issues – even regarding what should logically be in the province of a minister or lower-ranking official, such as the director-general of a ministry, director of a public office, or director of a specific department within a ministry. Dozens of persons are employed in the office of the *Ra'is* as assistants or advisors on various topics, including the director-general of the president's office, a media advisor, an advisor on Israeli affairs, an advisor on police affairs, an advisor on economic affairs, and an advisor on educational affairs. Advisors are supplemented by a large number of functionaries who bear the title "director-general in the president's office". The requirement of such a large number of personnel is unheard of in the offices of chiefs of state of western governments. What is more, these assistants and advisors only advise the *Ra'is*; they are not allowed, generally through oral instructions, to take any decisions or practical steps. That remains the exclusive privilege of the *Ra'is*, after he consults or ignores his advisors. Decisions are made by Arafat, and by him alone.

Cabinet meetings, with the participation of the ministers and the *Ra'is*, are merely a forum for Arafat or ministers to report about the activities of their ministries or at most for consultations. No truly significant decisions are taken there. Ministers have frequently reported that they learned about political moves by the Authority, such as talks with Israel or arrests of opposition figures, only from the media.

In addition to political decisions, appointments in the public service also tend to be the exclusive privilege of the *Ra'is*. It is he who proposes or at least confirms appointments in the various government ministries and agencies, such as the Broadcasting Authority and Central Bureau of Statistics, as well as of bodies and individuals that should be less dependent on political agencies, such as universities and research institutes, judges, and state attorneys.

The Palestinian institutions include some that operate as alternatives to institutions established under the Israeli occupation, as well as voluntary and nonprofit associations that focus on various issues. These institutions emerged during and after the *Intifada*. After the signing of the Oslo Accords, and since the establishment of the Authority, they have been subject to direct and indirect monitoring and supervision by Arafat, especially through the Office of National Institutions, which is affiliated with and directly subordinate to Arafat, who is also its honorary president. According to its acting director-general, Dr. Samir Shehada, this office was originally set up (in 1995) by the Fatah movement and was later confirmed by Arafat as an organ of the Authority.[1] However, the change in status did not bring with it the necessary personnel modifications to support democratic procedures; the result is a political movement turned into an organization that oversees all institutional activity in the Authority. In his preface to the first volume of the publication of the Office of National Institutions, *Al-Milad* (November 1995), Shehada noted that his agency was set up "in order to serve the national institutions without discriminating among them and according to the single criterion of patriotism and the extent of their contribution to building the homeland and its young Authority".[2] This reference to the homeland and the Authority, in a single breath, demonstrates that in practice this office has a single standard for judging contributions to the homeland – compatibility with the policies of the Authority. This is a broad opening for attacks and abuse of other organizations that are independent or affiliated with streams that have maintained their distance from the PNA, such as Hamas organizations.

In the preface, Shehada enumerated his agency's goals as follows: "The Office of National Institutions has general national objectives that can be defined as follows:

1   Organizational development of institutions that fall into the sphere of

its activities, by monitoring their performance and management and offering suggestions for improvements;

2   Drafting and implementing training programs to realise the level of performance of Palestinian agencies on the basis of an assessment thereof;

3   Establishing national institutions as needed, while preserving balance in spheres of responsibility;

4   Expanding the commitment to institutionalized activity and the transition from activity by individuals to organized and planned activity by institutions;

5   Expanding the democratic element in the operations of the national institutions by encouraging them to implement and develop internal working procedures and to permit newcomers to be members and participate in their activities;

6   Promoting the mechanism of elections within the national institutions to make them compatible with the previous principle;

7   Finding a format for coordination among government institutions;

8   Insisting that national institutions use public funds only under appropriate supervision and guidance."[3]

The Office of National Institutions has an honorary president, a secretary-general, a board of directors, a council, and departments, including those for finance and administration; for media, culture, and planning; the Palestinian center for management training; for institutional coordination; for elections; for nongovernmental institutions (voluntary organizations); for popular organizations; and for election strips. This structure provides for supervision of government agencies, voluntary organizations, and even popular organizations, such as local or regional associations, to promote various ends. In practice it is responsible for direct and indirect supervision of all organizations and institutions that are active in the Authority. The Agency has the right to intervene in their internal affairs and even to impose sanctions on organizations it considers are not contributing to the advancement of the homeland. These powers have been enumerated explicitly by the director-general of the office.[4]

The Office of National Institutions is an important tool through which Arafat monitors and guides the activities of all agencies under the Authority, including government and nongovernment offices, and popular organizations with various political objectives. This power is important to Arafat as a way to tighten his control and provides another significant manifestation of the consolidation of power in the Authority in his hands.

Economic Power

The second mechanism used by the *Ra'is* and his aides to concentrate power directly in Arafat's hands is the economic means available to the Authority. This is manifested chiefly in Arafat's personal control of expenditures and supervision of revenues, which are routed through three main channels – in addition to two others that belong to the PLO (the Palestinian National Fund) and the Fatah movement (its own finance ministry), both of which were controlled by Arafat before the establishment of the PNA by virtue of his position as chairman of the PLO and head of Fatah. The three main channels are: the PNA Finance Ministry, the Palestinian Economic Council for Development and Reconstruction (PECDAR), and special funds at Arafat's disposal.

The Ministry of Finance[5] is almost totally under Arafat's control, especially in everything associated with expenditures and the allocation of funds. The ministry is run by Arafat's right-hand man, Muhammad Zuhdi al-Nashashibi, who was Arafat's financial assistant before the establishment of the Authority and whose transfer to the position of finance minister continues his previous mission – helping Arafat to control the funds of the Authority, and to use them to assert political control of the field operatives of Fatah and Authority employees by their appointment or the allocation of funds to various objectives.

A short note scribbled on a scrap of paper by Arafat, and by Arafat alone, suffices for the transfer of funds to various persons or agencies, including some that have no logical connection with the regular operations of the Authority.

The Palestinian Economic Council for Development and Reconstruction (PECDAR) was created by a PLO decision in November 1993, just after the signing of the Oslo Accords, "to organize, administer and disburse international aid in an effective and efficient way".[6] The PNA later retroactively ratified the establishment of PECDAR. From the time of its establishment PECDAR became the only Palestinian institution empowered to oversee international financial assistance to the West Bank and Gaza Strip. According to its 1996 report, PECDAR has the following objectives and spheres of responsibility:

1   Formulating economic and social plans in accordance with the general policies established by the PNA;
2   Coordinating the flow of international assistance from donor states for the benefit of the Palestinian West Bank and Gaza Strip;
3   Selecting investment projects, administering and monitoring programs and projects and any other activities financed by the donor countries and approved by PECDAR;

4   Evaluating the impact of its programs and activities and reporting accordingly to the PNA;

5   Organizing the process of capacity and human resources building, and the agencies executing the basic activities of the council;

6   Undertaking any other task assigned by the PLO Executive Committee/PNA for achieving its purposes, particularly in the area of economic and social development.[7]

Each of the six departments of PECDAR is responsible for a specific area:

(1) *The Economic Policy Formulation and Project Review Department (ECON)* is responsible for: formulation of economic policies; evaluation of projects on the basis of their meeting special social and economic criteria before being presented to donors for funding; formulation of public investment programs and sectoral development; and proposing general macro-economic policies.

(2) *The Aid Coordination and Facilitation Department (ACF)* is responsible for: coordination of procedures and mechanisms of bilateral and international aid; keeping a record of the flow of donor pledges, commitments and real funding operations on a regular basis; coordinating donor activities to avoid overlapping in the process of project identification and fund allocation; participation in negotiating aid agreements between the PNA and donor countries and regional and international organizations; and distributing information on current and future projects and their funding.

(3) *The Project Monitoring Office (PMO)* is the department responsible for the implementation of projects and the execution of contracts. This includes: preparation of projects and programs according to PNA economic priorities as well as sectoral, geographic and demographic needs; indicating the financial feasibility of the projects, and their overall benefit to local communities as well as their national impact; adapting and updating programs according to political and social considerations as the peace process requires; acting as liaison between the PNA and the donor countries with regard to designated projects; monitoring and evaluating projects under implementation; recommending projects to donors in close coordination with the Aid Coordination Department; assisting other national Palestinian institutions (ministries, municipalities, etc.) in building their own implementation capacities; and informing donors on the stages of implementation of projects through the Aid Coordination Department.

(4) *The Technical Assistance and Training Department (TAT)* is responsible for: organizing relations with donors on matters of technical assistance proposals to ensure that training programs meet sectoral devel-

opment needs, with particular emphasis on the impact of the transfer of technology; supervising the planning and organization of special technical assistance programs and assisting other Palestinian institutions in the formulation of their technical assistance proposals; and defining procedures to ensure quality control in training and study courses.

(5) *The Department for Coordination with UN Specialized Agencies and NGOs (CSA)* is responsible for: coordinating PNA relations with UN specialized agencies and NGOs active in the field of assistance to the Palestinian people; reporting on financial and technical assistance to the Palestinian people provided by the United Nations Specialized Agencies directly or through local or international NGOs; mobilizing international nongovernmental aid; diffusing information on the programs, priorities and procedures of nongovernmental organizations; and supervising and coordinating UN and NGO activities according to the economic and social objectives and policies of the PNA.

(6) *The Department of Finance and Administration* is responsible for: the administrative, financial and personnel affairs of PECDAR; supervision of aid funds and their use according to conditions agreed upon with the World Bank and the major donors; financial execution of projects, contracts and payments to contractors; and accounts and financial resources generated by agreements signed between the PNA and the World Bank and other donor groupings (e.g. EU, Islamic Development Bank, Arab Fund for Economic Development).[8]

Officially, PECDAR is managed by a 14-member board, all of whom are members of the PLO executive committee and three of whom are also members of the PNA Council of Ministers; in other words, all of them are subordinate to Arafat in the PLO and/or the PNA. PECDAR itself is an extremely important instrument in Arafat's hands. He is the president of PECDAR and uses it to control the implementation of Authority economic policy. On paper, PECDAR reports to the PLO executive committee and PNA. In practice, it is subordinate to the *Ra'is* and his office, reports to him through its managing general, and follows Arafat's dictates as to how actually to implement policy and how to handle the international assistance transferred to the Authority by various countries, the World Bank, the Islamic Development Bank, the Arab Fund for Economic Development, and other sources.

Special funds controlled by Arafat. The unlimited powers confided to Arafat permit him to deal with special sources of revenues that are subject to his control – directly or indirectly, through those loyal to him – to serve whatever objectives he sees fit. This is done through two main channels.

Personal bank accounts in Arafat's own name: The Authority has bank accounts listed under Arafat's name. For the Authority, this is a legacy of the pre-Oslo period when funds had to be deposited under assumed names so as to camouflage PLO activities. Such accounts, however, should not exist after the establishment of the Authority; they allow Arafat personal control, hidden from the public eye, of a portion of the Authority's funds, for distribution to his intimates and supporters, or to finance other activities.

According to an investigative report in the Israeli daily *Ha'aretz* (April 4, 1997), a secret account of this sort, in Arafat's name, is maintained at the Hashmona'im Street branch of Bank Leumi in Tel Aviv. Vast sums that accrue to the Authority and Palestinian exchequer from a number of sources, including rebates of taxes from Israel and royalties from the franchises for the distribution of basic commodities in the West Bank and Gaza Strip controlled by the Authority, and special funds intended for the benefit of Palestinian people, are managed and allocated at the discretion of Arafat or one of his close associates. Muhammad Rashid (who is of Kurdish origin) confirmed the existence of the secret account to *Ha'aretz* reporters, and explained its questionable objectives. He stated that the account serves as an "insurance policy" for Arafat, in case there is a coup against him. These funds increase the odds of his political survival and continued control of the Palestinian political scene.

Corporate funds: Large sums reach Arafat's hands and are distributed without public accounting to his close supporters or to fund special needs. The funds come from profits of companies owned by the Authority, by Arafat confidants, or by private interests in partnership with the Authority or Arafat confidants. Money is then transferred to Arafat, or in accordance with his instructions. A conspicuous example here is the Palestinian Company for Trade Services, registered as a public corporation owned by the Authority but managed by Arafat's close associate and economic advisor, Muhammad Rashid. This company has a monopoly on the distribution of cement in the PNA areas; its profits have been applied to acquire a stake, on its own or in partnership, in mineral water, steel mills, hotels, food plants, insurance and financial management, and various other endeavors.

The company is run through the direct link between its head – Muhammad Rashid – and Arafat. It operates as an independent entity *vis-à-vis* Authority offices, even though it has established partnerships with a number of government ministries. Its revenues are managed separately and are under the direct control of Arafat, who spends some of them to finance special needs of the Authority, including financial grants to close supporters. This financial source has no public scrutiny.[9]

Security Forces

A third tool used by Arafat and his close associates to concentrate power in their hands is the security apparatus established under the Authority, chiefly before Arafat's arrival in Gaza in 1994. The security forces have continued to expand since that time. An appendix to the May 1994 Cairo ("Gaza–Jericho") agreement provided for the establishment of a Palestinian police force to handle security in areas controlled by the Authority. The 1995 Interim Agreement on the transfer of the Palestinian cities to the direct control of the Authority stipulated that "the [Palestinian] Council shall establish a strong police force", into which "the Palestinian police force established under the Gaza–Jericho Agreement will be fully integrated", and that it and the Israeli security forces would be the only security agencies present.[10] The accord between Israel and the Palestinians included agreement on the establishment of six security agencies to serve the Authority: civilian police, general security, preventive security, intelligence, presidential police, and civil defense. The fourth article of Annex I to the Interim Agreement enumerates the spheres of authority, composition, deployment, recruitment methods, and weaponry of the various forces.

These six forces, established by agreement between Israel and the Authority, soon mushroomed. Within less than two years they had turned into 11 separate security forces with distinct spheres of authority, each with its own commander reporting directly to Arafat and receiving instructions from him. These security forces derive their legitimacy from the *Ra'is* and implement his wishes in the arenas of domestic and external security. These 11 forces are: the civilian police, the Border Police, the Coast Guard, the campus police, the West Bank and Gaza branches of the Preventive Security service, the General Intelligence Service, military intelligence, Force 17, the Presidential Security service, the National Security Force, and the Special Security Force. The most important of these are detailed below:

1   *Civilian police*: This is the agency responsible for maintaining law and order for all Palestinians living under the Authority. It has a number of branches, including traffic police, park police, criminal investigation division, drugs division, riot-control division, special intervention force, and the Prisons Service. Its commander is Col. Ghazi Jebali, who arrived in Gaza along with Arafat. He is known to be an Arafat loyalist.

2   *General Intelligence Service*: This is the official intelligence agency of the Authority, set up when the Authority was established. It has about a thousand members. Its Gaza branch is commanded by Col. Amin al-Hindi, originally from Gaza and a long-time PLO activist. Although

he "vanished" in the 1970s and 1980s, he resurfaced to command the General Intelligence Service from its inception. The commander in the West Bank is Col. Tewfiq Tirawi. The origins of its members – recruited from the West Bank and Gaza Strip, or forces that arrived with Arafat from abroad – are not known.[11]

3   *Preventive Security*: This force, too, established after the Oslo Agreement on mutual recognition between Israel and the PLO, has two branches. That in the West Bank is commanded by Col. Jibril Rajoub; the Gaza division is commanded by Col. Muhammad Dahlan. The most active of the security forces in the West Bank and Gaza Strip, its responsibility extends to many spheres; or, to be more precise, there are no clear guidelines limiting its jurisdiction. It has offices in all Palestinian cities, including East Jerusalem (according to reports in the Israeli press and electronic media).

4   *Presidential Security*: This force, which numbers "a few hundred" members, is also divided into West Bank and Gaza branches. It is responsible for Arafat's personal security. Its mission and responsibility largely parallel those of Force 17, the PLO force set up to protect Arafat before the establishment of the PNA.[12]

All the security forces are directly controlled by Arafat, by virtue of his position as a commander of the Palestinian armed forces before the establishment of the Authority. In principle they can be divided into three categories: the Palestinian security forces/army, including the army, military intelligence, and Force 17; the police, including the civilian police and Civil Defense; and the special security forces, including Preventive Security and General Intelligence.

Surveillance (Intimidation)

The security forces enumerated above play a central role as the implementers of security activity, both internally and externally. They employ techniques and methods to impose a regime of surveillance and intimidation of oppositionist elements, activists of voluntary human rights organizations, and critics of the Authority – a regime that perpetrates violence against citizens not involved in political activity.

The frequency and variety of the assaults on people by the security forces have left the average Palestinian citizen with a sense of insecurity in daily life. These violent excesses range from random gunfire at citizens, illegal detentions, detention for prolonged periods, mistreatment of attorneys in ways that prevent them from doing their job, the use of fortune-tellers to identify criminals, failure to implement Supreme Court decisions, abduction and concealment of persons, and undermining the powers of the attorney-general.

Random Gunfire

There have been cases of gunfire directed by members of the Palestinian security forces at Palestinian demonstrators or chance passers-by.[13] There are many examples of this, including shooting at demonstrations or crowds of adults, teenagers, and even children. Other excesses include the premeditated killing of citizens who were protesting against Authority policy;[14] shooting indiscriminately or without warning at the general public during the pursuit of criminal suspects;[15] shooting at Palestinian vehicles by the security forces and gunfire from inside fortified positions of the Palestinian security forces;[16] and even wounding citizens as a result of members of the Palestinian security forces playing with their weapons.[17] Commentators have concluded that the Authority has been negligent with respect to giving clear instructions to the security forces and police concerning their treatment of citizens in cases of assembly or demonstrations, and the absence of security or safety rules governing how they handle their weapons. The public are concerned for the disregard shown by the security forces, and their willingness to injure citizens in order to achieve "security".[18]

Mistreatment and Wounding of Citizens by the Security Forces

The security forces intervened in the elections so as to guarantee the election to the Palestinian Legislative Council (PLC) of candidates favored by the Authority in general and by Arafat in particular. Members of the security forces entered polling stations even when requested not to by the precinct committee. They interfered with the activity of the committees, brought their weapons into polling stations and strolled around there, interfered with the distribution of leaflets supporting some candidates, urged voters to select particular candidates, assisted the illiterate in casting their ballot even when not asked for help, and confiscated identity booklets (on the pretext that their owners were not standing in line), which were returned to them later, stamped by the precinct committee as having cast their vote. All this demonstrates either that the security forces are not aware of the limits of their jurisdiction, or that they take these steps in accordance with the desires of senior officials of the PNC, led by Arafat.[19]

Citizens are frequently subjected to random abuse by the security forces. This includes persons who are summoned for questioning about a certain matter, only to have the charge against them modified at a later stage;[20] violent assaults on citizens by members of the security forces or government representatives;[21] brutal and humiliating treatment of passers-by and street vendors;[22] and even confiscation of property for the benefit and use of senior members of the security forces.[23]

Arrests of Citizens by the Security Forces

All branches of the Palestinian security forces arrest Palestinian citizens. Many of these arrests are problematic with regard to their excuse, legality or compatibility with the principles of a well-ordered society, let alone the rule of law. Those arrested are sometimes subjected to various forms of torture and violence.

All too often the security forces refuse to inform those arrested of the reason for their detention, even in cases of prolonged incarceration, and do not bring them before a judge for an extension of their remand or to present an indictment against them.[24] The security forces also use violent methods to try and compel detainees to confess to whatever crimes they see fit.[25] Sometimes they make unfounded accusations against the physically and mentally handicapped and arrest them, using their powers to confiscate property or money and use it for the benefit of police officers and investigators.[26] There are also cases where prisoners have continued to be held in detention even though the courts have ruled that they should be released.[27]

Prison Violations and Mortality

The rights of detainees and convicts in Palestinian prisons, under both international conventions and the norms of democratic society, are violated repeatedly. The Palestinian National Authority has committed itself to respecting human rights and has published statements and documents declaring its adherence to "the standards accepted by it and the principles of human rights and the rule of law".[28] These violations differ from one prison to another and according to the reasons for the prisoners' detention, but can be grouped under the following headings:

1   *Legality of the arrest*: Most arrests are made without a warrant. In addition, the authorities in Palestinian prisons lock up prisoners without completing the required paperwork and without receiving identifying documents issued by the authority responsible for the detention, such as a judge.[29]
2   *Visits by attorneys and relatives*: No one knows what authority is responsible for permitting visits to prisoners nor are there any specific guidelines. Usually, however, the prison authorities request the approval of the attorney-general or the chief of police, or both. Sometimes the district attorney refuses to permit lawyers to visit their clients without a permit issued by the chief of police.[30]

3 *Communication with the outside world*: There are no hard-and-fast
   rules about televisions, radios or printed matter for prisoners. As a
   result, many detainees are denied the right to receive information from
   the outside world. Similarly, there are no regular mail services to the
   prisons. Wardens have full freedom to decide what may be brought
   into the prisons.[31]

4 *Information about prisoners' whereabouts*: There is no central office
   responsible for notifying prisoners' families as to where they are being
   held. This means that family members have to conduct a search in the
   various prisons to locate their relatives. Because there are no defined
   procedures that must be followed after an individual is arrested, prison
   authorities sometimes deny that a particular prisoner is in their
   custody.[32]

5 *Food*: The quality and quantity of the food in the prisons is abominable
   and inadequate for prisoners' needs. Families are allowed to bring
   food to their relatives when they come to visit. Sometimes prisoners
   are allowed to go to a store to purchase food for themselves and
   others.[33]

6 *The right to complain*: Prisoners frequently lodge complaints about
   their harsh conditions of incarceration or brutal treatment by a guard,
   but these complaints are considered to be unofficial and are rarely
   responded to. In a testimony by "Hashem", he states: "I submitted a
   letter of complaint on November 19, 1996, to the office of the governor
   of Ramallah, in which I described everything that had happened to me.
   The governor's assistant received the letter and notified me that he
   would be in contact, but to date I have heard nothing from him."[34]

7 *Separation between categories of prisoners*: In some prisons there is no
   separation between minors and adults, the ill and the healthy, convicts
   and those awaiting trial, or criminal prisoners and political prisoners;
   in other prisons political prisoners and criminals are separated.[35]

8 *Medical treatment*: Only in rare cases do prisoners receive a medical
   examination when they are admitted to prison. In most cases there are
   no regular staff physicians and prisoners' families must purchase
   medications for their relatives, because there is no prison dispensary
   with an inventory of medicines. Treatment of prisoners who are ill
   before and during their imprisonment is not recorded in a medical file
   that accompanies them if they are transferred to a different prison or
   a hospital. Similarly, information about prisoners' health is not available to judges or prison wardens. In the case of A, he was interrogated
   for a number of days without being taken to a physician, even though
   he requires medication for a condition from which he suffered before
   he was brought to prison.[36] (Generally prisoners are treated in the security forces' clinics. Sometimes they are referred to government or

private hospitals, but prisoners are required to pay for any medications prescribed.)[37]

9   *Prison hygiene*: Prison authorities do not provide adequate facilities to allow prisoners to stay clean. In some prisons there are no showers, soap or other materials required for bathing. In a testimony, "Hashim" stated: "I did not take a shower for 13 days, even though I was bleeding from my face." Another prisoner from Gaza, who sent a letter to the office of the Palestinian Human Rights Monitoring Group, stated that "In such conditions disease spreads and cannot be stopped."[38]

10 *Attitude toward human rights organizations*: There are no clear rules about inspection of Palestinian prisons by Palestinian human rights organizations. The warden can decide whether or not to allow a human rights organization to visit a prisoner. The inspector-general of the police and district attorney can prevent such visits, even though they do not in fact have the authority to bar visits. In general, human rights organizations are allowed freedom of access in some prisons, except for visiting persons who are being interrogated. The difference in attitude, with freedom of access in some cases and a ban on visits in others, exists because there are no clear guidelines.[39] The Mandela organization has reported that it is not allowed to visit Palestinian prisons.[40]

11 *Clothing*: Prison authorities do not provide prisoners with clothing. As a result, prisoners who receive no visits from their relatives are unable to change their clothes and have to wear the same clothes they were wearing when arrested; some prisoners have no recourse to a change of clothing throughout their incarceration.[41]

12 *Prison buildings*: Palestinian prisons do not satisfy the minimum conditions for human life, because they are legacies of the past. Only the Tel al-Hawa prison was constructed under the Authority. It is said to have acceptable conditions, including lighting, ventilation, heating, and open spaces.[42]

Detainees and convicts, including children and teenagers, are tortured in Palestinian prisons.[43] Many different methods of torture are employed; most of them seem to derive from the methods used by the Israelis against Palestinian prisoners during the occupation. It seems likely that members of the Palestinian security services learned them when they were themselves held in Israeli prisons.

The most common forms of torture in Palestinian prisons include various forms of binding and blows, use of cold water, covering the head with a sack, and threats of murder or scandal. Such methods are used to get prisoners to confess to the charges against them. Other methods include burns on the body, causing strong pains in the back, sharp blows on the hands and feet, electric shocks, suspension by the arms from the ceiling, forcing the prisoner's head into a toilet bowl full of excrement, blows on the sex organs, and threats of death.[44] Table 6.1 reviews the incidence of various methods of torture at the hands of the Palestinian security forces. The data come from a study of 42 cases of torture in prisons in the West Bank and Gaza Strip.

Table 6.1 Torture: methods and frequency[45]

Method	Frequency
Beating with a thick cable or iron or plastic cord	15
"Al-farwaja" (hanging upside down with the two legs apart)	6
Cold water or cold air	5
Enclosure in a closet or confined space	3
Burns	4
Refusal of urgent medical treatment	2
Injury to sex organs	1
Threat of murder	1

Mortality in Prison

Death is common in Palestinian prisons. Inmates who were perfectly healthy when arrested, die in prison, evidently as the result of severe torture, or are taken to a hospital and die there. Between the establishment of the Authority in May 1994 and August 2000, at least 23 Palestinians died in Palestinian detention. The following case histories illustrate the extent of unacceptable and undemocratic behavior on the part of the Authority.

Farid Hashem Abu Jarbo'a was the first person known to die in a Palestinian prison. Aged 28 and married, a taxi driver who lived in Rafah in the Gaza Strip, Abu Jarbo'a was arrested in the street by the General Intelligence Service without a warrant. He died less than 10 days after his arrest, on July 4, 1994, in the Gaza central prison, as the result of torture. He had been charged with collaboration.

Media attention on Abu Jarbo'a's death brought about a declaration by the authorities that they would investigate the circumstances. The attorney-general summoned the dead man's sister and then made a deal with the father that he would release the daughter on condition that the father did not make any demands with regard to his dead son. In the event the daughter was released and the father kept silent about his son's case. An autopsy was performed on the body, and the family was permitted to see the body, but the pathology report was not made available to the family. Those who washed the body before burial noted a fractured spine. Three officers of the intelligence force were arrested but the incident was never investigated. Neither was the family paid compensation for wrongful death. The family was notified about the death by officers who came to their house that day.[46]

Suleiman Julaita, age 44, married and the father of seven, a resident of Jericho, was employed in Ein Feshkha. He died on January 18, 1995, three days after his arrest by the Preventive Security force, as a result of a heart attack he suffered in the Jericho prison. Before the autopsy his brother noticed bruises and scars on the corpse and a wound on the back of the neck. The pathology report was never published. Nor did the family ever find out whether any steps were taken against the perpetrators. Jibril Rajoub, the head of the Preventive Security service, said that a commission of inquiry was set up, but its findings were never published. Julaita was accused of murdering a member of Hamas in Jericho. The family was never compensated for his death, which they learned of only through rumors in the street. His death was confirmed only after Suleiman's brother Salim contacted the attorney-general.[47]

Muhammad al-Jundi, married and the father of seven, age 33, a resident of Gaza, died on April 2, 1995, after four Fatah Hawks took him from prison to al-Qitatwa in Jebalya. Al-Jundi was suspected of helping a group of Israeli undercover troops murder six Fatah members in 1994. Al-Jundi's wife heard from the neighbors that a detainee with the same name as her husband had died in prison. She went to the Gaza central prison, where she was told that the dead man was not her husband, and that she should go to Shifa Hospital to confirm this. But at the hospital she discovered that it was her husband. It is not known whether the four persons involved were ever put on trial. Justice minister Freih Abu Medein told the media that the responsible authorities would investigate the matter and bring the suspects to trial.[48]

Muhammad al-Amor, age 50, married and the father of 17, a resident of Khan Yunis in the Gaza Strip, was killed by the agents of the Preventive Security service on May 21, 1995.

Yussuf al-Sha'arawi, age 24, a resident of al-Zueida in the Gaza Strip, worked as a tailor. He died on May 23, 1995, two days after his arrest by the General Intelligence Service. His interrogator at the al-Nuseirat detention center, Khaled a-Zarid, shot al-Sha'arawi in the head and killed him because he refused to cooperate. Another version of his death, circulated by the General Intelligence Service, is that al-Sha'arawi worked for the service; while fooling around, a friend accidentally shot him in the head and killed him. The family learned of his death when 200 men representing all the security forces and local dignitaries came to their house in a convoy of

50 vehicles. The Authority gave al-Sha'arawi a military funeral and paid the expenses of the mourning period.[49]

Tawfiq Sawarqa, age 36, married and the father of seven, a resident of Gaza, employed as a watchman in a citrus orchard, died on August 27, 1995. The security forces arrested Sawarqa and tortured him at the Deir Balah detention center. That same night he was sent to the Deir Balah clinic. The physician who examined him notified the security official who had brought him there that Sawarqa had died. The doctor refused to comply with a request by the official to issue a certificate stating that Sawarqa had died of cardiac arrest. After his death, a hundred of Sawarqa's relatives demonstrated outside the offices of Chairman Arafat. The latter promised he would supervise the investigation personally, promised to appoint Sawarqa's son as a mechanic in the Gaza central prison, and gave them $3,000. The *Ra'is* kept his promise, but the family still does not know whether the matter was investigated, because the Authority has never published the findings of an investigation or informed the family about them. The Sawarqa family learned of his death from Israel Radio in Arabic.[50]

Azzam Masalah, age 52, married and the father of six, a pensioner, died on September 28, 1995, in the custody of the General Intelligence Service. Masalah, who held a US passport, was visiting his family in the village of Ein Yabrud, near Ramallah, when arrested by members of the Preventive Security service on a charge of murder. His body was taken to his birthplace in Yabrud by the legal advisor to the Preventive Security service, Fahmi Shabana, and received by his cousin, who placed it in his garage. The next day he informed the family. The family was never compensated. A special military tribunal was convened on the instructions of the *Ra'is* after intervention by the US consul. Three persons were tried for killing Masalah – Shassan Hassin Salim was sentenced to five years in prison, and Ali Abd el-Salim Hassan Abu Daya and Adnan Hamed Hamed Abu Aisha to one year in prison.[51]

Muhammad al-Jumayyel, age 26, a resident of Nablus, and a leader of the Fatah Hawks during the *Intifada*, was arrested on December 18, 1995, along with other Fatah Hawks – his brother Muwa'id, Nasser Juma'ah, and Ahmad Tabouq – and sent to the Jericho prison. On July 26, al-Jumayyel was taken to the naval police in Nablus for interrogation. That same night, after being brutally tortured, he was taken to the hospital, where he died three days later. Three persons were charged in court with torturing al-Jumayyel: Capt. Abd el-Hakim Daher Hajo, First Lieut. Omar Abdallah al-Qadoumi, and Sgt. Khaled Ahmad al-Labadi.[52] At their trial before the State Security Court, held three days after al-Jumayyel's death, the accused said that they had been questioning him about allegations of buying and selling weapons and reactivating the Fatah Hawks. The court president asked why the naval police were involved in the investigation. Capt. Hajo replied that he could not answer this question because he merely followed orders and the question should be directed to his superiors. But the issue was not followed up. The Jumayyel family, for their part, emphasized that they knew the secret reasons for their son's death. Al-Jumayyel's father told the media that "he knew too much" and that the affair involved activity during the *Intifada* and information about senior figures in the Authority. "We know who tortured him to death and that they still work at the prison." The al-Jumayyel file was officially closed. The father rejected the Authority's offer of a military funeral for al-Jumayyel and recognition as a *shahid* (martyr).[53]

Nahed Dahlan, age 24, married, a resident of al-Zuweida in the Gaza Strip, died on August 7, 1996. On August 7, Dahlan was summoned for questioning for the tenth time in 11 days. He was let out of a General Intelligence Service vehicle 50 meters from his home. He walked the rest of the distance but when he reached the door he was found to be trembling and spitting blood. His family took him to Nasser hospital in Khan Yunis, where he died within the hour. The attorney-general, who was notified, determined that Dahlan had committed suicide by taking poison, for personal reasons, and that the Palestinian security apparatus was not involved. He added that an autopsy had not found any indications of torture to Dahlan, internal or external, and no one had harmed him. Nor were there any signs of violence on his body. The authorities stated that the dead man had left behind a letter explaining why he committed suicide, but the family never saw the letter. Muhammad Dahman, the head of the human rights organization al-Damir Institute in Gaza, was also arrested after a press release issued by the organization demanded that the names of Dahlan's murderers be published. The Authority offered no compensation, because of the disagreement as to the circumstances of the death.[54]

Khaled al-Habel, age 65, married and the father of five, a resident of Kharbata near Ramallah, died on August 11, 1996. He was arrested on the evening of August 10 after a fight in the village between the Habel family and another family, during which a woman from the other family was killed. That same evening the Preventive Security service arrested Khaled al-Habel and his five sons. The next day the Authority announced that al-Habel had committed suicide. His sons emphasize that they were in cells near their father's and heard him screaming with pain, the result of a beating. An autopsy was performed on al-Habel's body at Abu Kabir on August 11. The pathology report found no signs of violence on the body, except for a bruise on the neck, indicating that death was caused by hanging with an electric cord. No compensation was paid to the family because of the disagreement concerning the circumstances of the death.[55]

Rashid al-Fitiani, age 26, a resident of Jericho, died in the Jericho prison on December 4, 1996, after a guard, Issam Julaita, shot him in a fight. The guard fired 13 bullets. The incident took place only one day before al-Fitiani was to be released. He had been arrested with his brother-in-law, Suleiman Julaita, on January 15, 1995, and accused, along with others, of murdering a Hamas member and collaborating with Israel. Al-Fitiani spent 23 months in prison and was due to be released on December 5, 1996. On December 4, one day before his release he was shot and died. Al-Fitiani's mother asked the minister for local government, Saeb Erekat, to pay for the funeral expenses and mourning expenses; he gave her 9,000 sheqels ($2,500). Afterward she stated that she was extremely angry because of the death of her son and would travel to London to file suit against the Palestinian Authority. The *Ra'is* heard about the case and asked to meet her. At their meeting he apologized for the death of her son Rashid and asked if there was anything he could do to calm her. He gave her a check for $2,500, payable at the Finance Ministry in Ramallah.[56]

Faiz Qumsiya, age 53, married and the father of six, a businessman from Beit Sahour near Bethlehem, died on January 17, 1997. The Authority announced that he had died of a heart attack at the detention center belonging to the police in Bethlehem. The police attempted to dismiss the matter as suicide and sent the body to the hospital, where his pants were found to be knotted around his neck. After the autopsy indicated that he had died of a heart attack the police refused to accept responsibility for his death. There is evidence that the heart attack was the result of torture, but the Authority still declines to investigate the matter and no one has been punished.[57]

Nasser el-Abd Radwan, age 28, married and the father of three, a resident of Gaza, worked as a building contractor. On June 20, 1997, one of the bodyguards of the operations officer of the presidential security apparatus (Force 17) came to his home and confiscated his identity card; he was told to report to the Force 17 headquarters in Gaza. On June 23, 1997, the same person returned to Radwan's home and asked him to come with him. He had no arrest warrant and told the family that he was summoning Radwan in order to solve a problem associated with the allegation by a member of Force 17 that Radwan was bothering his wife. On June 30, 1997, Radwan died of injuries caused by torture during his illegal detention at the headquarters of Force 17. On July 1, 1997, a large funeral was held for him. A military trial was held on July 3, 1997. The main defendants were Col. Muhammad Fathi Farihat (known as Abu Nasser), Staff Sgt. Mahmoud Ziyyad, and Staff Sgt. Wail Ghanem, charged with causing death by the use of excessive violence. They were sentenced to death before a firing squad, but the sentence was never carried out. After Radwan's death, Chairman Arafat sent the Reform Commission to the family's home and offered them $30,000 and a plot of land, but the family refused to accept compensation for his death.[58]

According to a medical report signed by Dr. Mu'awiya Salim on June 23, 1997, Nasser Radwan was brought by ambulance to Shifa Hospital at 11:45 p.m. on June 23, 1997, accompanied by members of Force 17, and admitted to the hospital as prisoner No. 10. The report conveyed initial information that he had fallen in his cell; the initial diagnosis was a serious head injury and unconsciousness with a suspected hemorrhage in the brain. According to the report, the clinical examination of the patient showed that he was totally unconscious; there was no movement of arms and legs, dilated pupils, and a discharge from the mouth. The medical examination found signs of bruises on the left and right arms, signs of binding with wire on the left leg, and that his beard and hair had been cut.[59]

Nafa Hassan Mardawi, age 50 and the father of seven, a resident of the village of Habla near Qalqilya, an unemployed construction worker, died of a heart attack on November 9, 1997. Mardawi was arrested illegally and held in the Nablus central prison after being accused of selling land to Israelis during the occupation. The Authority announced that he had died of natural causes after the prison warden had failed to provide him with the necessary medication for diabetes and high blood pressure that his family brought him. There were no signs of violence on the body and the Authority did not have an autopsy performed or investigate the incident.[60] One of Mardawi's relatives said that there were no signs of torture on the body, except for a blue mark in the chest region. His cardiologist told the al-Qanun Association that this was the result of the pooling of blood there.[61]

Ibrahim al-Sheikh, age 71, died in Nablus central prison on October 15, 1997, of a blood clot in the brain. In his case, too, they were no signs of violence on the body. He fell unconscious to the ground on October 13 and was taken to the National Hospital in Nablus that same day. Al-Sheikh, who suffered from diabetes and high blood pressure, did receive medical treatment while in custody. He had been arrested on July 10, 1997, by the Preventive Security service in Qalqilya. The family was forced to sign a statement that he had died of natural causes; no investigation was conducted.[62]

Nasser al-Haroub, age 26, married and the father of five, was arrested by police when two officers of the Criminal Investigation Division came to his house in the village of Deir Samet near Hebron, explaining that he was wanted to arrange a reconciliation with another man. This was on Monday evening at 5 p.m. When his relatives went to the Dura police two hours later, a policeman said that Nasser would be held at the station until the morning because the commander was not there. Despite promises by the family to bring Nasser back in the morning the policeman refused and said that he would be released in the morning.

The next morning al-Haroub's father went to the Dura police station and to police headquarters. At both places he was told that Nasser was at the other place. Finally he was told that Nasser had died of strangulation and was at the hospital in Beit Jala. Nasser died at 2 a.m. on February 3, 1998. Two autopsies were conducted; doctors were invited by the family to the second autopsy. The pathology reports agreed that death was caused by strangulation. No results of an investigation of the affair have been published. On February 14, 1998, the military court in Hebron sentenced Omar al-Haribat and Anwar Farraj of the Criminal Investigation Division of the police to six months in prison and dismissal from the force because of the affair.[63]

Yussuf al-Baba, a bachelor who lived in the al-Makhfiya neighborhood in Nablus, died while being tortured by military intelligence in Nablus on February 1, 1997. Al-Baba was summoned by military intelligence at 11 a.m. on Friday, January 3, 1997, for questioning about the sale of property to another resident of al-Far'ah. While in custody he was brutally tortured, which left marks on his body. As a result he was taken to Rafidiya hospital, where he died. The autopsy found unequivocally that he had been brutally tortured by the military intelligence authorities. The signs were most prominent on his left arm – red marks, burns, and holes, evidently the result of the use of an electric drill on his hand – along with signs of being bound on his arms and red marks all over his body as a result of sharp blows. In addition the investigators had forced his head into a pail of water. While they were doing this his arm was injured by the metal edges of the pail, which caused blood poisoning. The family heard about Yussuf's death on Israel radio in Arabic on January 31, 1997. The Palestinian police arrested the head of Palestinian military intelligence in Nablus, Hani Iyad, on charges of involvement in the murder; the chairman himself signed the detention order. Also arrested were Iyad's assistants and two nurses who helped conceal al-Baba's hospital file.[64]

Subhi al-Qamhawi died at the interrogation center of the Preventive Security service in Jericho on June 15, 1997. There were contradictory reports about the circumstances and cause of his death. The al-Qanun Association investigated the matter and discovered that during his questioning he was held for 12 days before his death. The medical examination showed that he died of a massive heart attack. His parents said that there were no signs of violence on his body.[65]

Jihad Abd al-Razek al-Majdalawi, age 40, from Nuseirat, died in the Gaza central prison on November 26, 1997, after being stabbed by another prisoner.[66]

Walid Mahmoud al-Qawasmi, age 40, father of eight children, manager of an insurance office in Bethlehem. Al-Qawasmi was arrested by General Intelligence in Hebron on 25 July, 1998; three days later he was taken to the General Intelligence detention area in Jericho. In August 9, 1998 al-Qawasmi was taken to Jericho hospital, the hospital transferred him to Rafidiya hospital in Nablus, but he died before reaching Rafidiya. Al-Qawasmi died from a hemorrhaging of the brain caused by a fracture in his skull which was caused by "severe beating to the head".[67]

Mohammed Shreiteh, age 33, maried with eight children. Shreiteh went on September 9, 1999, to the police station to complain against another person, but he was placed in prison without a warrant or a detention order. On the second night after his arrest he suffered a cardiac arrest. Members of his family came to the police station and demanded his release because of his deteriorating health condition; he was released and transferred to a hospital in Hebron, where he died the same night. Members of his family declared that "what caused his death was the beating he took from the Palestinian police".[68]

Mahmoud Mohammed al-Bajjali, age 33, a father of three children, from Bethlehem, died in Ramallah prison on December 6, 1999, after spending five years in prison without trial.[69]

Khaled Mohammed al-Bahar, age 35, from Biet-Ummar near Hebron, married with 6 children, was arrested on May 25, 2000, by the Preventive Security, which did not explain the reasons behind his arrest. After making contacts with officials in the Preventive Security the family was told that he would be released on June 6, 2000. Al-Bahar was found dead inside his cell on June 6, 2000.[70]

Nine citizens were killed during 1997 when they failed to heed warnings about shooting, or as the result of torture or failure to protect prisoners, or they died in Palestinian prisons and detention centers; the corresponding figure in 1996 was eight.[71] In total, twenty-three Palestinian citizens had been killed or died as the result of torture or excessive force by August 2000.

Repression of the Political Opposition by the PNA

The PNA does not view the political opposition and its activities in a favorable light or as elements of a democratic state. In many cases it treats the opposition and oppositionist organizations as an enemy to be put down with force. The Authority's attitude toward the political opposition is reflected in the campaigns of repression it carries out after every military action against Israeli objectives. In February and March 1996, more than 1,200 persons were arrested in the wake of suicide attacks inside Israel. A member of the General Intelligence Service told one of the detainees in the Ramallah prison: "You are here because you're divided into three types: type one are people that Israel wants arrested; type two are people that the

Authority wants arrested; type three are those arrested to placate Israel, and most of you belong to that type." During the wave of arrests in March 1996, Mustafa Atari, a student at Bir Zeit University, was arrested. He was released after 318 days, that is, in January 1997; no charge or indictment was filed against him, like most of those detained without trial or indictment and later released.

After the military action near Surda village on January 11, 1998 many activists of the Popular Front in the West Bank were arrested. In one case a brother of a member of the Popular Front was arrested and held hostage until the latter turned himself in. Also arrested after the wave of attacks was Ahmad Sadat, a member of the Popular Front in Ramallah; no indictment was presented against him and he was released on the day when the national debate in Nablus began, on February 27, 1998. The Preventive Security service held Dr. Ghazi Hamad, a member of Hamas, in the period between January 1 and 8, 1997. Later, and following the suicide attacks in Tel Aviv on March 21 of that year, many Hamas supporters and activists were detained briefly – in most cases for no longer than a few hours – during which the security forces attempted to collect information about Hamas policy in general and warned the detainees to restrain their behavior. The number of those detained, in both the West Bank and Gaza district, was estimated to be in the dozens. As a gesture of good will toward Hamas, the Authority released Dr. Ibrahim Maqadama, a Hamas leader, on March 11; no indictment was submitted against him. After the attack in Tel Aviv in March another arrest warrant was issued against Dr. Maqadama. This may be the only official and legal arrest made after the attack. After the two suicide attacks at Kefar Darom and Netzarim in the Gaza Strip on April 1, 1996 Israel accused the Islamic Jihad of perpetrating them. The Palestinian security forces arrested more than 200 activists of that organization. After the attacks on April 2, 15 students of a high school in Jebalya, near Gaza, were arrested; they were released later in stages after intervention by human rights organizations.[72] The Authority views military activity against Israeli objectives as a breach of the Oslo Accords, to which it is a signatory. Accordingly it believes that these operations are a challenge to its governing role.

The Authority is also sensitive to the pressure exerted on it by Israel and the United States to restrain the political opposition. On a number of occasions since the establishment of the Authority, repression has given way to rapprochement, especially when the Authority felt that public opinion would not tolerate further repressive measures. At such times it tries to improve its relations with the opposition by calling for a comprehensive national dialogue, releasing prisoners of the opposition, and improving their treatment inside prisons.

The Authority's position was evident in the reaction by General Ghazi

Jebali, the head of the Palestinian police, to a question about the arrest and persecution of members of the Palestinian opposition:

> We respect the Palestinian national opposition but it must be a Palestinian opposition and hold Palestinian opinions and not be controlled by other countries and receive instructions from them. We are a state with a government and there is no state in the world that tolerates a party that takes orders from outside and has sources of funding outside. We accept the Palestinian opposition that is funded by Palestinians and whose leadership is in Palestine; but if its leadership is in another capital or it is funded by another country – that is not a Palestinian opposition . . . it is an opposition that wants to sabotage the implementation of the agreements and we cannot allow that.[73]

The security forces have been making arrests in Gaza and Jericho ever since they were set up. Most of those arrested belong to the Islamic opposition groups that are opposed to the peace process (Hamas and the Islamic Jihad), but they also include members of the Popular Front and the Democratic Front, as well as journalists who were critical of the Authority, and a number of human rights activists.

The arrests made after attacks against Israel are conducted without indictments being filed or any particular action taken. Arrest warrants are not issued. Those detained are not brought before judges or allowed to contact attorneys to represent them.[74] The arrests began in May 1994. The number of those detained increased drastically in February 1995, when 400 supporters of Hamas, the Islamic Jihad, and the Democratic Front were taken into custody; and again in February, when some 200 supporters of the Islamic movements and the Popular and Democratic Fronts were rounded up. Most of these arrests were made after suicide bombings or military actions conducted inside Israel by the Palestinian opposition. Starting in February 1996, and continuing through October, the Palestinian security forces made large-scale arrests in both the Gaza Strip and West Bank, following the suicide attacks by Islamic groups opposed to the peace process. After the attacks in Tel Aviv, Ashqelon, and Jerusalem, more than a thousand persons were arrested in the West Bank and Gaza Strip. Most of the arrests were political and carried out without warrants and without any of the detainees being brought before a judge. The political prisoners were released in stages as a function of political developments or in response to Palestinian pleas. Some of the prisoners were held for lengthy periods. In August 1998, there were about 200 political prisoners in the West Bank and about 180 in the Gaza Strip, in addition to some 85 sentenced by the State Security Court in the West Bank and Gaza Strip.[75] All of these prisoners were released in October 2000, after the beginning of the Israeli attacks against Palestinian towns, following the "al-Aqsa *Intifada*", but many were rearrested a few days later.

Infringement of the Fundamental Rights of Assembly, Freedom of Expression, and Freedom of Information

The steps taken by the Palestinian security forces to intimidate the Palestinian population have included severe infringement of the fundamental rights of assembly, freedom of expression, and freedom of information. Spontaneous or planned demonstrations frighten the security apparatus, causing it to react apprehensively and with inadequate planning and forethought, the result of high-ranking officers' inexperience with and lack of awareness of public gatherings or meetings organized by political or voluntary organizations or rank-and-file citizens.

Already in the early days of the Authority, its representatives took unequivocal steps to prevent meetings organized by suspected opposition forces. The chief of police, Ghazi Jebali, summoned a member of the Democratic Front for the Liberation of Palestine on September 9, 1994, and announced his decision to ban the DFLP's third national congress, scheduled to take place at the YMCA in Gaza, on the grounds that the Front had not received prior permission, even though the PNA had not enacted any legislation on the subject.[76]

The Authority has used the police force to disperse meetings and assemblies. In 1996, the PNA used armed force and violence to disperse public gatherings. The most prominent cases included the use of "unjustified" violence against public gatherings on two occasions in Nablus and once in Tulkarm. The first time, force was used to disperse a press conference held by student factions at a-Najah University, at the invitation of the student council.[77] Force was used a second time against a protest assembly by families of political prisoners outside Tulkarm prison.[78] The third time was against the crowd attending a soccer match at the municipal field in Nablus. As a result of the use of force in Tulkarm and the Nablus field, two men were killed by gunfire.[79]

The orders to ban public assemblies, demonstrations and meetings are generally issued at the highest levels. Speaking on Israeli television, General Jebali ordered his officers in Nablus to break the bones of Palestinian citizens participating in a march to show solidarity with Iraq in January 1997. He described the marchers as "rabble".[80]

The Authority has also infringed freedom of the press and freedom of expression. It has "red lines" that periodicals, journalists, and citizens must not cross when it comes to freedom of expression. These red lines are not written down but exist in people's minds because of the assaults on most of those who have dared to criticize the Authority and its actions.[81] The freedom of reporting in newspapers is severely limited. Generally journalists are not allowed to write about corruption and favoritism by officials of the Authority.[82] Similarly, the Authority works to prevent and repress any media coverage of the activities of the political opposition.[83] The steps taken by the Authority against newspapers and the media include the confiscation of journalists' press passes or identity cards,[84] searches of cultural institutions and newspaper offices, and the confiscation of documents.[85] Journalists and editors who report on opposition activities, corruption, or anything not to the liking of officials of the Authority, have been arrested.[86] Newspapers have been closed, their printing banned, or distribution prohibited.[87] In addition to attempts to influence the content of reports in the daily and weekly press and a ban on the distribution of articles not to the liking of Authority officials, the infringement of freedom of information and expression has included the confiscation of books, and bans on the distribution of books that contain such materials.[88]

To sum up, the domestic activities of the security forces involve gross violations of human and civil rights under the terms of international conventions and even the laws of the PNA enacted since its establishment in April 1994. This conclusion has been reached by various organizations active in safeguarding human and civil rights in the Palestinian Authority areas, including the Palestinian Human Rights Monitoring Group, the al-Qanun Association, the Palestinian Commission for Human Rights, and B'tselem (the Israeli Information Center for Human Rights in the West Bank and Gaza Strip), as well as international organizations such as Amnesty International and the Agency for International Human Rights Cooperation, with its offices in Washington.

Buying Quiet (Bribery)

The Palestinian Authority and its chairman, Yasser Arafat, employ various and sundry ways to attract people to support the Authority. They generally target particular people, families or interests, "bribing" or neutralizing them. Direct financial support and jobs are the most important ways to attain this objective. The methods used by the Authority to buy quiet and hold the allegiance of various persons are detailed below.

Jobs

Various methods and actions are taken by the Authority and by its head personally to curry favor with individuals and groups. Arafat's intervention in the distribution of jobs demonstrates that the goal is not to strengthen the Authority and its activities, but to buy support. A close scrutiny of all the decisions taken by the Chairman of the Palestinian Authority and published in its official gazette, *al-Waqa'a al-Falistiniya*, reveals the large number of positions and appointments, as well as the creation of new posts, so that a particular person whose support the Chairman desires can be appointed to them, even if this means a duplication of jobs and positions.

The most conspicuous example is the large number of director-generals, of whom there are more than a thousand in the various PNA ministries and agencies. The Comptroller's Report demonstrates the hasty fashion in which these appointments are made.[89] This reaches absurd proportions; for example, all government ministries have, in addition to the minister, deputy ministers, assistants to the deputy minister, director-generals, directors, first directors, second directors, third directors, assistants to the director-general, etc.[90]

There are also many advisors in all ministries, with or without a title; the activity of some overlaps that of other executives.[91] In many cases the appointment circle is expanded by doubling a single position, with one incumbent for the West Bank and another for the Gaza Strip.[92]

Appointments to win support are frequently made retroactively; persons who actually begin working on a certain date receive a letter of appointment from the Chairman that stipulates an earlier effective date, which makes them eligible for financial compensation not actually due to them.[93] Some appointments apply to persons who have still not returned to Palestine, and are clearly made by the Chairman to guarantee that they will be loyal to his regime when they arrive in Palestine or to repay them for past loyalty.[94]

When he decides to set up particular agencies, the Chairman of the Palestinian National Authority is sometimes careful to leave jobs open so that he can later fill them with persons whose support he needs. An example of this is decision 94/4 on the composition of the Gaza town council, headed by A'wen a-Shawa, with nine other members. The fourth paragraph of decision states that "a number of independent representatives of the Palestinian organizations will be added to the council". Arafat has always exploited the term "independents" to gain the support of certain persons by appointing them to particular bodies or jobs (membership in the Palestine National Council is the best example of this).

The appointments made by Arafat include those of relatives or intimates of persons whose support Arafat desires. In many cases ministers or prominent persons in the Authority ask Arafat to appoint their daughter, son, or some other relative to a senior post. The Chairman also agrees to requests from close supporters whose relatives have tangled with the law or have been tainted by corruption to transfer them from one job to another without bringing them to trial or dismissing them on account of their illegal activities. Arafat is fully aware of the vast power he amasses as a result of acceding to these requests. In general Arafat exploits critical opportunities to get senior officials of the Authority to carry out and make decisions they dislike.[95]

Some of Arafat's appointments amount to gross interference in the independence of the legislative branch. This was reflected in the changes that Arafat made to the cabinet following the threats by the legislative council to vote no-confidence in his government after the publication of the Comptroller's Report on corruption in the Authority. Arafat co-opted a number of members of the legislative council as ministers, thereby guaranteeing their vote in favor of the government and neutralizing the no-confidence threat brandished by members of the council.[96]

Special appointments in Arafat's office are another currency used to buy quiet. An examination of the official gazette reveals a large number of advisors and director-generals in the office of the Chairman and office of the President; scrutiny of the names of these functionaries reveals that the intention behind their appointment is to amass power, and that some of them have "Jordanian" or "Egyptian" or religious proclivities. Some advisors have a specific mission and defined area of responsibility;[97] many others have no defined sphere of activity or assignment.[98] This suggests that the objective is to buy their support or that of larger social and political groups, and array them alongside the *Ra'is*. Still other persons have been named director-generals in the office of the President or office of the Chairman without defined assignments,[99] alongside others who do have a clearly defined job.[100]

Appointments of Members of the Opposition

The Chairman of the PNA works to win over members of the Palestinian opposition and makes them enticing offers to join the ranks of the Authority. This method has successfully neutralized some left-wing and Islamic opposition leaders. It has got them to end their hostility to the Oslo Accords and even to become supporters of Arafat and to work in the PNA institutions and ministries. Four individuals can be mentioned: two are from the left, namely Dr. Hanan Ashrawi, the minister of higher education, and Abd el-Jawad Salah, the minister of agriculture, who were among the most prominent opponents of the Oslo Accords and particularly critical of Arafat (especially Ashrawi, who together with a group of Palestinian academics and jurists founded the Independent Palestinian Authority for Civil Rights, which monitors the institutions of the Authority and notes its violations of Palestinian human rights).[101] The other two, formerly central figures in Hamas, are Imad al-Faluji, the minister of communications, and Talal Sidr, the minister of sports and youth. The former was the editor of the Hamas newspaper *al-Watan;* the latter was one of the Marj a-Zahour deportees. But under the heading of "reform from the inside" the two joined the Palestinian government and became Arafat supporters; in response, Hamas purged them from its ranks.

This concentration of power also occurs at lower levels, where opposition figures receive important positions. Prominent representatives of this category include Sheikh Tiyasir al-Tamimi, a Hamas leader in Hebron and one of the Marj a-Zahour deportees, who was appointed deputy chief justice of the Shari'a religious courts and then adopted a neutral stance; and Riyad al-Malki of Ramallah, a leader of the Popular Front for the Liberation of Palestine, recently named a member of the board of Orient House in Jerusalem.

Alongside government ministries and appointments to important positions, political power is also concentrated by means of financial support, in the form of money or a car, a house, a scholarship, or an airplane ticket given to political figures. In principle it is difficult to prove such things and no documentation can be provided, but the phenomenon is widely known and no secret. It has also been confirmed by a member of the Palestinian Legislative Council, Husam Khader of Nablus, in an interview with him.[102] He pointed a finger on three occasions when, he believed, politicians were "bought": first, the eighteenth session of the Palestinian National Council, in Algiers in 1988; second, the session of the Palestinian National Council in Gaza in April 1996; and third, the session of the Palestinian Legislative Council in Gaza in June 1996. In his opinion, "at the first meeting there was a flow of funds to the personal accounts of members of the PNC to buy their support for Resolutions 242 and 338; at the second, to buy their agreement to the repeal of parts of the Palestinian National Covenant; at the third, to ensure a vote of confidence in the cabinet, after a majority of the council had previously announced that it did not have such confidence".

Family Bribery

This method is used to attract large or well-to-do families to support the PNA, through the appointment of *Mukhtars*. Despite the ill repute that has come to be attached to the position of *Mukhtar* because of its holders' connections with the Israeli authorities under the occupation, the PNA, through the Ministry of Local Government, has recently appointed a number of *Mukhtars*, especially in regions with a tribal social structure, notably Gaza and Hebron.

Before the advent of the Palestinian National Authority there were about 120 *Mukhtars* in the Gaza Strip alone. After the establishment of the Authority, the Ministry of Local Affairs approved positions for 500 *Mukhtars*, according to Muhammad al-Fara, director of the Office for Municipal Officials.[103] There is no doubt that this number is impressive; it means that 500 families or villages have a direct link with the PNA through the *Mukhtar*s.

The Ministry of Local Government published the conditions and requirements for candidates to serve as *Mukhtar*.[104] These make it clear that the intention is to appoint those considered to be "notables", those with experience in society affairs and social problems, and those able to collect more than 200 signatures. Scrutiny of the local press and especially the society and congratulations pages give a picture of the significance of the appointment of *Mukhtar*s on a family basis in the Gaza and Hebron areas. For example, one can read the congratulations extended to a new *Mukhtar* on account of "the great confidence expressed in him by Chairman Arafat by appointing him *Mukhtar* of such-and-such a family". In other words, the family is declaring its loyalty to the Chairman.[105]

Economic Bribery

This refers to Arafat's policy of buying off businessmen and the well-to-do by granting them monopolies (concessions or franchises) and commercial agencies, or by turning a blind eye to their control of various sectors of the Palestinian economy. The report issued by the economic affairs committee of the Palestinian Legislative Council at its meeting of May 14, 1997, discloses many of the relevant facts. Monopolies, concessions and rigged tenders are enjoyed by ministers, Arafat's advisors, and employees of the office of the President. Examples include the monopolies on essential commodities such as cement, petroleum, flour, and cigarettes; special import permits and customs exemptions issued without the knowledge of the Finance Ministry; the distribution monopoly of commercial agencies; discrimination among registered companies; the establishment of dummy companies; the diversion of economic agreements to serve interested parties; and even the involvement of the security agencies in such matters.[106]

In addition to the granting of concessions for the distribution of commodities and monopolies, this category includes the allocation of government land to favored investors for the construction of projects with no restrictions attached or without fair competition. Already, 988 *dunams*, or 9 percent of all government land, has been awarded to a handful of persons for the establishment of 99 investment projects.[107]

The examples mentioned above can be classified as part of the financial, administrative and organizational corruption in the Authority, its institutions, and government. Because those who head them are close to Arafat and these things take place with his knowledge and with the objective of winning the support of investors, businessmen, and capitalists, they also fall under the heading of economic bribery.

Social Bribery

The Chairman of the PNA uses social bribery when he awards contracts and privileges to families. On the face of it these privileges constitute assistance by the Chairman to these families, but they are in fact a misuse of public assets, and privileges are given with no restriction or regulation. The decision is made by the Chairman personally and can be seen as a form of bribery. Examples include a decision by Arafat to refer someone for medical treatment abroad, in Israel, Jordan, or elsewhere, at the expense of the Palestinian Authority, without the knowledge of the Ministry of Health or a decision by the finance minister. A letter from Arafat is all that is needed to implement the decision; not even a medical examination is required.[108]

In its review of the first annual Comptroller's Report, the special committee appointed by the Palestinian Legislative Council noted that expenses for medical treatment in the period from January to the end of July 1995, amounted to $24 million, or 20 percent of the budget of the Ministry of Health. From the response to the committee's question to the deputy minister of health about "the form, method, and mechanism for treatment abroad", it was clear that there are "referrals made without going through the Ministry of Health, which come directly from the Chairman to the Finance Ministry and the expenses of which are then deducted from the Health Ministry budget".[109] This kind of bribery applies to various groups among the Palestinians in the West Bank and Gaza Strip, even those who do not come into direct contact with the Authority in their daily lives. Its objective is to expand loyalty to the Authority and its Chairman in these sectors and among all Palestinians ruled over by the PNA.

In addition to general assistance, similar to that for medical treatment abroad, there are other methods of using Authority funds to help Palestinians in need in exchange for their loyalty, such as assistance to the families of those studying abroad, or forgiving tax liabilities, and waiving fines for building infractions and traffic violations. A more direct method involves the financial assistance extended to supporters in the form of private cars or exemptions from customs duties on imported vehicles, and from other taxes. Sources allege that those with the right connections can receive vehicles from the Authority or acquire a private vehicle at a substantial saving if they present a letter from Arafat indicating his agreement that they be "exempted from paying taxes". The Comptroller's Report found that there is "an assault on public funds by customs exemptions that has caused severe financial loss to the Palestinian National Authority".[110] The special committee appointed by the legislative council to review the Comptroller's Report noted that "the total number of tax-exempt government vehicles used by government ministries and public institutions and agencies and security and military agencies, as well as private vehicles allowed to returning brothers, exceeds 4,300. Many of these vehicles that were allowed in without the payment of customs duties do not have the full documentation required by the conditions stipulated by the government."[111]

In addition to decisions made by Arafat, these customs exemptions on imported cars and other items, such as electrical appliances, furnishings, and household and office goods, are issued systematically and by decision from above. As such they represent a systematic practice for winning over and bribing families and individuals or rewarding those close to the Authority, related to ministers, security personnel, and government officials at various levels. According to the report of the special committee of the legislative council, the decisions are implemented through the personal intervention of the minister for civilian affairs, Jamil Tarifi: "The minister for civilian affairs assumes direct supervision of special decisions about customs exemptions, which include automobiles and furnishings as well as donations and scholarships that come into the territory of the PNA." This unequivocal conclusion is based on a statement by the deputy minister for civilian affairs and the director of the office for coordinating customs exemptions in response to the questions posed by the special committee.[112]

To sum up, the concentration of power in Arafat's hands and the methods of intimidation and bribery used by Arafat and his closest supporters are the main instruments they use to rule the Palestinians in the West Bank and Gaza Strip controlled by the Authority, and create the basis for the "partial democratic" regime founded in the West Bank and Gaza Strip after the establishment of the PNA. This undemocratic behavior has created a centralized political system that determines the lives of the Palestinians. This system exists parallel to the formal system described in chapters 4 and 5, but is more comprehensive and effectively overshadows and dominates the formal system, as will be demonstrated in chapter 7.

7

Conclusion: Contradictions within Palestinian Democracy

The Palestinian experience with democratization processes sheds light on such processes at a general level, and adds an important tier of information to what is already known about democratization on two specific levels.

First, the material presented in earlier chapters indicates that any attempt to classify states as democratic or undemocratic, based exclusively on formal criteria such as elections (even at regular intervals) or separation of powers, is misleading and inadequate. The literature emphasizes that essential components of democracy – such as the existence of a civic community with equality among its members in a defined geographic area where it wields exclusive sovereignty, the guarantee of basic liberties such as freedom of movement and freedom of association, accountability to all citizens, and the existence of a permanent and independent monitoring apparatus – are no less important than the basic formal features of regular elections and separation of powers. The detailed analysis of the Palestinian National Authority only partially meets some of the criteria for classification as democratic rather than authoritarian; other criteria it satisfies barely, if at all. It is for this reason that I have named it a "partial democracy". It will have to pass through fundamental processes in the future before it can be classified as fully democratic.

Second, the literature on democratization processes or democratic continuity emphasizes the need for certain conditions of socio-economic development as a precondition for democracy, and the existence of domestic conflict to lay the foundations for processes of democratization (see chapter 1). But the literature ignores the most important factor of all – the existence of a leadership group (or a paramount leader supported by a broad group of second-tier leaders) that believes that democracy is the "least bad" system for cultivating and preserving the political regime and consolidating society. Such a group can make an intelligent choice for a democratic regime and set in place the basic elements for its continuity.

In the Palestinian case, the quiet revolution that took place in the Middle East in 1993 (whose details were woven in Oslo) had two faces, though almost all the Palestinians, Israelis, and persons in other countries were aware of only one of them – the document of mutual recognition between Israel and the Palestinians, which recognized Israel's right to exist, on the one hand, and recognized the PLO as the legitimate representative of the Palestinian people, on the other. The signing of the mutual recognition agreement is one facet of the revolution. It is significant for Palestinians, Israelis, and other peoples in the region, and received wide attention as well as support and encouragement from various members of the international community. This process is not the subject of the present volume, though it certainly merits discussion, analysis, and understanding.

The other aspect of the revolution, of which most observers were unaware, took place within the Palestinian national movement. During the years of Israeli occupation, the first forms of a political entity began to emerge in the West Bank and Gaza Strip. This identity was democratic with respect to its basic characteristics, featuring rival parties and factions, voluntary organizations and institutions, representative leadership, community organization, and continual civil confrontation with the strictures of the Israeli occupation. This process was aimed at the construction of a future democratic political system.

In parallel to developments in the West Bank and Gaza Strip, which took place under the Israeli occupation and despite its severity, centralization in the PLO increased over the years, furthered by processes that affected the PLO as a result of the struggle with Israel, the experience in Lebanon, its forced departure from that country, and the experience of the *Intifada*. It involved political and legal measures that led to the takeover by the PLO, under Arafat, of the system that had begun to emerge in the West Bank and Gaza Strip, and the neutralization of the local leaders who, after the Madrid Conference, participated in the Washington talks with Israel aimed at reaching a peace agreement based on a resolution to the Israeli occupation of the West Bank and the Gaza Strip, and the ramifications of the Palestinian problem created during and after the 1948 war. This revolution entailed the gradual and agreed-upon transfer of land – agreed to by Israel and the PLO leadership in the name of Arafat – to the people of the West Bank and Gaza Strip and the establishment of a Palestinian political entity that aspired to control the territory.

A number of factors enabled the change. First among them was the weakness of the PLO after the Gulf War, the exhaustion of its financial resources, a decline of its organizational vigor, and the desire of its activists to revive it using whatever measures were available to them. Second came the signs of fatigue in the Palestinian national movement in the West Bank and Gaza Strip after years of struggling against the occupation. Third was the disconnection, after the PLO's departure from Lebanon, between the organization and its apparatus. The Palestinians living in refugee camps in the Arab world could not prevent the organization's leadership from signing peace agreements that made inadequate reference to their problem. Fourth was the Israeli assistance to the PLO leadership, especially Arafat, that made it possible for them to work the change and set up an alternative mechanism to "direct" Israeli control of the Palestinians living in the West Bank and Gaza Strip.

The last factor is crucial – or at least the only one without which the revolution could not have taken place. The Israeli leadership, headed by Yitzhak Rabin, wanted a peace agreement that was comfortable, cheap, and easy to market to the Israeli public – in other words, an agreement which contained no commitment whatsoever to find a genuine solution to the Palestinian problem, of the sort that had been demanded by the Palestinian negotiators in Washington. The Israeli side was also interested in the establishment of a "partner" within Palestinian society that could enjoy recognition and legitimacy on the part of the Palestinians, to rule them and to impose order where Israel had failed to do so. In the eyes of the then- (and current) Israeli leadership, the regime that would exert control on the ground was supposed to maintain tranquility, prevent anti-Israel protests by Palestinians, repress leftist and Islamic elements hostile to Israel, and prevent them from engaging in violence against Israel and Israelis. This agent was of course the PLO led by Arafat, which, during the course of the Oslo talks and later in all public contacts between the Israeli and Palestinian leadership, from Oslo on, demonstrated that it was willing to do the dirty work and satisfy Israeli expectations. There was an unwritten basic promise: the maintenance of quiet on the ground at any price, even if this required the denial of basic rights to the Palestinians controlled by the Palestinian entity.

The steps taken by the Palestinian leadership since its coalescence, and reinforced by Israeli support since the Oslo agreements, have produced a "partial democracy" marked by contradiction: on the one hand, processes that attest to greater democracy in the Palestinian national movement and the PNA after its founding; on the other hand, processes of de-democratization and restrictions on Palestinians' freedom of expression, movement and organization and an attempt to subject them to the exclusive control of Arafat. One facet of this is Arafat's attempt to impede the emergence of an alternative leadership in the West Bank and Gaza Strip, a crude attack on the principle of separation of powers in the PNA, and the existence and operation of a complex control mechanism.

Palestinian "Partial Democracy" before the Establishment of the PNA

The Palestinian national movement, which began to organize after the 1948 war in the aftermath of tragedy, developed in two parallel but interconnected channels: the creation of the Palestinian Liberation Organization (PLO) in 1964, and its institutions in the Palestinian diaspora; and, at the same time, the organization of the Palestinian community in the West Bank and Gaza Strip, where most Palestinians live. This distinction is important for understanding the different and sometimes antithetical experience of democratization processes by the Palestinians at home and by their national movement, even though in both cases the Palestinians and their leaders deemed it important to market themselves as a democratic and pluralistic society and national movement, unique in the Arab world.

In practice the PLO went through a slow process of de-democratization, epitomized in the transfer of decision-making authority from various power centers to the Chairman and the administrative apparatus that he fostered and consolidated. For many years, especially after Fatah came to dominate the PLO, and Arafat was named leader of the entire organization and not only of Fatah, Arafat cultivated a habit of consulting with close associates in the Fatah leadership and with the leaders of other factions in the PLO, such as the heads of the Democratic and Popular Fronts, other factions, and even prominent individuals in Palestinian organizations and communities.[1] This situation eroded gradually, starting after the Seventh Palestine National Congress meeting in June 1970, because of the establishment of the Central Committee, which was fully controlled by Arafat. This act neutralized the executive committee, and later during the PLO's heyday in Lebanon and construction of a Palestinian state-within-a-state there, brought about a situation of exclusive control by Arafat of decisions and their implementation. A number of factors made this possible, of which the most important were: the continuing state of war and climate of revolution, and the recurrent need to make rapid and secret decisions in Lebanese territory, near Israel; the absence of any law requiring the Chairman to consult with others or to obtain the consent of a defined majority; the absence of any mechanism to supervise finances and the Chairman's practical control of the organization's revenues and expenditures. These and other factors made it easier for Arafat to shake off any need to consult others. The process was gradual and moved ahead through the crises that beset the Palestinian national movement, such as clashes with Christians in Lebanon, with the Syrians, and with Israel. First Arafat suspended his dialogue with leaders of the opposition within the PLO, after that with independents, and finally he even turned a deaf ear to other Fatah leaders. He employed various means and pretexts to neutralize even his close associates, including the other founders of Fatah in Kuwait in the 1950s. Even while Arafat rid himself of the need to consult with others he gathered around him a set of yes-men as his advisors and assistants; over the years he appointed them to senior positions as advisors or department heads and even to senior positions within the PLO, including membership in the PNC.

At the same time as Arafat was tightening his control of the PLO and concentrating power in his own hands, he continued to champion tradi-tional methods of decision-making in the organization and its institutions (the PNC, the Central Committee, the executive committee, and other forums), especially the reliance on consensus and avoidance of formal votes to put majority support on record, as is the norm in a modern democratic system; the absence of a commitment to respect opposing opinions; and the absence of an apparatus to oversee the implementation of decisions. In practice, motions were submitted for debate whose results – which were whatever the Chairman wanted – were known in advance. Organizations or individuals who were not happy with the decisions or motions boycotted meetings or walked out, since the leaders of all factions knew that the final decision would always be whatever Arafat wanted, and that their opinions would have no impact on decisions or on their implementation.

Arafat's control of the apparatus, decision-making, and execution intensified over the years. It accelerated after the PLO's exodus from Lebanon, especially as a result of the consolidation of the new bureaucracy in Tunisia. Further rapid progress took place after the murders of Khalil al-Wazir (Abu Jihad) and Salah Khalef (Abu Iyad), leading figures since the founding of the organization, who were extremely close to Arafat and the decision-making apparatus. After their elimination Arafat promoted a new generation of aides and assistants who were subject to his authority. They helped him to take over the organization and its decision-making process and to shunt aside other figures such as Farouk Kadoumi (another founder of the organization). In practice the processes described reflect the concentration of power in the hands of the Chairman many years before his return to Palestinian territory in Gaza and Jericho, after the Oslo agree-ments, and coronation as the all-powerful sole ruler within the PLO and perhaps the entire Palestinian national movement. But the opposing devel-opments that took place on the ground in the West Bank and Gaza Strip brought with them contradictions that still have to be resolved.

Among the Palestinians who lived in the West Bank and Gaza Strip, a gradual process of democratization and pluralism took place after the Israeli occupation in 1967. Unlike the Jordanian interlude – when the king and his representatives acted to prevent all manifestations of pluralism and to put down oppositionist tendencies and any phenomenon that cast a shadow on the exclusive position of the Jordanian bureaucracy and royal authority – from the start of the Israeli occupation of the West Bank, and despite the attempts to suppress all expressions of pluralism or opposi-tionist organization, the Palestinians there, under the impact of global processes and the strengthening of the Palestinian national movement, were able to develop alternative political organizations and set up volun-tary organizations that worked to improve various spheres of life in the West Bank and Gaza Strip.

In parallel to the consolidation of the PLO and its growing acceptance in the Arab world and international community as the representative of the Palestinian people, various organizations appeared in the Occupied West Bank and Gaza Strip that supported this tendency and saw themselves as the representatives in the field of the PLO. In other words, there became established political organizations that reflected the existence of various streams in the Palestinian national movement, such as the Palestinian National Front, established in the summer of 1973 as a counterweight to Jordanian influence and Hashemite supporters in the West Bank. The 1976 local elections in the West Bank brought the nationalist current to the fore; its victories in many towns and authorities gave expression to local forces that had previously been repressed or not visible.[2] The results of the elec-tions and various other developments, such as the increased support for the PLO in the field and the growing support for it as the "sole legitimate repre-sentative of the Palestinian people", led to the establishment in 1978 of the National Guidance Committee, which set itself the goal of resisting Israeli attempts to foster an alternative leadership to the PLO and its supporters in the West Bank and Gaza Strip, and of mobilizing the Palestinians to struggle against the Israeli policy of land expropriation, construction of settlements, and various other hostile steps. This process reached its culmi-nation after the outbreak of the *Intifada* in December 1987, when the various secular forces got together and set up the United Command of the *Intifada*, while the Islamic stream set up its own alternative leadership. The two groupings directed the Palestinians' steps during the *Intifada* against Israel and its occupation.[3]

The establishment of political organizations that represented all politi-cal streams in the West Bank and Gaza Strip was accompanied by another positive development in terms of democratic process. This was the estab-lishment and operation of professional associations that represented the interests of various groups and political currents. These included organ-izations to represent the interests of workers, associations of engineers, lawyers, physicians, and other professionals, women's organizations, and student organizations on campuses and in Palestinian society. In addition to these, hundreds of groups that set their sights on improvements in various spheres were established, such as voluntary associations and research centers, educational and social services, help for youth and the elderly, and improving conditions in communities and neighborhoods in towns and large cities.[4]

These processes in the Occupied West Bank and Gaza Strip were the antithesis of the centralization of power that took place in the PLO in the Palestinian diaspora. The organizations and institutions established in the West Bank and Gaza Strip provided maximum representation for all strata, groups and actors in Palestinian society. Country-wide political organizations were established and run democratically while safeguarding pluralism, taking decisions on a majority basis, and preserving the right of the minority to express its opinion or promote its objectives in Palestinian society through democratic means. This was a difficult process, accompanied by severe problems that stemmed from the nature of Palestinian society, pressures exerted by the PLO leadership abroad, and especially the restrictions imposed by the Israeli occupation – its abuse of these actors, and repeated attempts to neutralize and immobilize them in the political, cultural, and social spheres, and to interdict their sources of funding.

"Partial Democracy" in the PNA

In a democratic regime the branches of government (legislative, executive, and judicial) should be independent and substantially separate from one another, whatever the practical overlap in various matters because of the need to promote the affairs of the various systems of state. The elections held in the Palestinian autonomous areas on January 20, 1996, were meant to strengthen the legislative branch *vis-à-vis* the executive branch.

A study of the degree of separation of powers in the Palestinian National Authority discloses a picture that is far from desirable. In practice the executive branch has real administrative and structural control, exerted especially by the *Ra'is* and his office, over the legislative and judicial branches. This is reflected in the clear and gross violation of the fundamental principles of the separation of powers and balance among them. In the relations between the legislative branch and the executive branch this violation is manifested in a number of ways.

The Executive Branch versus the Legislative Branch

Overall, relations between the legislative council and the executive branch have been tense; at best they can be described as "cold". Many of those close to the activity of the legislative council – such as the members themselves, human rights organizations, and researchers – attribute much of this tension to the executive's attitude toward the council, both as an institu-

tion and to its members as individuals. This treatment takes three forms –
attacking it, ignoring it, and interfering with its activity.

Attacking the Council. The executive attacks the legislative council on
two fronts – its individual members and its powers.

1   Members of the legislative council were beaten during the sit-down
     strike outside the house of the Awadallah family in el-Bireh on August
     25, 1998. The sit-down strike was staged to protest against the
     blockade imposed by the Palestinian security apparatus, and especially
     the Preventive Security service, on the Awadallah family, following
     Imad Awadallah's escape from Jericho prison. During the sit-down
     strike, Preventive Security agents attempted to disperse the demon-
     strators by force, which led to a confrontation with the members of the
     council at the site; an officer of the Preventive Security service began
     hitting the demonstrators. One legislator, Hatem Abd el-Qadr, was
     taken to hospital.
        Some members of the legislative council viewed this incident as a
     deliberate attempt to intimidate them and incite people against them.
     Even though two committees, one governmental (the military depart-
     ment) and the other parliamentary, were set up to investigate the
     circumstances of the assault, the matter was resolved through recon-
     ciliation. The minister for parliamentary affairs told the council, at its
     session of November 10, 1998, that the investigation had been
     completed and the officer who had been at the scene and another agent
     of the Preventive Security service would be tried in court. Nothing
     further has been heard of the matter.[5]
2   Some members of the legislative council have been harassed and
     attacked by the security forces. The legislative council set up commit-
     tees to investigate such cases and complaints submitted by its
     members. On March 30, 1998, the council requested two of its standing
     committees, Control and Internal Affairs, to deal with the complaints
     submitted by council member Hatem Abd el-Qadr alleging police
     harassment. On July 8, 1998, the committee investigated the harass-
     ment of council member Ma'awiya al-Masri by bureaucrats in the
     Nablus Strip. On July 10, 1998, a member of the security forces tried
     to attack two members of the legislative council and attempted to
     prevent them from entering the council building in Ramallah.[6]
3   Members of the legislative council were not allowed to visit the Juneid
     prison in Nablus. Details of this incident were contained in the report
     of the Control Committee to the council meeting on April 2, 1998. A
     special committee set up by the council to visit political prisoners who
     were staging a hunger strike in the prison asked to visit the prisoners

after coordination with General Haj Ismail Jabber, commander of the National Security Forces. But the committee – comprising Azmi Sha'ibi, Hassan Kharisheh, Ma'awiya al-Masri, Jamal Shati, and Kamal Afjani – was not allowed to enter the prison. Its gates were shut in their faces and a member of the National Security Force attacked them.[7]

4   Jibril Rajoub, the head of the Preventive Security service on the West Bank, verbally attacked members of the council and accused some of them of being thieves and gangsters. This was against the background of the Israeli authorities' arrest of council member Musa Abu Sabha while driving a Mercedes vehicle that turned out to have been stolen. Chairman Arafat set up a committee, headed by Tayeb Abd el-Rahim, along with Haj Ismail Jabber, Nasser Yussuf, and Abd er-Razek al-Majeida, to investigate Rajoub, but Rajoub refused to appear before the committee.[8]

Council member Husam Khader met with similar treatment. On one occasion he had a verbal confrontation with Yasser Arafat himself during a council session. Khader also noted that he was forbidden to give interviews to Palestinian radio or television.

Another way in which the executive branch attacks the legislative branch involves measures that infringe the powers and prerogatives of the council.

1   A ban was placed on direct broadcasts of sessions of the legislative council over al-Quds educational television, run by al-Quds University. The head of the station, journalist Daoud Kuttab, was arrested, following broadcasts of the council session that debated the affair of the spoiled flour in April 1997. The security forces also confiscated cameras and recording equipment in the council chamber in Ramallah; despite protests by members of the council its leadership proved unable to resolve the problem. I have been unable to locate documentation relating to this issue, but some newspapers covered Kuttab's arrest.

2   The executive works to curtail the powers of the legislative council. A basic principle of democracy is that constitutional amendments are the result of the legislative process. Despite this, on March 20, 1998, Presidential Decree No. 1998/54, which defined the responsibility of the State Security Court to try certain crimes, amended constitutional formulas for the West Bank. Similarly, on February 7, 1998, Presidential Decree 1998/7 permitted the establishment of a factory to supply the needs of the security forces and police, and gave it an independent legal status and budgetary responsibility. Again, on September 21, 1998, the *Ra'is* issued Legal Instruction 1998/1,

concerning the validity of the Tourism Law 45 (1965) on all Palestinian territory. All these cases infringed the exclusive prerogatives of the council.[9]

Ignoring the Council. During the last three years, in a series of actions and incidents, the executive branch has clearly ignored the legislative branch. The attempt to limit its powers and operation is noted clearly in the report of its speaker, Ahmad Qre'a, to the council at the end of its first year of operation. Below are several examples, from various sources, that explain how the executive branch ignores the legislature.

(1) *The PNA budget*: According to the General Budget and Fiscal Affairs Law, the council bylaws, and the draft Basic Law, the executive branch is supposed to submit a draft budget at least two months before the start of the fiscal year. But a review of executive branch behavior shows that it has submitted the budget several months late every year. The 1997 budget was submitted in May 1997;[10] the 1998 budget was submitted on March 31, 1998, and approved by the legislative council on June 29, 1998;[11] the 1999 and 2000 budgets were submitted by the executive branch to the council in August each year.

On November 14, 1996, the legislative council approved its own independent budget for 1997 and forwarded it to the finance minister for inclusion in the general budget of the PNA. But the executive branch did not submit the general budget to the council until May 1997, leaving the council without an approved budget. On November 15, 1997, the council decided that its budget for 1998 would be independent but did not set a figure.[12] For various reasons, some of them political and others the failure of the executive branch to heed the council budget, the council wound up dependent on assistance from the United States and Europe to finance its activities.

(2) *Draft legislation*: The head of the executive branch has ignored Bills passed by the council and sent to him for signature. Although the *Ra'is* did sign some laws after a long waiting period, others – especially the Basic Law – remained unsigned. It seems that he had no intention of approving them. By the end of 1997 – that is, two years after the election of the legislative council – the *Ra'is* had affixed his signature to only three laws.[13]

(3) *Council decisions*: One reason for the tense relations between the legislative and executive branches has to do with failure of the latter to implement decisions of the legislative council. By the middle of 1999 the council had passed some 378 resolutions; its members complain about the disregard for them demonstrated by the executive branch. One reaction to this is the discernible decline in the number of council decisions in its second year. Whereas it passed 135 resolutions in its first year (1996), the next year the total fell to only 96.[14]

(4) *Parliamentary questions to ministers*: At the start of June 1997, the legislative council assigned its Thursday session for the submission of questions to ministers by council members on pre-announced topics. The council began holding these sessions on June 19, 1997. By January 29, 1999, 136 such questions had been submitted to ministers, but only 64 had been answered.[15] That is, ministers' responses to questions were not at an appropriate level. Some ministers ignored invitations to appear before the council and answer questions, while others merely sent a representative – a low-level bureaucrat. Some did not even apologize for their failure to show up.[16]

(5) *Composition of the government*: The head of the executive branch brushed aside repeated requests by the legislative council that he present a new government after the report by the General Control Commission concerning corruption in the government service. Even though this council resolution was passed on July 31, 1997, the cabinet was not revamped until August 9, 1998, more than a year later.[17] In addition, the request to dismiss ministers accused of corruption and financial wrongdoing was ignored. Instead Arafat kept them in their posts and appointed additional ministers – which amounts to expanding rather than changing the government.[18]

(6) *Commissions of inquiry*: The executive agencies have not cooperated seriously with commissions of inquiry established by the legislative council to investigate incidents or complaints. Examples are the lack of cooperation by the Ministry of Agriculture with the special committee to investigate the forgery of factory documents in Nablus, the lack of co-operation by various executive-branch agencies with the committee set up by the council to investigate the information in the Comptroller's Report about corruption in the PNA, and the delay by other agencies in providing answers to questions posed by the Commission. It reached a point where the executive branch did not permit members of the Commission to meet with officials to receive information and documents. In its report, dated July 9, 1997, the Control Committee of the council also wrote about its displeasure with the refusal of the justice minister to meet with the committee, and saw this as contempt of the council and its committees.[19]

Another report issued by the Control Committee noted the lack of co-operation by the director-general of the Civil Defense Service, General Abd el-Hai Abd el-Wahad, with the committee during its investigation of corruption in that agency. This was despite the fact that the general had been officially subpoenaed by the legislative council and refused to appear; what is even more alarming is that the civil defense system is part of the Interior Ministry – a portfolio held by Arafat himself.[20] In addition, members of the committee set up by the council to investigate the murder of Muhi ed-Din Sharif threatened to resign because of obstacles put in their way by the executive branch, which did not allow them to determine the facts, as noted by council member Hatem Abd el-Qadr.[21]

(7) *Ratification of agreements*: The PNA has signed more than 25 agreements to receive loans from agencies and banks outside Palestine to finance projects. The executive branch is supposed to submit the documents to the legislative council for ratification but has never done so, except for one agreement signed with the Arab Fund for Economic and Social Development, in the amount of 11 million Kuwaiti dinars, ratified by the council in June 1997.[22] In this context, the economic committee of the council expressed its displeasure with the failure to submit loan agreements for ratification by the council.

(8) *Confidence in ministers*: Another example of the executive branch's contempt for the legislative council is the appointment of new ministers without requesting approval by the council. In 1997, the *Ra'is* appointed Talal Sadr as minister of sports and youth, without submitting the appointment to the legislative council. The council has passed many resolutions about this, such as Resolution 2/8/165, which demands that the activity and authority of the minister be suspended until he has been approved by the council. The executive branch (and the minister himself) ignored the council and he never appeared before it to receive its confidence.[23]

Interfering with the Council's Activities. Executive branch interference with the activity of the legislative council occurs in a number of ways. For example, the executive co-opts members of the legislative council or appoints them to executive functions as a way to guarantee their support.

(1) The Speaker of the council was invited to attend meetings of the Palestinian leadership. Many council members were opposed to his participation in meetings with the Palestinian cabinet, members of the PLO executive committee, the head of the PNC, the commanders of the security services, and the teams negotiating with Israel. Council members saw this as co-optation of the Speaker by the Chairman of the Authority and asked him to stop attending the sessions. Political commentators see this formula as evidence of the abrogation of the independence of the legislative branch.[24]

(2) Many council members are members of the cabinet. The government formed on August 9, 1998, included 23 ministers who were also members of the legislative council (76 percent of the 30-member cabinet). Even though this is in keeping with the Oslo Accords, the leaders of the executive branch thereby guarantee that these members will support it in council votes.[25]

(3) Some members of the legislative council hold senior positions and jobs under the Palestinian Authority. These include the head of the Civil Aviation Authority, Faez Zeidan; the director of the National Security Office, Hakim Balawi; the director of the Planning Center in the office of the Chairman, Fakhri Shukureh; Marwan Kanafani, advisor to the *Ra'is*; Ghassan Shaqa, a member of the PLO executive committee; and Hassan

Asfour and Saeb Erekat, members of the negotiating team. This participation and membership are not limited to jobs and assignments; they also affect the functioning of the council member as a legislator who is supposed to act independently of the executive branch.

The Executive Branch versus the Judicial Branch

An examination of the situation of the judicial branch *vis-à-vis* the executive branch reveals an even more clear-cut picture of gross infringement of the principle of separation of powers. In practice, the judicial branch is administratively and substantively subordinate to the executive branch. The violence to the independence of the judicial branch is strikingly evident, as the following indicates:

(1) *The appointment and dismissal of judges*: Judges, like most other functionaries in the PNA, are generally not appointed on the basis of fixed criteria nor by a system that preserves the independence of the judicial branch essential for a democratic system. The nature of the appointments represents gross interference by the executive branch in the affairs of the judicial branch and threatens the independence and future security of the judges. Referring to this, the first Palestinian Chief Justice, Qusi al-Abdallah, noted that he himself should have appointed judges after their selection by a special committee, though they would of course take office only after receiving a writ of appointment from the head of state. In his opinion, however, the appointment of judges, at all levels and courts, was done without his knowledge. Justice al-Abdallah charged that the Palestinian justice minister interfered in appointments in a manner contrary to the law, the principle of the separation of powers, and the independence of the judicial branch.[26]

The same principle applies to the dismissal of judges, which is usually done by actors outside the judicial system in a manner that constitutes a clear violation of the principle of separation of powers. The Chief Justice himself was dismissed by the appointments bureau, which is part of the executive branch. Of course in this and other cases where judges were dismissed there was no clear legal procedure to be followed. The judges were not relieved of office at their own request or because they had been impeached by a special commission that found them unfit for office, whether on the substantive level or because of actions unbecoming a judge, such as inappropriate conduct, accepting bribes, and the like.[27]

(2) *Courtroom conditions*: Since the establishment of the Palestinian National Authority and its assumption of responsibility for the judicial affairs of Palestinians, the number of cases on the courts' docket has risen sharply. There has not, however, been a corresponding growth in the system, including the number of judges, betterment of the physical condi-

tions of the courtrooms, extra auxiliary staff, and the like. In general, the number of workers and conditions in the courtroom are inadequate for the caseload. According to the report of the al-Qanun Association, which monitors the judicial system and its operation, there are too few bailiffs to bring defendants and witnesses to court, even though this position does not require any particular skills. In the Nablus Strip, which covers the northern part of the West Bank, there are only four bailiffs. According to attorneys in various regions, the system is collapsing under the overload and the situation is exacerbated by the physical condition of the courtrooms, which seriously undermines the system, its operation, independence, and freedom from superfluous pressures – all of which are indispensable for its proper operation.[28]

(3) *Failure to implement court decisions*: A factor that adds to the fatigue and frustration of the judicial system, including lawyers, is that court decisions are frequently not implemented and are even disregarded and treated with contempt by the agencies supposed to implement them. Many court decisions, particularly those of the Supreme Court relating to the release of prisoners, are ignored or countermanded by police commanders, who believe that the courts erred in their decision, which should accordingly not be implemented. (The annual report on the status of justice in the West Bank and Gaza Strip of the PNA by the al-Qanun Association presents a number of cases in which those supposed to implement court decisions ignored or derided them.) In many cases, senior PNA officials, such as commanders of the police, security services, governors, and so on intervene and try to resolve problems awaiting judicial resolution. As senior functionaries they take upon themselves the right to mediate and implement their decisions, as if there were no applicable court decisions.[29]

As has been described, the formal system of the PNA operates in a manner that is quite different from the desired situation of separation of powers, which should reflect a democratic political structure and behavior. In addition, the executive branch, which is also part of the formal structure, during and since the establishment of the PNA after the withdrawal of Israeli forces from Gaza and Jericho and the subsequent expansion of the territory under its control, has amassed so much power as to leave the formal structure in its shadow. It employs various techniques of control to rule Palestinian institutions and population, namely: concentration of power, security supervision (intimidation), and benefits to buy quiet and supporters (bribery).

The system is totally under the control of Arafat, who built it up, step-by-step, in the early stages of the reconstruction of the Palestinian national movement. This began for all practical purposes in the mid-1960s; Arafat continued to cultivate and strengthen it during the ensuing years until the establishment of the Palestinian National Authority. It was possible for him to expand and strengthen his system of control because of the fact that it operates in a defined territory, which permits the institutionalization and continuity of control.

In summary, on the formal level the Palestinian regime is supposed to function as a democratic system like those in the West, where "the people is the source of legitimacy of the regime that exists in the legislative, executive, and judicial branches, based on the principle of separation of powers, in a manner clarified in a constitution".[30] This is supposed to include structural arrangements for the separation of powers (legislative, executive, and judicial), intended to guarantee democratic behavior on the substantive level, including equal treatment of all citizens, equality before the law, maintenance of a reasonable level of welfare, the liberty and freedoms appropriate to a democratic regime, government transparency, the accountability of the authorities to citizens, freedom of information, and all the procedures and conduct associated with a democratic system. The degree of separation of powers in the PNA is far from ideal, not to mention the infringements enumerated above that undermine the independence of the judiciary.

Conclusions for the Future

The price that the Palestinian leadership paid Israel for allowing it to return to the West Bank and Gaza Strip and establish an administrative apparatus and a Palestinian political entity for the first time in history was paid in the coin of anti-democratic measures that consolidated into the authoritarian-led situation described above. But is the Israeli factor a sufficient explanation? I think not. The current situation is the outcome of a number of factors, such as the nature of Palestinian society itself, which for the most part was willing to accept the new regime, and also the undemocratic nature of the Palestinian leadership that set up the Palestinian National Authority.

For many years Palestinian society in the West Bank and Gaza Strip was mobilized for the struggle against the Israeli occupation. Under Israeli occupation this society experienced many torments and difficulties, on both the collective and individual levels. The entire society was subject to collective punishment, land expropriation and underdevelopment, including the devastation of the basic services left behind by the Jordanians (in the West Bank) and Egyptians (in Gaza Strip) after their own 20-year occupation of the West Bank and Gaza Strip. On the individual level, too, Palestinians suffered greatly from persecution, arrests, unemployment, and various other cruel steps taken by the occupying power. The years of unrelenting mobilization, which reached their pinnacle during the *Intifada*, produced many signs of exhaustion and fatigue among the Palestinians in the West Bank and Gaza Strip, and a desire for a personal existence. This situation made it easier for the Palestinian leadership to move with only rare manifestations of opposition. Even the elites and intelligentsia were willing to waive a struggle against the signs of incipient dictatorship in return for payoffs to their members by Arafat and his henchmen.

The Palestinian leadership – Arafat and those who arrived with him, along with his loyalists in the West Bank and Gaza Strip who were co-opted to the bureaucratic establishment after the founding of the PNA – are for the most part people who have led lives of perpetual struggle to survive. Their formative years were dominated by risk-taking, and they grew up in a traditional and undemocratic Arab society. They had no democratic tradition, no basic commitment to the construction of a democratic regime, and no understanding of the importance of preserving the fundamental principles of democracy. They viewed manifestations of pluralism, democracy, and the free play of ideas as a threat to their exclusive control of the Palestinian people in the West Bank and Gaza Strip. They played a decisive role in the consolidation of the centralized regime that leaves no room for democratization processes and even seeks to impose greater centralization. It rejects all manifestations of pluralism and the basic traits of a democratic system.

In practice, a new political order emerged with the establishment of the PNA. Arafat created an authoritarian regime of the sort described in the literature as centralized "totalitarian democracy", which he controls directly by means of well-known techniques such as the concentration of power, intimidation, and bribery. In parallel he shoved aside the forces that had shaped the emerging autochthonous political order in the West Bank and Gaza Strip during the last years before the establishment of the PNA. This order, which incorporated political pluralism, struggle, protest on behalf of change, and voluntary organizations that were the first sign of the appearance of a Palestinian civil society, was shunted to the sidelines by Arafat and his entourage or incorporated into the new political structure, if that was more convenient to the heads of the new regime and could serve the new order in the West Bank and Gaza Strip.

It is not true, however, that these characteristics of the pre-PNA Palestinian order have totally vanished. They still exist and fight against the continuing Israeli occupation and the regime established by the PNA. Some have surrendered to the new order and are attempting to adapt themselves to it; others are still using legitimate means to bring about the democratic changes needed to turn the clock back and resume the construction of a democratic system in which the Palestinians will rule themselves. This system is barely alive, and functions as a weak shadow of Arafat's centralized regime. Thus at present, there are two systems in the West Bank and Gaza Strip, one of which is active, undemocratic, and dominant, while the other is passive, democratic, and overshadowed by the first.

A serious attempt to deal with the factors that produced the decisions by the PLO leadership, headed by Arafat, concerning the Palestinian political entity in the West Bank and Gaza Strip will lead to an inverse development in the democratic context and the start of an opposing process of democratization in the political life of the Palestinians subject to PNA rule. By this I mean that there will be a serious and effective confrontation with the issue of the orderly succession of leadership and the rise of forces committed to a democratic system in Palestine. This must be expressed in meaningful changes in leadership, including and especially intergenerational issues. Democracy and democratization exist only where the political, social, economic, educational, and cultural leadership is strongly committed to it. The current leadership of the PNA, at the highest levels, lacks a democratic tradition and has no understanding or internalization of the principles of democracy. I would cautiously assert that it cannot lead the desired process of democratization. The solution must involve a change in the leadership and the rise of new forces that have a basic comprehension of the importance of democracy for the future of the PNA and of the Palestinians in general. Only a new leadership generation can spearhead a process of democratization and perhaps even market it in neighboring Arab states and societies.

The change in leadership must take advantage of two other developments. The *first* is the final end of the Israeli occupation in the West Bank and Gaza Strip. This, along with Palestinian political and economic independence in a sovereign state with international recognition, is a necessary condition for eliminating the perpetual pressure exerted by Israel and its government for the PNA to deal with anti-Israel elements among the Palestinians in the West Bank and Gaza Strip. Such a development would remove a key obstacle to the democratization of the Authority.

The *second* development is the reorganization of Palestinian society around a firm demand for democracy, manifested in active political life. This must include a return to vigorous partisan political activity, the operation of an active opposition, the operation of the political institutions of the Authority, the establishment and rational operation of voluntary organizations, and the active political participation of Palestinian citizens. An organized political society is a hallmark of democracy; hence there is a vital need for a political awakening among the Palestinians, and not just acquiescence with steps taken by the Authority in both foreign and domestic affairs.

The above conditions may be essential for democratization of the Authority, but they are not sufficient. What is also needed for the process to succeed is a desire to realize such a process, as well as ample time and patience. Only then will it be possible to transfer the PNA from the rubric of a centralized authoritarian state to the category of a pluralistic democracy.

Appendixes

APPENDIX NO. 1
The Palestinian Authority's Political Program, May 28, 1994

APPENDIX NO. 2
Basic Law: The Palestinian National Authority

Chapter 1   Preface
Chapter 2   Public Rights and Freedoms
Chapter 3   The Legislative Branch
Chapter 4   The Executive Branch
Chapter 5   The Judicial Branch
Chapter 6   Provisions for a State of Emergency
Chapter 7   General and Transitional Provisions

APPENDIX NO. 3
Standing Orders for the Palestinian Legislative Council

Preamble
Title I
Chapter 1   The Initial Meeting
Chapter 2   The Presidium of the Council
Chapter 3   Vote of Confidence, No Confidence, and Withdrawal of Confidence

Title II
Chapter 1   Meetings of the Council
Chapter 2   Minutes of the Meetings
Chapter 3   Secret Meetings
Chapter 4   Rules of Order at Meetings
Chapter 5   Termination of Membership

Title III
Chapter 1   Committees of the Council
Chapter 2   Committee Procedures
Chapter 3   Interpellations and Motions for the Agenda

APPENDIX NO. 4
Draft Law, Independence of the Judiciary

APPENDIX NO. 1

The Palestinian Authority's Political Program, May 28, 1994

Nature, Definition, Mandate and Methodology of the Palestinian Authority

The Authority was established by virtue of a decision by the PLO – the sole legitimate representative of the Palestinian people – as the authorized agent of the PLO. The Authority will derive its legitimacy from the PLO, which will remain the source of its political and legislative power. The Palestinian Authority is a temporary interim authority that will operate until general democratic elections are conducted in the Palestinian lands. The Authority is responsible for implementing the interim programs during the interim phase in order to consolidate a national program to link the interim period to the permanent solution.

The Authority will exercise its executive and legislative mandate temporarily until the general elections.

The Palestinian Authority will design its internal system, which will define them for implementing its programs and tasks. The Authority is committed to performing its tasks according to clear criteria that are compatible with the national commitments and utility. This will be accomplished through specialized institutions, systems, and framework, which the authority will establish in cooperation with Palestinian centers of power wherever they exist.

The Authority's Interim Work Program – Tasks and Mechanisms

Implementing and exercising governmental authority in the Palestinian lands, starting with the Gaza District and Jericho, through its mandate and responsibilities, and through a Palestinian definition of the legitimacy and obligations of the Authority.

Tracking everything related to the Authority's responsibilities – issues that have been deferred for future negotiations – finalizing them, and to see to the restoration of the rest of the occupied lands.

Fighting for the final release and return of all the prisoners and expellees.

Drafting and executing plans and special programs for dealing with the detainees, the fighting cadres, and martyrs' families, in addition to approving a comprehensive plan for youth.

Drafting a special program for the return of the expellees.

Preparing for local and parliamentary elections and ensuring their free nature and legitimacy.

Planning and formulating an active local-government structure that includes a new framework for local, municipal, and village councils.

Implementing economic and other agreements with the Arab states, especially Jordan, Egypt, and Tunisia, with whom agreements have already been signed.

Drafting laws and special decrees for the National Authority's institutions. These will regulate various aspects of life [in the territories of the Authority], in a fashion that will entrench the concepts and principles of democracy and elections. The laws will continue the protection of civil rights, general freedoms, the independence of the judiciary, separation of powers, achievement of equality between men and women, and equality of opportunity, so as to create a foundation for a free-market economy and guarantee the private sector a primary role.

Coordinating with international institutions and the donor countries with regard to development programs, in accordance with international procedures for activity with the Palestinian Authority.

The Authority is committed to continue the implementation of all agreements concerning it and to ensuring their implementation through laws and regulations in accordance with the public welfare.

Reorganizing political life by licensing political parties and movements, and defending political freedoms, including the freedom of opinion and freedom of political organization.

Rehabilitating the judicial system, in a fashion that will lead to judicial independence, so that the judiciary will be based on a foundation of justice and guarantee the supremacy of law in all aspects of life.

Preparing a modern, efficient monetary system distinguished by transparency, auditing, and accountability to secure the usage and management of public funds.

Completing or establishing central institutions such as a monetary authority, investment bank, employment bureau, chamber of chartered accounts, public ombudsman, economic council, and statistics bureau.

Accelerating implementation of development programs by giving priority to infrastructure projects, creating job opportunities, and providing basic services in order to create an active incentive for the productive sector.

Implementing an emergency development program to mobilize all the resources and capabilities of the Palestinian people in this field; binding the Gaza Strip to the implementation of this plan and giving priority to solving its problems and economic deficiencies.

Continuing to guide and organize the executive branch and its leadership through the demarcation and definition of its mandate, in order to make it an agency that energizes development and reconstruction.

Reorganizing the service sectors including their development, improvement of their human resources, and raising the educational level and skills of the work force.

Supporting and encouraging Palestinian community institutions, including cultural and artistic institutions, and defending the Palestinian heritage and identity.

Supporting and assisting the improvement of the capabilities of the security forces, in order to protect the security of the citizens, their property, and individual freedom, as well as maintaining stability and social security and preserving and enforcing the law in order to defend its supremacy.

Fostering resources and incentives to ensure women's active participation in the economic, social, and political fields, in addition to drawing up programs to train them and create opportunities for them.

Creating an appropriate mechanism for implementing cultural and economic agreements in addition to artistic cooperation with friendly neighboring states and international organizations.

APPENDIX NO. 2

Basic Law:
The Palestinian National Authority

Name of Draft Law: Basic Law
Submitted by the Minister of Justice

Council's Reading: Third Reading

No. of Draft Bill:

Date: October 2, 1997

CHAPTER 1: Preface

Article (1)
Palestine is part of the larger Arab World, and the Arab Palestinian People are part of the Arab Nation. Arab unity is an objective that the Palestinian People shall work to achieve.

Article (2)
The People are the source of all power that may be exercised through the legislative, executive, and judicial authorities, based on the principle of separation of powers, and in the manner set forth in this Basic Law.

Article (3)
Jerusalem is the Capital of Palestine.

Article (4)
Islam is the official religion in Palestine. The dignity and sanctity of all other heavenly religions shall be respected.
   The principles of Islamic Shari'a shall be the main source of legislation.
   Arabic shall be the official language.

Article (5)
The governing system in Palestine shall be a parliamentary democracy, based on political and party pluralism. The President of the National Authority shall be directly elected by people. The Government shall be responsible to the President and to the Palestinian Legislative Council.

Article (6)
The principle of the rule of law shall be the basis of government in Palestine. All

authorities, powers, agencies, institutions, and individuals shall be subject to the law.

Article (7)
Palestinian citizenship shall be regulated by law.

Article (8)
The flag of Palestine shall be in four colors, and in accordance with the dimensions and measurement approved by the Palestinian Liberation Organization. It shall be the official flag of the country.

CHAPTER 2: Public Rights and Freedoms

Article (9)
All Palestinians are equal under the law, with no distinction on account of race, sex, color, religion, political views, or disability.

Article (10)
Basic human rights and freedoms shall be respected.
    The Palestinian National Authority shall act to join regional and international declarations and covenants that protect human rights.

Article (11)
Personal freedom is a natural right and shall be guaranteed and protected.
    It is unlawful to arrest, search, imprison, restrict the freedom, or prevent the movement of any person, except by judicial order in accordance with the provisions of law. The law shall specify the period of detention for the purpose of interrogation. Imprisonment or detention shall be permitted only in places that have been defined by the prison system regulations.

Article (12)
Every arrested or detained person shall be informed of the reasons for his arrest or detention. He shall be promptly informed, in a language he understands, of the nature of the charges made against him. He shall have the right to contact a lawyer and to be tried without delay.

Article (13)
No person shall be subject to any duress or torture. All persons deprived of their freedom shall receive proper treatment.
    All statements or confessions obtained through violation of Paragraph (1) of this article shall be considered null and void.

Article (14)
The accused is innocent until proven guilty in a legally constituted court of law that guarantees him the right to an adequate defense. Any person accused in a criminal case shall be represented by a lawyer.

Article (15)
Punishment shall be imposed upon individuals only. Collective punishment is prohibited. Crime and punishment shall be determined according to the law only. Punishment shall be imposed only by order of a judge and shall apply only to actions committed after the promulgation of law.

Article (16)
It is unlawful to conduct any medical or scientific experiment on any person without his prior legal consent. No person shall be subject to medical examination, treatment, or surgery, except in accordance with the law.

Transplantation of human organs, and new scientific developments shall be regulated by law to serve legitimate humanitarian purposes.

Article (17)
Homes shall be inviolable; thus, they shall not be subject to surveillance, entrance or search, except in accordance with a valid judicial order, issued in accordance with the provisions of the law.

Any consequences resulting from violations of this article shall be considered invalid. Individuals who suffer from such violation shall be entitled to fair compensation guaranteed by the Palestinian National Authority.

Article (18)
Freedom of religion, belief, and ritual is guaranteed to all, provided that this does not disturb the public order or offend public morals.

Article (19)
Every person shall have the right to freedom of thought, conscience, and expression, and shall have the right to publish his opinions orally, in writing, or in any form of art, or through any other form of expression, provided that it does not contravene any provisions of law.

Article (20)
Freedom of residence and movement shall be guaranteed within the limits of the law.

Article (21)
The economic system in Palestine shall be based on the principle of a free market economy. The Executive Branch may establish public companies that will operate in accordance with the law.

Freedom of economic activity is guaranteed. The law shall regulate the principles for the supervision and limitation of economic activity.

Private property shall be protected. Real estate and movable property shall not be confiscated or expropriated except in the public interest, and for fair compensation in accordance with the law, or pursuant to a judicial order.

Expropriation shall be in accordance with judicial order only.

Article (22)

Social, health, disability, and retirement insurance shall be regulated by law.

The welfare of the families of martyrs and prisoners, concern for the injured, wounded, and disabled shall be regulated by law. The National Authority shall guarantee them education, health services, and social insurance.

Article (23)

Every citizen has a right to suitable housing. The Palestinian National Authority shall act to guarantee housing for those without shelter.

Article (24)

Every citizen has the right to education. It shall be compulsory until at least the end of elementary school and shall be free in public schools and institutions.

The Palestinian National Authority shall supervise all levels of education and institutions and shall strive to upgrade the educational system.

The independence of universities, institutions of higher education, and scientific research centers shall be guaranteed by law, in a manner that guarantees the freedom of scientific research, as well as of literary, artistic, and cultural creativity. The Palestinian National Authority shall encourage and support such creativity.

Private schools and educational institutions shall comply with the curriculum approved by the Palestinian National Authority and shall be subject to its supervision.

Article (25)

Work is the right, duty and honor of every citizen. The Palestinian National Authority shall strive to provide it to any individual capable of performing it.

Labor relations shall be organized in a manner that guarantees justice for all. Safety, health, and social insurance shall be guaranteed for all workers.

The organization of unions and guilds is a right that shall be regulated by law.

The right to strike shall be exercised within the limits of law.

Article (26)

Palestinians shall have the right to participate in political life as individuals and in groups. They have the following rights in particular:

To establish and join political parties in accordance with the law.

To establish unions, guilds, associations, societies, clubs, and public institutions in accordance with the law.

To vote and nominate candidates who will be elected in general elections in accordance with the law.

To hold public office and positions in accordance with the principle of equal opportunity.

To conduct private meetings without the presence of the police and to conduct public meetings, processions, and assemblies, within the limits of law.

Article (27)

The right to establish newspapers and other forms of media is guaranteed by this

Basic Law. However, the financial sources of the media shall be subject to monitoring in accordance with the law.

Freedom of audio, visual, and written media, as well as the freedom to print, publish, distribute, and broadcast, together with the freedom of individuals working in this field, is guaranteed by this Basic Law and other related laws.

Censorship of the media shall be prohibited. No warning, suspension, confiscation, cancellation, or restrictions shall be imposed on the media except by law, and in accordance with a judicial order.

Article (28)

No Palestinian shall be deported from the homeland, or prevented from returning to it. No person shall be prohibited to leave it, be deprived of his citizenship, or surrendered to any foreign entity.

Article (29)

Maternity and childhood welfare is a national duty. Children shall have the following rights:

Comprehensive protection and welfare.
Freedom from exploitation for any purpose, including engaging in work that might harm their safety, health, or education.
Protection from harm and cruel treatment.
Laws prohibiting the beating or mistreatment of children by their parents.
To be segregated from adult offenders during imprisonment and treated in a manner that is appropriate to their age and rehabilitation.

Article (30)

Litigation is a right guaranteed to all. Every Palestinian shall have the right of access to the legal system. Litigation procedures shall be regulated by law to guarantee prompt settlement of cases.

Laws shall not include any text that would provide immunity from judicial review for any administrative decision or action.

Judicial errors shall result in compensation by the National Authority. The conditions and methods of such compensation shall be regulated by law.

Article (31)

An independent commission for human rights shall be established by law. The law shall specify the manner of its formation, duties, and jurisdiction. The commission shall submit its reports to the President of the National Authority and to the Palestinian Legislative Council.

Article (32)

Any assault against any personal liberty, against the privacy of another person, or against any of the rights or freedom that have been guaranteed by the law or by this basic law, shall be deemed a crime. Any criminal and civil case resulting from such infringement shall not be subject to any statute of limitations. The National Authority shall guarantee fair indemnity for those who suffer such damages.

Article (33)
A balanced and clean environment is a basic human right. The preservation and protection of the Palestinian environment from pollution, for the sake of the present and future generations, is a national duty.

CHAPTER 3: The Legislative Branch

Article (34)
The Palestinian Legislative Council is the elected legislative authority.
Without prejudice to any provision of this law, the Legislative Council shall exercise its legislative and oversight duties, as prescribed in its Standing Orders.
The term of this Council shall be the interim period.

Article (35)
The Legislative Council shall be composed of 88 Members elected in accordance with the law.
If the position of one Member or more becomes vacant due to death, resignation, or disability, by-elections shall be conducted in the concerned constituency to elect a successor in accordance with the law.

Article (36)
Before taking office, every Member shall swear the following oath before the Council:

"I swear by Allah Almighty to be faithful to the Homeland, and to preserve the rights and interests of the people and nation, and to respect the law and perform my duties in the best manner, as Allah is my witness."

Article (37)
At its first meeting, the Council shall elect the its presidium, which shall consist of the Speaker, two deputies, and the Secretary General. Members of this presidium shall not serve as the President of the National Authority, a member of the Cabinet, or hold any other governmental position.

Article (38)
The Council shall accept the resignation of its Members, and establish its own Standing Orders, as well as rules of interrogating its Members, in a way that does not contravene the provisions of this Basic Law, or with the general constitutional principles. The Council shall be solely responsible for maintaining order and security during sessions and meetings of its committees. Security personnel shall not be present in the Council, unless requested by the Speaker, or by the Chair of a Committee, according to the situation.

Article (39)
The President of the Palestinian National Authority shall open the first ordinary session of the Council and deliver his opening statement.

Article (40)

Members of the Council shall not be interrogated, through either a civil or criminal procedure, because of their actions, opinions, or votes in the Council's sessions and committee meetings, or because of any action they undertake outside the Council in the course of their function as Members, in order that they may perform their parliamentary duties.

No Member of the Legislative Council shall be disturbed in any manner, nor shall any search be made of his luggage, house, accommodations, car, or office, and in general any private property of his, whether real or movable, throughout the period of immunity.

No Member of the Legislative Council shall be asked during the period of his membership or subsequently, to testify on any subject related to his actions or statements or information he obtained as a result of his membership in the Council, unless he agrees to do so, with the prior consent of the Council.

No legal steps shall be taken against any Member of the Palestinian Legislative Council, except when there is suspicion of criminal activity. The Council shall be notified immediately about steps taken against a Member, so that the Council may take whatever action it deems proper. The Presidium of the Council shall assume this responsibility if the Council is not in session.

A Member of the Legislative Council shall not relinquish his immunity without the prior permission of the Council. After the end of a term of office, immunity shall not be nullified with regard to the period of time included in the membership period.

Article (41)

A Member of the Legislative Council shall not exploit his membership in the Council to conduct any other type of private business, or in any manner whatsoever.

Every Member of the Legislative Council shall submit a financial statement for himself, his wife, and his children, detailing the property they own, both real and movable, both inside Palestine and abroad, and their debts, to the Speaker of the Council. This financial statement shall be confidential and kept at the Supreme Court of Justice, and shall not be examined except with the approval of the Court, within the limits it allows.

Article (42)

Members of the Legislative Council shall receive a monthly salary determined by law.

Article (43)

Each Member of the Council shall have the right to:

Submit to the Executive Authority all necessary and legitimate requests, which will enable him to perform his parliamentary duties.

Propose laws. Rejected proposals shall not be resubmitted within the same annual session.

Address inquiries and questions to the Government or to any Minister. Parliamentary questions shall be discussed only seven days after submission, unless the addressee agrees to reply promptly or within a shorter period. However, this period can be curtailed to three days in case of urgency, with the approval of the President of the National Authority.

Article (44)
Ten Members of the Council may submit a request, after a parliamentary question, to withdraw confidence from the Government or from any Minister. However, voting on the request shall be at least three days after submission. A decision shall be taken by a majority vote of the Members of the Council.

The withdrawal of confidence shall result in termination of the incumbency of the party from whom confidence was revoked.

Article (45)
The Council may form special committees or charge one of its permanent committees to gather information on any public matter or public institution.

Article (46)
The Legislative Council shall approve the General Development Plan. The method of preparing and presenting the Plan to the Council shall be stipulated by law.

Article (47)
The law shall regulate the special procedure for the preparation, approval, and utilization of the regular budget, as well as the subsidiary budgets, development budgets, the budgets of public institutions and agencies, and the budget of every project in which the government's investment is 50% or more of its capital.

Article (48)
Taking into consideration the provisions of Article (81) of this Basic Law:

The Government shall present the draft budget to the Legislative Council at least two months before the beginning of the fiscal year.
The Legislative Council shall convene a special session to discuss the annual draft budget. It shall either ratify the budget prior to the start of the new fiscal year, or send it back to the government within one month of receiving the budget. The returned budget shall include the Council's comments, in order that the Government may make the necessary amendments and return it to the Council for approval.
Voting on the general budget by the Council shall be chapter by chapter.
Transfer of funds among the budget's chapters is not permitted, unless the Legislative Council and Executive Branch agree on this.

Article (49)
The final accounts of the National Authority's budget shall be presented to the Legislative Council no later than one year after the end of the fiscal year. The Council shall vote on the final accounts chapter by chapter.

CHAPTER 4: The Executive Branch

Article (50)
The Executive Branch is the supreme executive and administrative body and is responsible for developing programs that must be approved by the Legislative Authority for implementation. The President of the National Authority and the Council of Ministers shall assume the responsibility of the Executive Authority in the manner prescribed in this Basic Law.

First: The President
Article (51)
The President of the Palestinian National Authority shall be elected directly by the Palestinian People in general elections held in accordance with the Palestinian Election Law.

Article (52)
Before assuming office, the President shall take the following oath before the Legislative Council, in the presence of the Chairman of the Palestinian National Council and the Chief Justice of the Supreme Court:

> "I swear by Allah Almighty to be faithful to the Homeland and its sacred values and to the people and its national heritage, and to respect the Constitutional system and the law, and to safeguard the interests of the Palestinian people completely, as Allah is my witness."

Article (53)
The term of the President shall be the Transitional Phase, after which the President shall be elected in accordance with law.

Article (54)
The office of the President shall be considered vacant in any of the following cases:

By death.
By resignation submitted to the Palestinian Legislative Council and accepted by two-thirds of its Members.
By a ruling of legal incompetence issued by the Supreme Constitutional Court, and subsequently approved by two-thirds of the Palestinian Legislative Council.
If the office of the President of the National Authority becomes vacant due to any of the above causes, the Speaker of the Palestinian Legislative Council shall temporarily assume the powers and duties of the President of the National Authority, for a period not exceeding sixty days (60), during which time free and direct elections to choose a new president shall take place in accordance with the Palestinian Election Law.

Article (55)
The President is the Commander-in-Chief of the Palestinian Forces.

Article (56)
The President of the National Authority shall appoint the National Authority's representatives to foreign countries, international organizations, and foreign agencies, and decide upon the termination of their service. The President shall accept the credentials of foreign representatives to the Palestinian National Authority.

Article (57)
The President of the National Authority shall issue laws that have been ratified by the Palestinian Legislative Council within thirty days (30) of those laws' being referred to him. The President may return the laws to the Council within the same specified period, together with his comments and objections. If the President does not return a law to the Council with thirty days (30), the law shall be considered issued and published immediately in the official gazette.

If the President of the National Authority returns the proposed law within the deadline and conditions set forth in the previous paragraph, and the Council debates the proposed law and passes it again with a two-thirds majority, the proposed law shall be considered ratified and shall be published in the official gazette.

Article (58)
The President of the National Authority and the Council of Ministers shall have the right to propose laws, issue regulations, and take the necessary actions to execute laws.

Article (59)
The President of the National Authority shall have the right to pardon or commute sentences. General amnesty, however, shall not be granted except through a law.

Article (60)
The President of the National Authority shall have the right, in exceptional cases that cannot be deferred, when the Legislative Council is not in session, to issue decrees that have the force of law. However, those decrees shall be presented to the Legislative Council in the first session convened after their issuance; otherwise they will cease to have the force of law. If these decrees are presented as specified above but are not approved by the Legislative Council, then they shall cease to have the force of law.

Article (61)
The President's salary, allowances, and compensations shall be determined by law.

Second: The Council of Ministers
Article (62)
The President of the National Authority shall appoint Ministers, discharge them, accept their resignations, and preside over the meetings of the Council of Ministers.

Article (63)
The President shall be assisted by the Council of Ministers in the performance of

his duties and the exercise of his powers in the manner set forth in this Basic Law.

Article (64)
After the selection of the members of the Council of Ministers by the President of the National Authority, the President shall present the Council of Ministers to the Legislative Council in the first session for a vote of confidence. The vote of confidence shall be taken after the delivery of the ministerial statement that defines the Government's policy and program.

If an absolute majority of the members of the Legislative Council do not vote confidence in or vote to withdraw their confidence from all the members of the Council of Ministers, or any one or more of them, the President of the National Authority shall present a replacement at the next session, provided that this session takes place within two weeks of the date of the first session.

In the case of a change in the Council of Ministers, or the addition of a Minister, or the filling a portfolio vacant for any reason, the new Minister or Ministers shall be presented to the Legislative Council in the first session it convenes for a vote of confidence.

No Minister shall assume his duties before obtaining the confidence of the Legislative Council.

Article (65)
The Council of Ministers shall consist of no more than 19 Ministers. The decision of appointment shall specify the Ministry that each Minister shall be responsible for.

Article (66)
Before assuming their offices, the Ministers shall take the oath stipulated in Article (52) of this Basic Law before the President of the National Authority.

Article (67)
Every Minister in the Cabinet shall submit a financial report for himself, his wife, and dependent "minor" children, detailing what they own in real estate, transferable property, stocks, bonds, cash, and debts, whether inside Palestine or abroad, to the President of the National Authority, who shall make the necessary arrangements to keep it secret. This information shall be kept in a confidential manner, and will be disclosed only by a permit issued by the Supreme Court when necessary.

No Minister may purchase or lease any government property or that of any public legal or juridical person, or have a financial interest in any contract concluded with governmental or administrative entities. Nor may a Minister, during his term of office, be a Board Member in any company, or practice commerce or any other profession, or receive a salary or any other financial reward or remuneration from any person in any capacity, other than the one salary determined for the Minister and its allowances.

Article (68)
Ministers are responsible to the President of the National Authority, each within his jurisdiction, for the actions of his Ministry.

The Council of Ministry is collectively responsible before the Legislative Council.

Article (69)
The President of the National Authority has the right to initiate an investigation of any Minister for criminal acts he is suspected of committing during or due to the performance of his duties.

Article (70)
A Minister who has been indicted shall be suspended from his duties immediately upon the issuance of an indictment. The suspension of a Minister's duties shall not prevent the continuation of the investigation and procedures against him.

The Attorney General, or his representative from the prosecutor's office, shall conduct the investigation and submit the indictment. A Minister's trial shall be conducted before a special court and shall follow the provisions and rules prescribed in the penal law and in the criminal procedure law.

The above provisions shall apply to Deputy Ministers, ministry director-generals, and their subordinates.

Article (71)
The President of the National Authority may request a vote of confidence in the Cabinet, a Minister, or some Ministers, by the Legislative Council. A vote of no-confidence requires an absolute majority of the Council Members and shall result in the termination of the duties of those who lose a confidence vote.

Article (72)
The Council of Ministers shall have the following functions:

Devising the general policies within the limits of its jurisdiction, taking into consideration the Ministerial program approved by the Legislative Council.
Executing the general policies set forth by the relevant Palestinian authorities.
Preparing the general budget to be presented to the Legislative Council.
Preparing the administrative apparatus, designing its structures, and providing it with the necessary means, as well supervising and monitoring it.
Overseeing the implementation of laws and compliance with their provisions, and taking necessary actions in this regard.
Overseeing the performance of different Ministries and all other components of the administrative apparatus, their duties and functions, and coordination between them.
Discussing the proposals and policies of different Ministries concerning the implementation of their functions.
Any other functions entrusted to it by this Basic Law, or by any other law or resolution.

Article (73)
Every Minister shall exercise the following powers and functions within his Ministry:

Proposing the general policy of the Ministry and supervising its implementation after approval.

Supervising the conduct of business and affairs within the Ministry, and issuing the necessary instructions for this.

Implementing the general budget within the funds appropriated for his Ministry.

Proposing bills and legislation related to his Ministry and presenting them to the Council of Ministers.

Delegating some of his powers to the director-general or other senior officials in his Ministry, within the law.

Article (74)

Every Minister shall submit detailed periodic reports to the Council of Ministers on the activities, policies, plans, and achievements of his Ministry in comparison with the objectives specified for his Ministry within the framework of the General Plan, and on his Ministry's proposals and recommendations concerning its future policies.

These reports shall be submitted regularly every three months, to give the Council of Ministers sufficient information about the activities and policies of each Ministry.

Third: Security Forces and Police

Article (75)

The Security Forces and the Police are a regular force. They are the armed forces in the country. Their functions are to defend the homeland, serve the people, protect the community, and maintain public order, security and morals. These forces shall perform their duties within the limits prescribed by law with complete respect to fights and freedom.

The Security Forces and the Police shall be regulated by law.

Fourth: Local Administration

Article (76)

The country shall be organized, by law, into local administrative units, with each unit having independent legal status. Each unit shall have a council elected directly as prescribed by law. The law shall determine the jurisdiction and functions of the administrative units, their financial resources, their relations with the central authority, and their role in the preparation and implementation of development plans. In addition, the law shall determine the manner of oversight over these units and their various activities. Demographic, geographic, economic, and political factors shall be taken into consideration at the time of dividing the country administratively, to provide for the territorial integrity of the homeland and interests of the communities.

Fifth: Public Administration

Article (77)

The appointment of all public officials and government personnel, and their conditions of employment, shall be in accordance with the law.

Article (78)
All affairs related to the civil service shall be regulated by law. The Civil Service Commission shall coordinate with the concerned governmental entities to upgrade and improve the public administration. Its point of view shall be taken into consideration on draft legislation, laws, and regulations that deal with the public administration and its personnel.

Sixth: General Finance
Article (79)
General taxes and levies shall not be imposed, amended, and repealed except by law. No one shall be totally or partially exempt from paying these taxes, except in circumstances prescribed by law.

Article (80)
The law shall state the procedures for the collection and expenditure of public funds.

Article (81)
The beginning and the end of the fiscal year, and the general budget shall be regulated by law. If the general budget is not approved by the beginning of the new fiscal year, expenditures shall continue on the basis of a monthly allocation of 1/12 of the fiscal year's budget.

Article (82)
All revenues collected, including taxes, levies, loans, grants, and profits accrued to the Palestinian National Authority from managing its property or activities, shall be paid to the Public Treasury. No part of the Public Treasury funds shall be allocated or spent for any purpose whatsoever except in accordance with the law.

The Palestinian National Authority may establish a strategic financial reserve to address fluctuations and emergency situations in accordance with the law.

Article (83)
Public loans shall be regulated by law. It is prohibited to engage in a project that requires spending funds from the Public Treasury during a future period unless approved by the Legislative Council.

Article (84)
Regulations relating to the monetary authority, banks, securities market, foreign exchange, and insurance companies, and all financial and credit institutions, shall be regulated by law.

The Governor of the Monetary Authority shall be appointed by a resolution issued by the President of the National Authority and approved by the Palestinian Legislative Council.

Article (85)
The law shall determine the rules and procedures for granting franchises or commitments related to the exploitation of natural resources and public services. The law

shall also set forth the methods for dealing with real estate owned by the state and other public and legal persons, and the rules and procedures organizing them.

Article (86)
The law shall determine regulations for paying wages, salaries, compensations, subsidies, and rewards from the public treasury. The law shall also regulate those entities responsible for implementation of these regulations. No exceptional funds shall be spent other than within the limits prescribed by law.

Article (87)
A Financial and Administrative Auditing Bureau shall be established to provide financial and administrative oversight of all entities of the Executive Branch, including the collection and spending of public revenues within the framework of the general budget.

The Bureau shall submit to the President of the National Authority and to the Legislative Council an annual report, or when requested, concerning its work findings.

The head of the Financial and Administrative Auditing Bureau shall be appointed through a decision issued by the President of the National Authority and approved by the Legislative Council.

CHAPTER 5: The Judicial Branch

Article (88)
The Judicial Branch shall be independent, and shall consist of courts of different types and level. The law will determine the structure and jurisdiction of the courts. Their verdicts shall be in accordance with the law. The rulings shall be announced and executed in the name of the Palestinian Arab People.

Article (89)
Judges shall be independent, and shall not be subject to any authority other than the authority of law while exercising their duties. No other authority may interfere with the judiciary or with the exercise of justice.

Article (90)
The appointment, dismissal, grant of authority, promotion, and questioning of judges shall be as prescribed in the Law on the Independence of the Judiciary.

Judges may not be dismissed and their services terminated other than as stipulated in the Law on the Independence of the Judiciary.

Article (91)
A Supreme Judicial Council shall be created. The law shall specify its structure, jurisdiction, and operating rules. The Council shall be consulted about draft laws that regulate any affairs of the Judicial Authority, including the public prosecution.

Article (92)
Shari'a affairs and personal status shall be handled by Shari'a and religious courts
in accordance with law.

Military Courts shall be established by special laws. These courts shall not have
any jurisdiction beyond military affairs.

Article (93)
Administrative courts may be established by a law, to handle administrative
disputes and disciplinary claims. Other duties and functions of administrative
courts, and their procedures, shall be determined by law.

Article (94)
A High Constitutional Court shall be established by law to:

Ensure the constitutionality of laws, regulations, rules, and the like.
Interpret the text of the Basic Law and legislation.
Resolve jurisdictional disputes which arise between judicial entities and adminis-
    trative entities that have judicial jurisdiction.

The law shall determine the structure and composition of the High Constitutional
Court, its operating procedures, and the impact of its rulings.

Article (95)
The Supreme Court shall temporarily assume all duties assigned to the administrative court and to the High Constitutional Court, unless those duties fall within
the jurisdiction of other judicial entities in accordance with applicable laws.

Article (96)
Court hearings shall be public unless the court decides to make them secret due to
considerations related to public order or public morals. In all cases, verdicts shall
be pronounced in open court.

Article (97)
It shall be mandatory to implement judicial rulings and judgments. The non-implementation or deferral of implementation of a ruling or judgment shall be considered
a crime subject to imprisonment, or dismissal from office if the accused individual
is a public official or servant. The plaintiff may file his case directly with the
concerned court, and the National Authority shall guarantee full compensation for
him.

Public Prosecution
Article (98)
The Attorney General shall be appointed through a decision issued by the President
of the National Authority, based on a recommendation submitted by the Supreme
Judicial Council, and approved by the Legislative Council.

The Attorney General shall operate in the name of the Palestinian Arab People.
The jurisdiction, functions, and duties of the Attorney General shall be determined
by law.

Article (99)

The jurisdiction, functions, structure, and composition of the Public Prosecution shall be regulated by law.

The appointment, transfer, removal, and questioning of members of the Public Prosecution shall be determined by law.

Article (100)

Death sentences issued by any court shall not be implemented unless approved by the President of the Palestinian Executive Authority.

CHAPTER 6: Provisions for a State of Emergency

Article (101)

The President of the National Authority may decree a state of emergency when there is a threat to national security caused by war, invasion, armed insurrection, or natural disaster, for a period not to exceed thirty (30) days.

The state of emergency may be extended for another period of thirty (30) days after approval by two-thirds of the Legislative Council.

The decree declaring a state of emergency shall state its purpose, the territory to which it applies, and its duration.

The Legislative Council shall have the right to review all or some of the procedures which have been implemented during the state of emergency at the first session of the Council to be convened after the announcement of the state of emergency, or during the session convened to extend the state of emergency, whichever comes first, and to conduct the necessary discussion in this regard.

Article (102)

It is prohibited, when a state of emergency is declared, to impose restrictions on basic rights and freedoms, except to the extent necessary to achieve the objective stated in the decree of the state of emergency.

Article (103)

Any arrest based on the declaration of a state of emergency shall be subject to the following minimum requirements:

Any arrest made in accordance with the decree of the state of emergency shall be reviewed by the Attorney General or by the appropriate court within a period not exceeding fifteen (15) days from the date of detention.

The detainee shall have the right to appoint a lawyer of his choice.

Article (104)

The Palestinian Legislative Council shall not be dissolved or suspended during the state of emergency, nor shall the provisions of this chapter be suspended.

Article (105)

All laws that regulate a state of emergency prevailing in Palestine prior to the implementation of this Basic Law are repealed, including the Mandate Civil Defense (Emergency) Regulations issued in 1945.

CHAPTER 7: General and Transitional Provisions

Article (106)
The provisions of this Basic Law shall apply during the transitional period, and may be extended until the new constitution of the Palestinian State takes effect.

Article (107)
Laws shall be promulgated in the name of the Palestinian Arab People, and shall be published immediately in the Official Gazette. These laws shall come into force 30 days from the date of their publication unless the law states otherwise.

Article (108)
The provisions of any law shall apply only to matters occurring after the date on which that law came into force, unless the law provides otherwise if the articles are not punitive.

Article (109)
Laws, regulations and decisions in force in Palestine before the implementation of this law shall remain in force to the extent that they do not conflict with the provisions of this Basic Law, until they are amended or repealed in accordance with law.

Article (110)
All laws which are in contravention of the provisions of this Basic Law shall be repealed.

Article (111)
The provisions of this Basic Law shall not be amended except by a two-thirds majority of the Members of the Legislative Council.

Article (112)
This Basic Law shall take effect as of the date of publication in the Official Gazette.

APPENDIX NO. 3

Standing Orders for the Palestinian Legislative Council

Revised by the Legal Department on April 28, 1997

Preamble
The Palestinian people in Palestine have expressed, through general free and direct elections, their determination to follow democratic rules in building their institutions and in exercising their national sovereignty. Those elections have led to the birth of the first Palestinian Legislative Council of the Palestinian National Authority.

On that basis, it is necessary to establish the principles for the elected Legislative Council to operate, based on the principle of separation of powers, which guarantees the independence of the legislative authority and its right to legislate and to control and inspect the actions of the Palestinian Authority.

These Standing Orders have been established in order to organize the functioning of the Council, and regulate its actions, including the election of its committees, its decision-making process, and its legislative procedures, as a first and necessary step toward national independence, the construction of an advanced democratic society, and the exercise of sovereignty on the soil of the homeland.

The provisions of these Standing Orders guarantee freedom of opinion and expression, freedom of opposition and constructive criticism, and the achievement of comprehensive cooperation between the Council and the other constitutional institutions.

Article (1)
Definitions
In these Standing Orders, the following expressions shall have the meanings stated below, unless noted otherwise:

The Council: The Palestinian Legislative Council
The President of National Authority: The President of the PNA
The Speaker: The Speaker of the Palestinian Legislative Council
The Council of Ministers: The Council of Ministers of the PNA
The Presidium of the Council: The Presidium of the Palestinian Legislative Council
The Constitution: The Basic Law of the Authority for the transitional period
The Secretariat: The Secretary General and his or her assistants
Member: An elected member of the PLC
Committees: Committees of the PLC
Temporary Speaker: The Speaker of the session before the election of the Presidium of the Council

Title I
CHAPTER 1: The Initial Meeting

Article (2)
The President of the PNA shall summon the meeting of the first ordinary session to take place at the beginning of the second week following the publication of the official results of the elections. He shall open the meeting and make a general speech to the Council.

The Council shall at its first meeting elect the Presidium of the Council. The position of the Temporary Speaker shall be filled by the oldest member.

No debate shall be held before the election of the Presidium of the Council.

Article (3)
Each Member individually shall swear the oath of office before the Council at the first meeting, as follows:

> "I swear before Almighty God to be loyal to the nation of Palestine, to keep the rights and interests of the people and nation, to respect the Constitution and to fulfill my duties to the best of my ability, as God is my witness."

CHAPTER 2: The Presidium of the Council

Article (4)
The Presidium of the Council shall consist of the Speaker, two Deputy Speakers, and the Secretary General, who shall be elected by the Council by secret ballot.

The Presidium shall serve until the beginning of the next regular term of the Council. Vacancies shall be filled by election to be held according to articles (9, 10) of this Standing Order.

Article (5)
Three elected members of the Council shall be responsible for counting the votes. Each Member of the Council shall be given a paper on which to write the name of the candidates of his or her choice. The Temporary Speaker shall call members one by one to deposit their ballots. The candidate who receives an absolute majority of votes, i.e., half of the members present plus one, shall be declared elected. Otherwise, the Council shall proceed to a second round of voting, between only the two candidates who received the most votes in the first round. The Candidate who receives more votes shall be declared elected. A tie shall be resolved by lot, and the Temporary Speaker shall announce the result of the Speaker's election.

Article (6)
The two Deputy Speakers and the Secretary General of the Council shall then be elected, following the same procedure as for the election of the Speaker. The Temporary Speaker shall then invite the Presidium of the Council to assume its responsibilities.

Article (7)
The Speaker shall entrust his two deputies to supervise one or more departments, such as the legal, media, foreign relations, and public relations. The Secretary General shall be responsible for administrative, financial, and protocol affairs, and will be responsible for the minutes of sessions, record keeping, implementation of the Council's decisions, and notification of concerned parties.

The Presidium of the Council will conduct periodic meetings, at least once a month, to discuss and prepare the Council's agenda, evaluate progress of sessions and committees, listen to reports of the Presidium staff regarding progress of work in the departments which they supervise, and generally to draw up and develop legislative and oversight policies which are proposed for the Council.

Article (8)
The Speaker shall represent the Council and speak on its behalf, and shall open, preside over, direct, control and announce the close of its meetings. The Speaker shall give the right to speak, decide the agenda of the Council, and authorize the Secretariat to publish the decisions of the Council. Generally, the Speaker shall ensure that the work of the Council progresses well, and supervise all of its relations. The Speaker may participate in the discussions. S/he shall vacate the chair while doing so.

Article (9)
If the Speaker is absent, or is participating in the discussions of the Council, the chair shall be taken by his First Deputy Speaker; if the First Deputy Speaker is also absent, the chair shall be taken by the Second Deputy Speaker, or in his/her absence by the oldest Member of the Council.

Article (10)
No Member of the Presidium of the Council shall be eligible to serve as a Minister or to hold any governmental position.

CHAPTER 3: Vote of Confidence, No Confidence, and Withdrawal of Confidence

Article (11)
After the President of the PNA selects the members of the Council of Ministers, they will be presented in a special session for a vote of confidence after their ministerial statement, which specifies the program and policy of the government, has been heard.

In case the Council votes by absolute majority against giving confidence to the members of the Council of Ministers, or to any of them, the President of the National Authority will submit a replacement in a second session, which shall not be later than two weeks from the date of the first session.

In the event of a change in Ministerial positions or the filling of a position vacant due to resignation or death, the new Ministers will be presented to the Council in an extraordinary session to be convened for a vote of confidence.

Article (12)
Ten members of the Council may request the withdrawal of confidence from the Government or from any Minister. Voting on this request shall be at least three days after submission. A decision shall be taken by a majority vote of attending members of the Council.

The withdrawal of confidence will result in the termination of office of the individual in whom confidence was lost.

Title II
CHAPTER 1: Meetings of the Council

Article (13)
The Council will convene its ordinary annual session in any of its two temporary locations. Each such session shall last for four months. The first period shall start on the first Tuesday of March, and the second shall start on the first Tuesday of October.

The Council may convene in an extraordinary session upon the request of the Council of Ministers, or one-third of its members.

If the Council is not called to convene, the Council shall be considered as convened at the time and place specified in the first paragraph, or at the request of the members or the Council of Ministers.

The President of the National Authority shall open the ordinary term with a comprehensive speech addressed to the Council.

Article (14)
The Council shall meet in public, and shall meet on Tuesday, Wednesday, and Thursday every two weeks unless it decides otherwise.

Article (15)
The quorum required to open a meeting of the Council shall be the presence of more than one half of its members. Decisions shall be made by an absolute majority of votes of its members present, except as provided otherwise. If a meeting does not have the quorum at the time specified for its start, the Speaker shall delay the start for 30 minutes. If the meeting remains without quorum, the Speaker shall adjourn it and shall announce the date and time for the next meeting, which shall be no more than one week later.

Article (16)
The Secretary General shall distribute the decisions and minutes of the Council's previous session 24 hours prior to the next meeting. Decisions and minutes shall be considered as approved unless a Member raises an objection to them.

Article (17)
The Speaker shall present the agenda of the meeting to the members of the Council. The agenda shall be communicated to the members of the Council at least two days before the meeting.

The Council shall not discuss any subject not on the agenda of the meeting, except upon the request of the President of the PNA or the Speaker, or the written request of a minimum of 10 members. Except as provided otherwise in these Standing Orders, the Council shall decide to include any new subject added to the agenda by a simple majority after having one speech in favor and one speech against. Such speeches will not exceed five minutes in duration.

Article (18)
The Speaker, following the approval of the Council, shall announce the interruption or adjournment of the meeting, and the date and time of the next meeting. The Speaker may, however, call the Council to meet before the agreed date and time in the case of urgency or pursuant to a request by the Council of Ministers.

Article (19)
The Council shall convene an extraordinary "emergency" session based on a request submitted by the President of the PNA, the Speaker, or per a written request submitted by one fourth of the Council Members. If the Speaker fails to call a duly requisitioned extraordinary session, the Council shall be considered as convened at the time and place made in the requisition.

CHAPTER 2: Minutes of the Meetings

Article (20)
Minutes shall be recorded for each meeting of the Council, including discussions held, issues debated, and decisions made by the Council.

Article (21)
Following approval of minutes of a meeting, the Speaker and the Secretary shall sign them. The minutes shall be kept in the files of the Council, and a summary shall be published in a special publication of the Council.

CHAPTER 3: Secret Meetings

Article (22)
The Council may in exceptional cases be called to meet in closed session, following

a request from the President of the PNA, the Speaker, or one fourth of members. The Council shall decide whether or not to meet in closed session, following a debate in which only two speakers in favor and two speakers against shall be heard.

Article (23)
When such a closed session is convened, unauthorized persons shall evacuate the Council chamber and visitor's gallery. No person except the members of the Council shall be present when the Council meets in camera, except with the permission of the Council.

No employee of the Council shall attend the Council when it meets in closed session, except by permission of the Speaker.

When the justification for the Council to meet in camera has ended, the Speaker shall propose to the Council that the closed session end; upon the agreement of the Council, the Speaker shall reopen the meeting to the public.

Article (24)
The Secretary General shall take the minutes when the Council is meeting in camera. Such minutes shall be kept by the secretariat of the Council. Access to such minutes shall be restricted to the members of the council, unless the Council by majority vote decides to publish such minutes or any part thereof.

Article (25)
The Council may call a special meeting for the purpose of inviting any personality or guest to address the Council. There shall be no other item on the agenda of any such meeting.

CHAPTER 4: Rules of Order at Meetings

Article (26)
No member shall speak unless he requests to speak, and after recognized to do so by the Speaker. The Speaker may deny a request to speak only in accordance with these Standing Orders. In case of conflict, the Speaker shall put the question to the Council, which shall take a vote without discussion.

Article (27)
The Secretary General shall record the requests to speak as per the order and sequence he receives them. A request to speak upon a subject selected for consideration by a committee shall not be accepted until the report of the committee has been submitted.

Article (28)
No Member may speak on any issue more than twice: once during the general discussion, and once during the debate on proposals and draft decisions.

Article (29)
The right to speak shall be given by the Speaker, in the order in which members request it. Any Member who has been recognized to speak may yield in favor of another member. In the event of disagreement, the right to speak shall be given in turn to a Member seeking an amendment to the proposal, to an opponent of the proposal, and to a supporter of the proposal under discussion.

Article (30)
The Speaker may give the Ministers the right to speak about a subject within the competence of their Ministries.

Article (31)
The right to speak shall always be given in the following cases:

To request that the provisions of the Constitution or of these Standing Orders be respected.
To propose that discussion on the subject under debate be postponed.
To correct any facts.
To reply to a statement which affects the requester to speak in person.
To move that the discussion be terminated.
To propose that the discussion on the subject under debate be postponed until the Council has dealt with another related item of business. Any such request shall take priority over the main subject under discussion; discussion of the main topic shall cease until the Council reaches a decision about it. The right to speak in such cases shall not be given until the Member speaking has finished his/her statements, except in cases related to the respect for the provisions of the Constitution or of these Standing Orders, or to correct facts.

Article (32)
No Member may use impolite language or incite against public order.

Article (33)
If a Member does not comply with the provisions of Article 32 above, the Speaker may call him/her by name and draw his/her attention and request him/her to maintain order, or may rule that s/he may no longer speak. If the Member challenges any such ruling, the Speaker shall refer the matter to the Council, which shall decide without discussion.

Article (34)
No member may interrupt the speech of another or express comments about it. Notwithstanding the provisions of article (31), the Speaker only may request a Member speaking to comply with these Standing Orders at any time during his or her speech.

Article (35)
No speaker may repeat any point s/he has made, or that has already been made by another Member, or go beyond the subject submitted for discussion. Only the

Speaker may draw the attention of the Member speaking to this, and inform the Member that his/her point is sufficiently clear and requires no further explanation.

Article (36)
The Council may discipline a Member who fails to comply with these Standing Orders, or who does not comply with a decision of the Council forbidding him or her to speak, by imposing any of the following penalties:

To prevent the Member from speaking for the remainder of the meeting;
To instruct the Member to leave the Council chamber and withdraw from the remainder of the meeting;
To exclude the Member from participating in meetings of the Council for a period not exceeding two weeks.

Article (37)
If any Member refuses to comply with a decision of the Council, the Speaker may adopt all measures necessary, including the adjournment or postponement of the meeting, to enforce the decision. In such case, any penalty imposed on the Member shall be doubled.

Article (38)
The Speaker may announce his/her intention to suspend the session, and may so suspend it for up to 30 minutes in the case of disorder. If order is not restored when the meeting is reconvened, the Speaker may adjourn the meeting and announce the date and time for the next meeting.

CHAPTER 5: Termination of Membership

Article (39)
Membership is terminated in the following cases:

Death
Conviction by a competent Palestinian court for a felony or infamous crime.

Article (40)
Any motion to deprive a person of membership under article (39 B) above shall be signed by 10 members of the Council and submitted to the Speaker. The Speaker shall notify the Member concerned and shall bring the question before the Council at its first subsequent meeting.

Article (41)
The Council shall refer any proposal under article (39) above to the Legal Committee, which shall discuss it at its next meeting. The Council shall, unless it decides otherwise, take its decision on the proposal in the same session.

The Member concerned shall have the right to defend himself before the Committee and before the Council.

Article (42)
If the report of the Committee recommends expulsion from membership, the Council shall upon the request of the Member concerned or upon a vote of the Council postpone the decision to a subsequent meeting.

Article (43)
The Member who is subject to a motion for expulsion from membership may attend the meeting and participate in the debate on such proposal, but shall leave the meeting while the Council votes.

Article (44)
The Council shall decide on a proposal for the expulsion of a member by a majority of two-thirds of the attending members. The vote on any such proposal shall be secret.

Title III
CHAPTER 1: Committees of the Council

Article (45)
The Council shall establish the following standing committees, which shall discuss and report on any proposals referred by the Council or by the Speaker:

Jerusalem and Settlements Committee
Political Committee, Refugee and Palestinians Abroad Affairs (negotiations, Arabic and international relations, exiles, displaced persons, and overseas residents)
Legal Committee (constitution, law, and justice)
Budget and Financial Affairs Committee
Committee for Economic Affairs, Natural Resources, and Energy (industry, commerce, housing, investment, tourism, planning, water, agriculture, rural, environment, energy, animal resources, and fishing)
Committee for the Interior (interior, security, and local government)
Education and Social Affairs Committee (education, culture, media, religious affairs, historic sites, social affairs, health, work and labor, prisoners, martyrs, injuries, war veterans, childhood, youth, and women)
Committee for Human Rights and Public Freedom
Committee for Council Affairs

The Council may form any other *ad hoc* Committees to fulfill temporary or permanent purposes and specific objectives.

The Council shall determine at the start of each ordinary term the number of members in each of its standing committees to ensure that the committees perform their work in a suitable manner.

Article (46)

The selection of the committees' members will be conducted in the first session of the Council. Each Member may submit a request to be appointed to any Committee. The Presidium of the Council shall coordinate and consult with all applicants, following which the Speaker shall submit the final list of appointments to the Council for approval.

On the proposal of the Presidium of the Council, or of the Council Affairs Committee, the Council may change the composition of any committee at the beginning of the term of each year.

Article (47)

No Minister may sit on any committee or be a Member of the Presidium of the Council.

Article (48)

Taking into consideration the provisions of the previous articles, a Member may participate in one of the Council's committees. The Member may participate, with the approval of the Council, in a second committee, only to benefit from his experience and specialty.

Article (49)

Each Committee shall elect a Chairman and Secretary from among its members. In the absence of either, the remaining members of the Committee shall elect a temporary substitute.

CHAPTER 2: Committee Procedures

Article (50)

A meeting of a Committee shall be convened by its chairman, or at the request of the Speaker in coordination with the Chairman, or at the request of a majority of the members. The meeting shall be called with at least 24 hours' notice. The notice shall be accompanied by the agenda of the meeting.

Article (51)

Committees shall meet behind closed doors. The quorum for a Committee shall be a majority of members. Decisions of Committees shall be made by absolute majority. In the case of a tie, the Chairman shall have a casting vote.

Committees may decide to hold public meetings.

Article (52)

Minutes shall be kept of each meeting of each Committee, which shall include the names of those members present and those members absent and a summary of discussions held and decisions taken. The Chairman and the Secretary of the Committee shall sign the minutes.

Article (53)
The Speaker shall refer to the relevant Committee all documents related to the subject referred to it and within its scope.

Article (54)
Committee Chairmen may request any Minister or responsible person within the PNA to give information on or clarify any point related to the subjects referred to it, or that lie within its scope.

Article (55)
Ministers may attend Committee meetings. Committees may request any Minister or concerned person to attend any of their meetings.

Article (56)
Members of the Presidium of the Council may attend any meeting of any Committee and participate in its debate.

Any Member of the Council may attend any meeting of any Committee of which he is not a Member to hear the discussion, but shall not express any opinion or comment, unless given the permission to do so.

Article (57)
Each Committee shall submit a report regarding the subject that has been referred to it, within a period determined by the Council. If it fails to do so, the Speaker may ask the Chairman of the Committee to explain the reasons for the delay, and to determine the time that the Committee deems necessary to complete its report. The Speaker may bring the question before the Council for decision. The Council may include this subject in its agenda.

Article (58)
The report shall be submitted to the Speaker for inclusion in the agenda of the Council. The report shall be printed and distributed to the members of the Council at least 24 hours before the meeting that will discuss it.

Article (59)
The report shall include the opinion of the Committee on the subject referred to it, with reasons, and minority opinions. The report shall be accompanied by the recommendations of the Committee and draft decisions, with explanatory memoranda.

Article (60)
The report of any committee shall be presented to the Council by its Chair. In his or her absence, the Speaker shall ask the Secretary of the Committee to present the report, or shall ask the attending members of the Committee to elect one of their number to do so.

Article (61)
Any Committee, through its Secretary, may request to withdraw its report for

further review, even if the Council has started to discuss it. Any such request shall be subject to the agreement of the Council.

Article (62)

The Council of Ministers shall submit the text of any draft law to the Speaker, accompanied by a preamble that shall explain its purpose. The Speaker shall refer any such law to the relevant Committee.

The relevant Committee shall refer the draft law accompanied by its report and recommendations no later than thirty days from the date the Committee received the draft law.

Based on a request from the relevant Committee, the Speaker may extend the above period for a maximum of fifteen days.

The Council may decide to commence the general discussion of the draft law if the relevant Committee does not submit its report within the above deadline.

The Secretary General shall distribute to each Member of the Council a copy of any draft law to be submitted to the Council, accompanied by a preamble, three days in advance of such submission.

The Council of Ministers may request to withdraw any draft law it has submitted to the Council, provided that the Council has not voted on acceptance of such law.

Article (63)

After the general discussion of the draft law, the Council will put it to a vote.

If the Council does not vote to approve the draft law, it shall not be considered.

If the Council votes to approve the draft law, the Council shall refer it to the relevant Committee to make the appropriate amendments in view of the general discussion, after which it shall be returned to the Speaker.

The Speaker shall refer the draft law (after inclusion of amendments by the relevant Committee) to the Legal Committee for legal opinion.

Article (64)

Any Member or Members of the Council may submit a proposal for a new law, or to amend or repeal an existing law. Any such proposal shall be referred to the relevant Committee to express its opinion. It shall be accompanied by a description of the general principles and by a preamble. The Council shall hear the report of the Committee. If the Council approves the proposal it shall be forwarded by the Council to the Legal Committee, which shall put it into the form of a complete draft law and resubmit it to the Council during the same or the following term.

Article (65)

Each draft law submitted to the Council shall be debated in two separate readings as follows:

In the first reading articles shall be debated, each article in turn. Following such debate, the Council shall vote on each article in turn and then on the draft law as a whole.

The second reading shall take place for the sole purpose of discussing and voting on proposed amendments.

A third reading (limited to discussing the proposed amendments) shall take place based on a written request of the Council of Ministers, or of one fourth of the members of the Council, provided that the request is submitted before referring the proposal to the President of the National Authority for ratification.

Article (66)
Draft laws shall be ratified by an absolute majority of the members of the Council (unless stated otherwise).

Article (67)
Upon ratification of the draft law in the third reading, or within two weeks after its ratification in the second reading, the Speaker shall forward it to the President of the PNA for his consent and publication.

Article (68)
The President of the PNA shall issue the laws within thirty days after they are forwarded to him, and shall return them to the Council within the above period, accompanied with his comments, or justification of his rejection. Otherwise the proposal shall be considered to be law and shall be published immediately in the official gazette.

If the President of the PNA returns the draft law as per the provisions of the above clause, it shall be re-discussed in the Council. Then, if the draft law has been ratified by two thirds of the members, it shall be considered to be law and shall be published immediately in the official gazette.

Article (69)
The Speaker shall inform the Council of Ministers at the beginning of each legislative term about the draft laws that have been submitted by the Council of Ministers and rejected by the Council as per article (63B). If the Council of Ministers does not request to discuss them, the draft laws will be considered to be non-existent. However, if the Council of Ministers requests a discussion they will be referred to the relevant Committee.

Article (70)
Any proposal to amend the Basic Law shall be submitted by articles in a written form, accompanied by a preamble, and shall be signed by at least one-third of the members of the Council.
    Upon receipt of any such proposal, the Speaker shall inform the Council and refer it to the Legal Committee
    After the Committee returns it to the Council, the Council shall decide by a majority of the members to accept it or reject it.
    Any amendment or revision to the Basic Law shall require the approval of two-thirds of the members of the Council.

Article (71)
The Council of Ministers shall submit the draft annual budget to the Council at

least four months before the beginning of the budgetary (fiscal) year.

The Council shall refer this draft budget to the Budget and Finance Committee for study. The Committee shall submit its detailed report and recommendations to the Council no later than one month from the date of referral to the Committee.

The Council shall hold a special meeting to discuss the draft budget in view of the Committee's report and recommendations. The Council may approve the budget or refer it back to the Council of Ministers within two months of its submission to the Council, accompanied by the comments of the Council. The Council of Ministers shall make the required amendments and resubmit the budget to the Council for approval.

CHAPTER 3: Interpellations and Motions for the Agenda

First section:
Article (72)
The Council shall reserve one hour at the beginning of its ordinary meeting every two weeks, for interpellations addressed by its members to the Ministers, to inquire about the affairs of their Ministries.

Any Member of the Council shall have the right to address an interpellation to the Council of Ministers, or to a Minister, to ask about any subject, which is related to their scope, to ask about a fact which he doesn't know, or to clarify measures that have been taken or could be taken to deal with any subject.

Article (73)
The interpellations shall be submitted by one member, and shall be related to a subject of public interest. The interpellation shall be void of improper and indecent expressions. The interpellations shall be submitted without any critical comments and shall not be related to a subject referred to any Committee of the Council, before such Committee submits its report.

The Member shall not address more than one interpellation in the same session.

Article (74)
The interpellation shall be submitted in written form to the Speaker, who shall in turn read it to the concerned Minister. The Member who raised an interpellation shall have the right to ask the Minister for clarification, and to comment on the answer once only.

The answer to the interpellation shall be in a verbal form, unless the inquiring Member asks for a written answer.

The Member submitting the interpellation may withdraw it at any time. Other members shall not have the right to hold on to it, unless it is adopted by the Council. The interpellation shall be dropped upon the termination of the position and capacity of the addresser and addressee, or upon the recession of the term during which the interpellation was submitted.

Article (75)
The provisions relating to interpellations do not apply to questions made orally by the members to Ministers in the course of debate by the Council.

Article (76)
Any Member of the Council shall have the right to direct an interpellation to the Council of Ministers, or to an individual Minister or the like, in affairs related to their scope.

Second section:
Article (77)
The interpellation shall be submitted in writing, and shall specify the matters that will be raised without any comment.

It shall not include any improper expressions, or any matters that violate law.

It shall be related to the public interest and relevant to the scope of the Council of Ministers or to the concerned Ministers.

It shall not refer to a subject that has been discussed and resolved previously by the Council in the same term, unless new facts arose to justify it.

It shall not refer to a subject that has been referred to any Committee of the Council, and pending the submission of its report in this matter.

The Member who submits the interpellation shall not have any personal or private interest in the interpellation.

Article (78)
The interpellation shall be submitted to the Speaker. The Speaker shall pass it to the Council of Ministers or to the concerned Minister within forty-eight hours. The Speaker shall include it in the agenda of the first possible session of the Council, provided that it has been communicated to the concerned party at least one week before the session, unless the object of the interpellation party agrees to answer it or discuss it sooner. This period of time can be curtailed to three days with the approval of the President of the PNA.

Interpellations shall have priority over all other items on the agenda except for interpellations.

A Member may, through the Presidium of the Council, and in writing, request the relevant Minister or the like to inform him/her of any documents related to his/her interpellation.

Article (79)
Taking into consideration the provisions of article (78), and in case there is more than one interpellation submitted in one subject, or in subjects which are correlated to each other, they will be all included in the agenda, and discussed at the same time. The right to speak for those who submitted the interpellation shall be given to the original applicant, followed by the earliest one in registration.

Article (80)

The absence of the Member who submitted the interpellation from the session scheduled to discuss his interpellation shall be considered as a forfeiture of his request, unless his absence is justified by an excuse accepted by the Presidium of the Council. The Council shall postpone the interpellation to the next session only and for one period only after hearing the opinion of the Minister.

Article (81)

The interpellation shall lapse upon the termination of the position and capacity of the submitter and recipient, or the adjournment of the term during which the interpellation was submitted.

Article (82)

Before the start of the discussion, the Member submitting the interpellation shall explain it to the Council. After the Minister or the like has replied, other members may participate in the discussion. If the Member submitting the interpellation is not satisfied, s/he may explain his or her reasons; s/he or any other Member may propose a motion of no confidence in the cabinet, or in any individual Minister.

The Member submitting the interpellation may withdraw it, in which case it shall not be discussed except on the request of five or more members of the Council.

CHAPTER 4: Urgency

Article (83)

The Council may decide to adopt urgency procedure to deal with any subject, including any motion of confidence or motion of reprimand to any Minister or to the Executive Authority as a whole. Any proposal to adopt urgency procedure shall be made by:

Any five members, submitted in writing;
A written request submitted by the Council of Ministers; or
A written request submitted by the relevant Committee
– and shall be decided without discussion.

Article (84)

The Council and its Committees shall deal with subjects taken under urgency procedure before other subjects. Any such subject shall not be subject to time limits as laid down in these Standing Orders. The Council may decide to discuss a subject to be taken under urgency procedure at the meeting to which it is submitted, in which case the relevant Committee shall report to the Council immediately, orally or in writing.

Article (85)

Any subject discussed by the Council under urgency procedure may be discussed again in the cases provided under these Standing Orders, and shall not be subject to the relevant time limits.

Article (86)

If the subject to be discussed under urgency procedure is a draft law, the Council shall refer it to the relevant Committee. Such Committee shall determine first whether it believes the draft law can be discussed, and second shall examine the content of the draft law, and report to the Council on both matters. The subject shall be presented to the Council, which will first express its opinion whether to discuss the proposal. If it so decides, the Council shall proceed to debate the draft law.

In cases of necessity, the Council may decide by a vote of two-thirds of its members to discuss a draft law directly without prior reference to the relevant Committee.

Article (87)

Any subject that the Council has declined to discuss under urgency procedure can be submitted again to the Council only one month after the date of rejection. However, the subject may be submitted again in less than one month by a vote of two-thirds of the Members of the Council.

CHAPTER 5: Cloture

Article (88)

The discussion on any matter before the Council shall be closed upon the decision of the Council, provided that at least two supporters and at least two opponents of the proposal have spoken, in the following cases:

1. Upon the proposal of the Speaker, if s/he believes there is no need for further discussion; or
2. Upon the proposal of at least five members.

The relevant Minister shall always be given the right to reply to the discussion.

Only one supporter and one opponent of any motion for cloture shall be called to speak for a period not to exceed five minutes each. Priority shall be given to the Member who requested to speak on the original subject, following which the Council shall vote on whether to close or continue the debate on such proposal. If such proposal is agreed, the Council shall proceed to the substantive original question.

Article (89)

No Member may request to speak after the discussion has been closed and before a vote has been taken, except to determine the form of the proposal to be voted on.

CHAPTER 6: Council Votes

Article (90)

Only the Speaker may call a vote of the Council.

Article (91)

The decisions of the Council shall be made by absolute majority. In the case of a tie, the Speaker shall cast a second vote. If the tie is not resolved, the Speaker shall have a casting vote.

The provisions of paragraph "A" above shall not apply where these Standing Orders specifically provide otherwise.

Article (92)

If the proposal presented for discussion contains several questions, any Member may request, with the agreement of the Speaker, for it to be divided and each part will be voted on separately.

Article (93)

A Member may abstain. Any such Member may explain his/her reasons for doing so after the vote and before the announcement of the result of the vote.

Article (94)

Abstentions shall not be counted either with votes in favor or with votes against. If the total of votes in favor and votes against is less than the quorum, the vote shall be postponed to a further meeting. In the second meeting, decisions shall be taken by absolute majority of those who actually vote, even though their number is less than a majority, due to abstention of others.

Article (95)

The quorum shall be verified immediately before any vote is taken.

Any proposal related to the Basic Law shall be put to a roll call vote.

Except as provided in paragraph "B" above, any vote shall be by show of hands, or by asking members to stand or sit, or by secret ballot if a majority of members so requests.

Article (96)

The Speaker shall announce the decision of the Council as per the result of voting. No discussion may take place on a question once decided except as provided under these Standing Orders.

Title IV
CHAPTER 1: Immunity of Members

Article (97)

A Member shall not be interrogated, in either a civil or criminal procedure, because of his or her actions, opinions, or votes in the meetings of the Council and its Committees, whether open or secret, or because of any action outside the Council in the course of his or her function as a member, to enable them to perform their parliamentary mission.

No members shall be disturbed in any manner, nor shall any search be made of his or her possessions, house, car or office, and generally any real estate or movable property, during the period of his or her immunity.

No Member shall be asked, during the period of membership or subsequently, to testify on any subject related to his or her opinions or actions, or to information received in the course of his or her membership, unless he agrees to do so, and with the prior consent of the Council.

Members shall possess such immunity during the term of the Council. No penal measures shall be taken against any member, unless apprehended in a criminal act. However, the Council shall be notified immediately about the measures taken against the member, so that the Council shall take the proper action in this regard. The Presidium of the Council shall assume this responsibility if the Council is not convened.

A Member shall not relinquish his/her immunity without prior permission of the Council. Immunity shall not lapse after an individual ceases to be a Member of the Council, within the limits which have been included during the membership period.

Article (98)
Any request to deprive a Member of immunity shall be submitted in writing to the Speaker by the President of the Supreme Court of Justice, accompanied by a memorandum including details of the alleged crime, its place and date, and the requisite proof for criminal proceedings to be initiated.

The Speaker shall inform the Council of any such request and shall refer it to the Legal Committee.

The Committee shall study the request and submit a report to the Council within fifteen days. The Council shall decide to deprive a Member of immunity only by the vote of two-thirds of its members.

The Member who has been deprived of immunity shall have the right to attend sessions and meetings of Committees, as well as participate in debates and vote.

Only the Council or the Committee shall have the right to examine the integrity and seriousness of any request to deprive a Member of immunity, to ensure that it does not have any malicious or vexatious ground, and without having to study the subject of the case in terms whether there is a condemnation or not.

Article (99)
No Member shall be summoned before a Civil Court on the day of any meeting of the Council, whether as a plaintiff, defendant, or witness.

Article (100)
Except for the position of Minister, a Member of the Council shall not accept appointment in any public position whether in an executive or consultative capacity.

A Member of the Council shall not combine his membership with presiding or joining any local Palestinian organization, nor holding the office of Governor.

CHAPTER 2: Petitions

Article (101)
Every Palestinian citizen has the right to submit a petition concerning public affairs to the Council. Any such petition shall be signed by the petitioner, and shall include his or her name, profession, and full address. Any petition submitted on behalf of an organization or group shall be signed by a legal entity or a juridical person. No petition may include impolite or improper language.

Article (102)
Every petition shall be registered in the order of its submission, and shall be given a serial number; the name, address, and profession of the petitioner shall be recorded, together with a summary of its subject. The Secretary General may maintain possession of any petition that does not meet the requirements established in the archive, and shall so inform the petitioner.

Article (103)
The Speaker shall refer any petition to the General Monitoring and Petitions Committee, or to the Committee within whose purview the petitions falls.

The General Monitoring and Petitions Committee shall examine the petition referred to it, and shall decide to refer it to the Council of Ministers or to a relevant Committee, or to reject it.

Article (104)
The Council may ask the relevant Minister or Ministers to provide clarifications to any petition referred to them within one month from the date of referral. Otherwise, the subject of the petition shall be debated in a subsequent session of the Council, right after the deadline.

Article (105)
The Secretary General shall communicate the response to the petition of the petitioner.

CHAPTER 3: Absence of Members

Article (106)
No member of the Council may be absent without informing the Speaker and giving a reason. No Member may be absent for more than three consecutive meetings without the consent of the Speaker. In the event of necessity, the Speaker may give any Member leave for one month, and shall so inform the Council.

Article (107)
Any Member who is absent from the meetings of the Council or of its Committees, or is absent for a period longer than the leave he or she has been given, shall be considered as having forfeited his/her allowances for the period of his or her

absence. The Speaker may call the attention of the Council to any such absence; the Council may, upon the proposal of the Speaker, reprimand such member.

If a Member of any Committee is absent without permission or a justified reason for three consecutive or five non-consecutive meetings of that Committee during the same term, s/he shall be considered to have resigned from that Committee. The Secretary of any Committee shall inform the Speaker of any such occurrence.

CHAPTER 4: Order in the Council

Article (108)
The Council shall be responsible for maintaining its own order and security. For these purposes, a special police force for the Council shall be established, according to rules drawn up by the Council. The Speaker shall control the exercise of this function on behalf of the Council.

No security force or police force shall enter the precincts of the Council, unless the Speaker decides otherwise.

Article (109)
No person may enter the chamber of the Council for any reason while it is meeting, with the exception of its staff and employees.

Article (110)
Any person permitted to observe any meetings of the Council who causes disturbances or refuses to obey the rules shall be asked to leave the meeting. If s/he refuses to do so, the Speaker may order that the person be removed from the meeting and that appropriate measures be taken against him or her.

CHAPTER 5: General Provisions

Article (116)
If the Council needs to elect a representative delegation, the proposed number of members shall be determined and selected by the Presidium of the Council, which shall then submit their names to the Council for approval. If the Council does not agree to such proposal, the members of the delegation shall be elected by and from the Council. If the Speaker or either of the Deputy Speakers is a Member of any delegation, s/he shall preside it. Otherwise, the Council shall appoint the president of the delegation.

Article (117)
These Standing Orders may be amended only pursuant to a motion submitted by the Speaker or by one-third of the members of the Council. Any such proposal shall be submitted to the Council, which shall refer it to the Legal Committee. That Committee shall study this proposal and submit its recommendations to the Council within a period not exceeding one month. Otherwise, the Council may

consider the proposal directly, and shall not accept the amendment unless it is approved by two-thirds of the members.

Article (118)
The Council shall issue supplementary regulations to these Standing Orders to explain the duties, rights, and privileges of the members.

Article (119)
These Standing Orders shall enter into force upon approval, and shall be published in the Palestinian Official Gazette. Any other related legislation or rules previously in force in Palestine shall be repealed by these Standing Orders.

APPENDIX NO. 4

Draft Law, Independence of the Judiciary

IN THE NAME OF GOD, THE MOST GRACIOUS, MOST MERCIFUL

The Palestinian Legislative Council (PLC)

Legal Department, Gaza

Draft Proposal No. —— for 1997 Concerning the Independence of the Palestinian Judicial System

The Chairman of the Executive Committee of the Palestinian Liberation Organization, President of the Palestinian National Authority

After reviewing the Palestinian constitution of 1922;
After reviewing the Basic Law of Gaza Strip no. 255 for 1955;
After reviewing the declaration of the constitutional law of Gaza Strip for 1962;
After reviewing the Courts' law of 1940 and its amending articles afterwards;
After reviewing the Independence of Judiciary Act no. 19, for 1952, currently valid and implemented in the West Bank;
After reviewing the Courts Formation Act no. 26, for 1952, currently valid and implemented in Gaza Strip;
After reviewing articles 96 & 97 of the Palestinian Basic Law Proposal of the Palestinian National Authority;
After securing the consent of the Palestinian Legislative Council in its session held on ____/____/1997;
In view of the public interests, and powers vested in us, we issue the following Act:

CHAPTER 1: General Provisions

Article No. (1)
Judicial authority is assumed by courts. It is an independently functioning self-existing entity. It shall have its own budget, which will be part of the general budget of the Palestinian National Authority and attached to it. The Supreme Judicial Council shall prepare the budget proposal and submit it to the Minister of Justice, who shall take the necessary legal procedures for ratification and issuance as appropriate.

Article No. (2)
Judges are independent and shall not be subject to any authority other than the

authority of law while exercising their duties. No authority may interfere in the judiciary or in judicial affairs.

CHAPTER 2: Courts

Section One
Court Levels, Types, and Organization

Article No. (3)
The regular courts comprise the following:

The Supreme Court, which comprises:
Supreme Court of Justice
Supreme Court of Appeal
Supreme Criminal Court
Central Courts (Courts of First Instance)
Conciliation Courts (Courts of First Instance)

Article No. (4)
The headquarters of the Supreme Court shall be located in Jerusalem. It may convene its sessions outside Jerusalem as per a decision issued by the Head of the Supreme Court, "The Chief Justice".

Article No. (5)
The Supreme Court is composed of the Chief Justice and a number of justices as may be required. It shall have different departments such as the supreme justice department, the criminal affairs department, civil, commercial and personal affairs departments, etc. Each of these departments shall be headed by either the Head of Court or by the most senior justice.

Article No. (6)
The creation, establishment, and revision of the various types and levels of courts, together with specification of their scope and domain, shall be initiated and implemented in accordance with law.

CHAPTER 3: Jurisdiction of Regular Courts

Article No. (7)
Regular courts shall settle and resolve all types of conflicts and crimes which have been assigned to them by law, except for those that have been excluded by special provision.

Article No. (8)
The sessions of the courts shall be public, unless the court or one of the litigants

asks that the proceeding be confidential in conformity with public morality or public order. The verdict shall be announced in public session, which shall be chaired and run by the Head of the Court.

Article No. (9)
Arabic is the official language used in the courts. The court shall hear witnesses and litigants who do not speak Arabic via an interpreter after asking him to take the appropriate oath.

Article No. (10)
Verdicts, accompanied with appropriate reasoning and rationale, are issued and executed in the name of the Palestinian People.

CHAPTER 4: Judges' Appointment, Promotion, and Seniority

Article No. (11)
The person nominated to assume a judicial position shall possess the following:

Palestinian nationality and complete civil eligibility.
Not less than twenty-seven years old.
A degree from a law school.
Not convicted by any court or any disciplinary council whatsoever of an infamous
    crime, even if he/she received clemency afterwards.
Reputable, of good conduct, well qualified, and competent to assume such posi-
    tion.
Medically fit.
Does not belong to any political party or organization.

Article No. (12)
Judges may be appointed from the following bodies:

Attorney General Deputies
Advisors from Legal Departments
Attorneys who practiced actually before regular courts for at least five years

Article No. (13)
Judicial positions shall be filled either through appointment or promotion via a decision issued by the President of the Palestinian National Authority based on nomination and endorsement by the Supreme Judicial Council.

Article No. (14)
The person nominated to assume the position of Chief Justice should possess the following qualifications:

At least 20 years of experience in the judicial field;
Membership on the Supreme Court bench.

A person nominated to the Supreme Court bench should possess the following qualifications:

At least 17 years of experience in the judicial field;
Membership on the Central Court bench.

A person nominated to serve as a judge in the Central Court should possess the following qualifications:

At least 7 years of experience in the judicial field;
Membership on the Conciliation Court bench.

A person nominated to serve as a judge in the Conciliation Court should possess the following qualifications:

Prosecuting Attorney with at least three years in the position.
Legal advisor in a legal department with at least five years in the position.
Attorneys who have practiced law for not less than five years.

Article No. (15)
The promotion of judges is based on their qualifications and competence. Thus if two or more candidates have similar qualifications, the most senior one in the grade shall have priority over the other. Seniority is also determined according to the most recent and latest grade; however, if two or more candidates have the same grade, priority shall be determined according to the date of the previous grade (who received the grade first) and so on. If the dates shown on all previous grades were similar for two or more candidates, their competence shall be determined according to the date of appointment. If they have a similar appointment date, reference should be made to the graduation date.

Article No. (16)
The seniority of judges is based on the date of their appointment or promotion date, unless the appointment or promotion notice specifies another date, as per the consent of the Supreme Judicial Council.

If two or more judges have been appointed or promoted in one decree, the seniority of each of them shall be based on the sequence in which their names were stated in the decree. The seniority of judges who are reappointed to their position shall be based on the date of their first appointment.

CHAPTER 5: Judges' Salaries and Remuneration

Article No. (17)
Judges' salaries and remuneration scales are determined in accordance with the table and annex attached hereto. It is prohibited to allocate any allowance to any judge on personal grounds or deal with him/her in any exceptional way.

Article No. (18)
The resignation of a judge shall not result in any way in the forfeiture of his/her rights to pension or compensation. The resignation shall be considered to be in force as of the date it has been endorsed by the President of the Palestinian National Authority, after being approved by the Supreme Judicial Council.

Article No. (19)
The pension of a judge is calculated on the basis of the rules and regulations included in the pension act, after replacing the thirty-year period with a twenty-five-year period, i.e., replacing the one to thirty ratio with a one to twenty-five ratio in all parts of the pension act, provided that the judge has completed actual service of not less than fifteen years in the judicial field.

Article No. (20)
Regardless of the provisions of any statute, no person aged more than seventy-two years may retain or be appointed to any judicial position, unless approved by the Supreme Judicial Council for exceptional circumstances of public interests.

CHAPTER 6: Transfer, Secondment, and Lending of Judges

Article No. (21)
Judges shall not be transferred, seconded, or lent other than in cases specified and outlined in this act, and as per the consent of the Supreme Judicial Council.

Article No. (22)
Transfer of judges shall take place as per a decision issued by the Chief Justice after securing the consent of the Supreme Judicial council. The decision shall specify the court to which the judge has been transferred. The date of transfer shall be identical to the date of notification.

Article No. (23)
Should the position of Chief Justice become vacant, or in case of his absence or incapacity to perform his duties, the most senior judge or justice shall assume his duties. In case any judge is absent or is prevented from assuming his/her duties, the Chief Justice shall second another judge to replace him.

Article No. (24)
A judge may be temporarily seconded to perform judicial or legal tasks other than his work, or in addition to it, as per a decision issued by the Chief Justice, with the consent of the Supreme Judicial Council, and based on a request by the Minister of Justice. However, the Supreme Judicial Council alone shall determine the remuneration which the judge deserves on account of these tasks, after completion.

Article No. (25)
A judge may not act as an arbitrator, even without pay, without the consent of the

Supreme Judicial Council, even though no case has been filed in this connection, unless any of the opponents is one of his relatives up to the fourth degree.

Further, a judge may not be seconded without the consent of the Supreme Judicial Council to act as an arbitrator on behalf of the government or any other public body if he/she is part of the conflict. In case of approval, the Supreme Judicial Council shall determine the remuneration the judge deserves.

Article No. (26)
The period of judge secondment shall not exceed three months in one year unless approved by the Supreme Judicial Council. Also, this secondment shall not exceed three consecutive years.

Article No. (27)
The President of the Palestinian National Authority may second judges to international governments or bodies following nomination and approval by the Supreme Judicial Council. The period of secondment shall not exceed three consecutive years. However, this period may be extended if the President of the Palestinian National Authority considers that the national interest necessitates such extension. In all cases, the secondment should in no way have a negative impact on the course of judicial performance in Palestine.

CHAPTER 7: Judges' Immunity and Protection against Dismissal

Article No. (28)
Judges cannot be dismissed and their services cannot be terminated other than in the following cases:

Death
Resignation accepted by the Supreme Judicial Council
Reach the age of retirement
Evident disability to render duties due to health reasons. Such disability is determined by a decision from a specialized medical committee
Appointment to other non-judicial positions
Disciplinary dismissal in accordance with the rules stipulated hereinafter.

CHAPTER 8: Judges' Duties

Article No. (29)
Judges must take the following oath, before assuming their duties and responsibilities for the first time:

"I swear by the Almighty God that I shall perform my duties in a faithful, honest and sincere manner, and that I shall respect the provisions of the constitution and law, and work for the realization of justice."

The Chief of Justice shall take the oath before the President of the Palestinian National Authority. The judges of the Supreme Court and the remaining judges shall take oath before the Chief of Justice in the presence of Supreme Judicial Council members.

Article No. (30)
A judge may not practice any commercial activity, or any other activity that contradicts or is not in keeping with the independence and pride of the judicial system. The Supreme Judicial Council may decide to prevent a judge from practicing any activity that contradicts the duties of the position, or its correct performance.

Article No. (31)
Judges are prohibited from engaging in political activity, or expressing political opinions. A judge may not stand for election, including for the Palestinian Legislative Council or any political party or organization, unless he/she resigns and the Supreme Judicial Council accepts such resignation.

Article No. (32)
Judges who are related (up to the fourth degree) may not work in the same legal department. Further, a judge may not be related (up to the fourth degree) to the attorney-general, or with the attorney of any of the litigants. Any power of attorney given to a lawyer related to any member of the bench with such a relationship is not accepted, if such power of attorney was given after the judge receives the case.

Article No. (33)
A judge shall not leave his place of work without notifying and seeking the permission of the Chief Justice or his/her deputy in writing. Except for emergencies, a judge shall not interrupt his work without written permission. However, if the judge does not abide by this rule, he/she shall be warned in writing by the Chief Justice or his/her deputy.

If a judge's unauthorized absence lasts for more than seven days, the period, in excess of seven days, shall be considered part of his ordinary leave, and shall be deducted from his/her accrued leave.

A judge shall be considered to have resigned if he/she is absent from work for thirty consecutive days without permission, even if such absence occurs after the end of his/her vacation, or secondment.
If the judge returns and submits justifiable excuses accepted by the Supreme Judicial Council, then he/she will not be considered to have resigned. The period of his absence is considered as the previous leave, or as ordinary leave, depending on the conditions.

Article No. (34)
A judge shall never disclose confidential deliberations.

CHAPTER 9: The Supreme Judicial Council

Article No. (35)
The Supreme Judicial Council is composed of the Chief Justice, along with:

The three most senior judges of the Supreme Court
The Attorney General
The head of the Ramallah Appeals Department and the next senior judge from the Supreme Court (whose rank is second after the head of Ramallah Appeals Department). The Supreme Judicial Council shall hold its sessions in the Supreme Court Headquarters, and shall have its own secretariat, which will operate in accordance with regulations issued by the council.

Article No. (36)
Should the position of Chief Justice become vacant, or in case of his absence; or whenever there is anything that prevents him/her from assuming his/her duties, he shall be replaced by the next most senior judge, or by the most senior judge in the Supreme Court. In such case, the most senior judge, other than those referred to in the previous article, shall join the membership of the Council.

Should the position of any member of the Council become vacant; or in case of his absence; or whenever there is anything that prevents him/her from assuming his/her duties, the next most senior shall replace the judges of the Supreme Court.

Article No. (37)
The Supreme Judicial Council is responsible for all matters pertaining to judges' appointment, promotion, transfer, and secondment along with any other matters and affairs related to judges and the judicial system. The Supreme Judicial Council should be consulted in developing draft proposals pertaining to the judiciary and public prosecution. However, consultation and coordination with the Minister of Justice in this regard shall be taken into consideration, in order to hear his point of view.

Article No. (38)
The Supreme Judicial Council holds its sessions in the Supreme Court Headquarters when convened by the Chief Justice or upon a request by the Minister of Justice. The sessions shall not be considered valid unless five of its members attend. The deliberations of the sessions shall be confidential and the decisions shall be taken by majority vote. In case of a tie, the Chief Justice shall have the casting vote.

Article No. (39)
The Supreme Judicial Council shall develop its internal policies and procedures, including the rules and regulations applied in the exercise of its duties. The Supreme Judicial Council may form a committee or more from its members, and authorize it to assume some of its jurisdiction, except in matters related to appointment, promotion, or transfer.

Article No. (40)
The Supreme Judicial Council shall assign every year, one or more Supreme Court justices to inspect the activities and performance of judges in lower courts, such as the Central and Conciliation courts. The assigned justice(s) shall submit a report to the Supreme Judicial Council in this regard. The competence and efficiency of judges shall be evaluated and given any of the following grades: Competent, Above Average, Average, or Below Average.

The Minister of Justice shall receive a copy of the report for information, which shall be kept in the file of the concerned judge.

CHAPTER 10: Grievances, Petitions, and Appeals against Decisions Related to Judges

Article No. (41)
After delivering the inspection reports to the Supreme Justice Council, the Chief Justice shall notify judges whose inspection reports show an "Average" or "Less than average" assessment. The notified judges shall have the right to respond and submit his grievance against the report, within fifteen days of the notification date.

Article No. (42)
Petitions and grievances shall take the form of a petition to the Chief Justice, who, in turn, shall forward it to the Supreme Judicial Council. The latter shall form a committee of three or more members to study the grievance. In doing so, the committee shall examine documents and listen to the defense and arguments of the appealing judge. The decision of this committee concerning the competence of the appealing judge, after the Supreme Judicial Council endorses it, shall be considered final and conclusive. The concerned party shall be notified of the decision via registered mail.

Article No. (43)
Should a judge receive a "Below Average" grade, a re-inspection shall be performed before his grade can be promoted to a higher position, or one year after the previous inspection. If the findings of the new inspection point to a similar assessment, the Supreme Judicial Council, after consultations with the Minister of Justice, shall consider transferring him to another non-judicial position. The transfer decision shall be made by the Minister of Justice based on the decision and consent of the Supreme Judicial Council. Such a decision shall be considered final and not subject to appeal.

Article No. (44)
Regular inspection checks of the judges' performances shall be conducted at least once every two years. The findings shall be submitted to the concerned party no later than two months after the end of the inspection.

Article No. (45)
Decisions made by the Supreme Judicial Council concerning appointment, transfer or secondment, after consultations and verification with the Minister of Justice, shall be final and not subject to appeal before any party.

CHAPTER 11: Vacations and Judicial Leave

Article No. (46)
In every calendar year, the judicial vacation shall start in the middle of July and continue until the end of August. However, there shall be one judge available for urgent matter at each court during that period.

Article No. (47)
The Supreme, Central, and Conciliation Courts shall continue during the judicial vacation to adjudicate urgent cases. Such cases shall be determined as per a decision made by the Chief Justice.

Article No. (48)
Judges shall be entitled to a forty-five-day vacation. Such vacation shall be specified in accordance with the rules and regulations related to the vacations of civil servants. The Chief Justice shall be responsible for organizing the vacations of the judges.

CHAPTER 12: Judges' Accountability and Disciplining

Article No. (49)
The Minister of Justice shall have the right to exercise administrative supervision of all courts. On the other hand, the Chief Justice shall have the right to supervise and oversee the performance of judges, judicial employees, court organization, and the progress of work. Further, the Chief Justice shall have the right to warn judges either verbally or in writing whenever they fail to perform their duties.

Article No. (50)
The disciplining of judges falls within the purview of the Supreme Judicial Council. The Council shall do whatever it deems necessary to interrogate the judge being investigated. Further, the Supreme Judicial Council may authorize any of the Supreme Court judges to do so. The authorized judge shall enjoy the powers vested in the court for summoning witnesses and conducting any other procedure.

Article No. (51)
If the Supreme Judicial Council decides that there are grounds to proceed with legal actions against the defendant judge, the defendant judge shall be summoned to appear before the court, at least one week prior to the intended date, pursuant to

an order issued by the Chief Justice. The summons shall include sufficient details about the matter of the indictment and evidence.

Article No. (52)
When the Supreme Judicial Council decides to proceed with disciplinary proceedings, the Council may also order the suspension of the defendant judge from his activities or place him on involuntary leave until the legal proceedings come to an end. The Council may reconsider the suspension order or involuntary leave at any time.

Article No. (53)
Sessions of the disciplinary court shall be confidential and in camera, unless the accused (defendant) judge requests otherwise. The defendant shall appear in person before the Supreme Judicial Council. He may present his defense in writing, or ask any of his colleagues or advocates to defend him.

Article No. (54)
Disciplinary proceedings may be initiated and pursued by a judge from the Supreme or Central Court, provided that he has been delegated to do so by the Chief Justice, via a written memorandum including the charges as arrived at by the interrogation committee. The memorandum shall be kept by the secretariat of the disciplinary council, in order to issue a summons for the judge to appear before it. The summons shall include sufficient details about the matter of indictment and evidence. If the defendant judge does not appear before the court or does not authorize some one to represent him, it will be lawful to pass a judgment in absentia against him.

Article No. (55)
The Supreme Judicial Council shall review the disciplinary proceedings after hearing the arguments of the prosecution and the defense. The verdict shall state the grounds upon which it is based. These grounds shall be pronounced even if the sentence is passed in a confidential and in camera session.

Article No. (56)
A temporarily suspended judge may earn not less than fifty percent of his salary. However, if the legal proceedings and interrogations initiated against him/her did not result in his conviction, the judge may demand complete reimbursement of his salary as of the date of suspension.

Article No. (57)
Disciplinary proceedings shall be terminated upon the resignation of the defendant judge and the acceptance of such resignation by the Supreme Judicial Council. However, the disciplinary proceedings shall not have an effect on criminal or civil proceeding resultant from the same incident.

Article No. (58)
The disciplinary penalties which may be implemented against Judges include:

Reprimand; Suspension of salary; Postponement of annual increment; Salary reduction for a certain period of time; Demotion; Dismissal from office

Article No. (59)
In cases other than flagrant delicto, a judge may not be arrested or detained without a warrant from the Supreme Judicial Council. If a judge is caught in the act, the Attorney General shall obtain the consent of the Chief Justice to arrest or detain the judge. The Chief Justice shall refer the issue to the Supreme Judicial Council within the next twenty-four hours. The Council may decide, after listening to the suspected judge, to continue his detention or order his release, with or without bail.

The Council may conduct necessary and appropriate investigation, and may assign three of its members to do this.

Article No. (60)
The Supreme Judicial Council is authorized to consider provisional detention, or renew an arrest warrant, unless the case has been brought before the criminal courts authorized to handle such cases.

Article No. (61)
The detention and arrest of a judge shall result in the immediate suspension of his judicial activities and tasks. The Supreme Judicial Council may suspend the judge's activities during interrogation and investigation of a crime (at the request of the Minister of Justice). However, such a suspension shall not result in the suspension of salary during the interrogation period, unless the Supreme Judicial Council decides to deprive him of his salary in whole or part. The Supreme Judicial Council may, at its sole discretion or upon the judge's request, reconsider the denial of salary.

Article No. (62)
The Supreme Judicial Council shall establish a disciplinary council of Supreme Court justices to discipline judges (at least three justices, headed according to seniority) by adopting a resolution in this regard.

CHAPTER 13: Office of the Attorney General (Public Prosecution)

Section One
Appointment, Promotion and Seniority

Article No. (63)
The Office of the Attorney General (Public Prosecution) is composed of:

The Attorney General (Public Prosecutor)
Assistants to the Attorney General, one in the West Bank and another in the Gaza
   Strip

Chief Attorneys
Prosecutors
Assistant Prosecutors

Article No. (64)
A person nominated to serve as Assistant Public Prosecutor shall meet the conditions and requirements stipulated in article 11 of this act, including being not less than twenty-one years old.

Article No. (65)
The appointment of a Deputy Public Prosecutor, Assistant Public Prosecutor, or Technical Staff in the legal departments of governmental bodies or other institutions, shall take place via immediate promotion from the previous degree. Candidates for a Deputy Public Prosecutor position may, however, be selected from the technical staff employed at least for three years in the legal departments of governmental bodies, or from attorneys who practiced their professions before courts for at least four years.

Article No. (66)
The Attorney General shall be appointed as per a presidential decree, issued by the President of the Palestinian National Authority. He shall be selected from the Supreme Court judges. The Attorney General may request to return to work in the judicial field. In such case, his seniority is determined on the basis of his status when appointed to the Attorney General position, together with keeping his salary and other forms of remuneration as is.

The appointment of the Assistant Attorney General (Assistant Public Prosecutor) and other public prosecution members shall be in accordance with a presidential decree issued by the President of the Palestinian National Authority, after consultation with the Supreme Judicial Council.

If the appointment is conceived as a promotion or if the appointed person has never held a judicial or prosecutorial position, the appointment shall be approved by the Supreme Judicial Council. The appointment or promotion date shall be effective from the date of approval or consultation with the Supreme Judicial Council.

Article No. (67)
Members of the public prosecution shall take an oath before the Minister of Justice and the Attorney General, before assuming their duties, in accordance with the text contained in Article No. 31 herein. The Attorney General shall take oath before the President of the Palestinian National Authority.

Article No. (68)
The location of work for members of the public prosecution, and their transfer, shall be determined by a decision made by the Minister of Justice, based on recommendations of the Attorney General. However, the Attorney General shall have the right to transfer the members of the public prosecution within the boundaries of the

court they work, as well as the right to second any of them outside the boundaries of the courts, for a period not to exceed six months.

Article No. (69)
The Supreme Judicial Council shall assign a number of judges and public prosecutors, whose grades are not less than chief public prosecutor, to inspect and check the performance of the members of the public prosecution for a period of one year, which can be renewed. Inspection rules and regulations shall be issued in accordance with a decision made by the Supreme Judicial Council to regulate inspection and specify the jurisdiction of those who implement it.

The members of the public prosecution shall be notified of any remarks or documents placed in their files.

The assessment scale will be: Competent, Above Average, Average, or Below Average. Public Prosecutors shall be evaluated at least once every two years by the Chief Prosecutor. The evaluation report shall be submitted within two months (at most) from the date of completion.

Article No. (70)
Salaries of members of the public prosecution of all grades shall be determined in accordance with the salary scale attached herein. The seniority of members of the public prosecution shall be determined in accordance with the prescribed rules and regulations, as per article 17 of this act.

Section Two
Disciplining Members of the Public Prosecution

Article No. (71)
Members of the public prosecution shall report to their direct supervisors. They shall all report, together with the Attorney General, to the Minister of Justice. The Minister shall have the right to exercise administrative supervision of the Office of Attorney General. On the other hand, the Attorney General shall have the right to supervise and control the activities of all members of the public prosecution.

Article No. (72)
Disciplining members of the public prosecution, regardless of their degrees, is a function of the Judges' Disciplining Council referred to in Article No. 62 of this act.

Article No. (73)
Sanctions for disciplining members of the public prosecution shall be similar to those applied for disciplining judges.

Article No. (74)
The Attorney General shall initiate the disciplinary proceedings against suspected members of the public prosecution, based on a request from the Minister of Justice.

The Minister of Justice and the Attorney General may suspend the activities of the suspected member of the public prosecution until the disciplinary legal proceedings are concluded. Rules and regulations adopted for taking legal actions against judges shall be implemented.

Article No. (75)
Members of the public prosecution are not subject to dismissal, except for their assistants.

Notes

1 Introduction: Political Development and the Transition to Democracy

1 See Ronald Chilcote, *Theories of Comparative Politics* (Boulder: Westview Press, 1981).
2 See the discussion in ibid.; Gabriel Almond and James Coleman, eds, *The Politics of the Developing Areas* (Princeton: Princeton University Press, 1960).
3 Robert Dahl, *Polyarchy: Participation and Opposition* (New Haven: Yale University Press, 1971).
4 Samuel Huntington, *The Third Wave: Democratization in the Late Twentieth Century* (Norman: University of Oklahoma Press, 1991).
5 See the discussion in Guillermo O'Donnell and Phillip Schmitter, *Transitions from Authoritarian Rule: Tentative Conclusions about Uncertain Democracies* (Baltimore: Johns Hopkins University Press, 1986).
6 David Collier and Steven Levitsky, "Democracy with Adjectives: Conceptual Innovation in Comparative Research", *World Politics* 49 (April 1997): 430–51.
7 See, for example, the extensive discussion, with a wealth of examples and case studies, in Yossi Shain and Juan Linz, *Between States: Interim Governments and Democratic Transitions* (Cambridge: Cambridge University Press, 1995).
8 See, for example, Larry Diamond, *Political Culture: Democracy in Developing Countries* (Boulder and London: Lynne Rienner Publishers, 1993); Seymour Martin Lipset, "Some Social Requisites of Democracy: Economic Development and Democracy", *American Political Science Review* 53 (1959); Huntington, *The Third Wave*.
9 See Huntington, *The Third Wave*.
10 See Lipset, "Some Social Requisites of Democracy".
11 Dankwart Rustow, "Transitions to Democracy", *Comparative Politics* 3 (1970): 337–63.
12 Nancy Bermeo, "Myths of Moderation: Confrontation and Conflict during Democratic Transitions", *Comparative Politics* 29 (3) (1997).

2 The Palestinian National Movement: A Historical Overview

1 Yehoshua Porath, *The Emergence of the Palestinian–Arab National Movement 1918–1929* (London: Frank Cass, 1974), pp. 223–50.
2 Salah Abd el-Jawad, "The Development of the Palestinian National Movement from the Beginning of the Zionist Settlement until the Partition",

in *The Palestinian Society* (Beirut: The Center to Revive the Palestinian Heritage, 1990), pp. 479–95 (Arabic); Yehoshua Porath, *The Palestinian Arab National Movement: From Riots to Rebellion. Vol. 2, 1929–1939* (London: Frank Cass, 1977), pp. 69–104.

3 See Abd el-Jawad, "The Development of the Palestinian National Movement", pp. 486–92.

4 Charles Cayman, "After the Catastrophe: The Arabs in the State of Israel 1948–1950", *Notebooks for Research and Criticism* 10 (1984): 5 (Hebrew).

5 Majid al-Haj, "Adjustment Patterns of the Arab Internal Refugees in Israel", *International Migration* 24 (1986): 651–74; Majid al-Haj, "The Arab Internal Refugees in Israel: The Emergence of a Minority within the Minority", *Immigration and Minorities* 7 (1988): 149–65.

6 Pamela Ann Smith, *Palestine and the Palestinians, 1876–1983* (New York: St. Martin's Press, 1984), p. 82.

7 Ibid., pp. 83–4.

8 Ibid., pp. 84–7.

9 Benny Morris, *The Birth of the Palestinian Refugee Problem 1947–1949* (Cambridge and New York: Cambridge University Press, 1987), pp. 21–42.

10 Ibid., pp. 382–96.

11 As'ad Abd el-Rahman, ed., *The PLO: Its Roots, Founding, and Activity* (Beirut: PLO Research Center, 1987), pp. 30–2 (Arabic).

12 Several references maintain that the movement originated in the early 1950s. But since it was dormant until after 1957, that date seems better for marking the start of its activity.

13 Abd el-Rahman, *The PLO: Its Roots*, pp. 39–40; Guy Bechor, *The PLO* (Tel Aviv: Ministry of Defense Publishing House, 1995), p. 283 (Hebrew).

14 Abd el-Rahman, *The PLO: Its Roots*, pp. 40–1.

15 Bechor, *The PLO*, pp. 274–82.

16 On earlier attempts to establish Arab political parties in Israel, all of them unsuccessful, see Habib Qahwaji, *The Arabs in the Shadow of the Israeli Occupation since 1948* (Beirut: The Research Center of the Palestine Liberation Organization, 1972), pp. 423–5 (Arabic); See also Yaakov Landau, *The Arabs in Israel: Political Studies* (Tel Aviv: Ma'arkhot, 1971), pp. 90–4 (Hebrew).

17 Sabri Jeryis, *The Arabs in Israel* (Beirut: The Institute for Palestinian Studies, 1973), p. 316 (Arabic).

18 See As'ad Ghanem, "The Popular Arab Front and the Struggle against Land Expropriation", *Qadaya* 3 (1990): 50–8 (Arabic).

19 Jeryis, *The Arabs in Israel*, p. 318; Qahwaji, *The Arabs in the Shadow*, p. 446.

20 Jeryis, *The Arabs in Israel*, pp. 318–19; Qahwaji, *The Arabs in the Shadow*, pp. 447–72.

21 Jeryis, *The Arabs in Israel*, pp. 319–20.

22 Qahwaji, *The Arabs in the Shadow*, p. 459.

23 Jeryis, *The Arabs in Israel*, pp. 324–8; Qahwaji, *The Arabs in the Shadow*, p. 473.

24 Abd el-Rahman, *The PLO: Its Roots*, pp. 42–6.

25 Ibid., pp. 63, 82.

26 Ibid., pp. 93–101.

27 Ibid., p. 139.
28 See Maher al-Sharif, *In the Wake of the Entity* (Nicosia: The Center for Socialist Studies and Research in the Arab World, 1995) (Arabic).
29 Bechor, *The PLO*, pp. 30–9; the text of the Covenant is cited from Bernard Reich, ed., *Arab–Israeli Conflict and Conciliation: A Documentary History* (Westport and London: Praeger, 1995).
30 Al-Sharif, *In the Wake of the Entity*, pp. 181–2.
31 Ibid., p. 184.
32 Ibid., p. 188.
33 Ibid., pp. 188–9.
34 Ibid., pp. 238–9.
35 Bechor, *The PLO*, p. 318; Reich, *Arab–Israeli Conflict*, p. 128.
36 Al-Sharif, *In the Wake of the Entity*, p. 311.
37 Ibid., p. 346.
38 Bechor, *The PLO*, p. 85; Reich, *Arab–Israeli Conflict*, p. 214.
39 Al-Sharif, *In the Wake of the Entity*, p. 371.
40 Ibid., pp. 408–9.
41 Ibid., pp. 413–18.
42 See Yossi Beilin, *Touching Peace: From the Oslo Accord to a Final Agreement* (London: Weidenfeld and Nicolson, 1999).
43 See Uri Savir, *The Process: 1,100 Days that Changed the Middle East* (New York: Random House, 1998).
44 See, for example: Beilin, *Touching Peace*; Savir, *The Process*; Mahmud Abbas (Abu Mazen), *The Road to Oslo* (Beirut: Printing and Distribution Co. 1994) (Arabic); Marek Halter and Eric Laurent, *Les Fous de la paix: histoire secrète d'une négociation* (Paris: Plon, 1994).

3 Democracy and Centralism in the Palestinian National Movement, 1967–1993

1 See the discussion in Ali al-Jarbawi, *The Legal System and Democratic Change in Palestine* (Ramallah: Mowaten – The Palestinian Institute for Democracy Studies, 1999) (Arabic).
2 Manual Hassassian, "Policy and Attitude Change in the Palestine Liberation Organization, 1965–1994: A Democracy in the Making", in Avraham Sela and Moshe Ma'oz, eds, *The PLO and Israel: From Armed Conflict to Political Solution, 1964–1994* (New York: St. Martin's Press, 1997), pp. 73–94; Emile Sahliyeh, "The PLO and the Politics of Ethnonational Mobilization", ibid., pp. 3–22.
3 Abd el-Satar Qasim, *The Road to Defeat* (privately published, 1998) (Arabic); see also Assad Abd el-Rahman, *The PLO: Its Roots*; Al-Sharif, *In the Wake*; Helena Cobban, *The Palestinian Liberation Organisation* (Cambridge: Cambridge University Press, 1984), chs 1 and 11.
4 Said Aburish, *Arafat: From Defender to Dictator* (London: Bloomsbury, 1998), chs 10 and 11.
5 *Palestinian Encyclopedia* I, vol. 4, pp. 317–20 (Arabic).
6 Azmi Bishara, "What is the Meaning of the Discourse about Palestinian Democracy?" in *Palestinian Democracy: A Position Paper* (Ramallah:

Mowaten – The Palestinian Institute for Democracy Studies, 1995), p. 139 (Arabic).

7   Musa al-Budiri, "Democracy and the Experience of National Liberation: The Palestinian Case", ibid., p. 43 (Arabic).

8   Ibid., pp. 52–3.

9   Jamil Helal, "The Problems of Democratic Institution in Palestinian Public Life", in *Palestinian Democracy: A Position Paper* (Ramallah: Mowaten – The Palestinian Institute for Democracy Studies, 1995), p. 94 (Arabic).

10 Ibid., p. 44.

11 *Palestinian Encyclopedia* I, vol. 4, p. 108.

12 Ibid., p. 118.

13 Ibid., p. 110.

14 Naji al-Khatib, *A Discussion of Palestinian Democracy: A Dialogue* (Paris: The Civil Alternative Association, 1993) (Arabic).

15 Al-Budiri, "Democracy and the Experience", p. 52.

16 Bishara, "What is the Meaning of the Discourse", p. 138.

17 *Palestinian Encyclopedia*, p. 104.

18 Ibid., p. 320.

19 Ibid., p. 321.

20 Helal, "The Problems of Democratic Institution", p. 94.

21 *Al Ayam*, June 1, 1999.

22 *Palestinian Encyclopedia*, pp. 322–5.

23 Anis Sayegh, *September 13* (Beirut: Beisan Library, 1994), p. 30 (Arabic).

24 Ibid., pp. 126–7.

25 *Palestinian Encyclopedia* I, vol. 3, p. 61.

26 Ibid., p. 3.

27 Qasim, *The Road to Defeat*, p. 162.

28 Ibid., p. 159.

29 Ibid., p. 160.

30 Ibid., p. 160.

31 *Palestinian Encyclopedia* I, vol. 3, p. 470.

32 Sayegh, *September 13*, pp. 72–4.

33 Ibid., pp. 75–6.

34 Mamduh Nofal, *The Oslo Stew* (Amman: The Civilian Institution for Publication and Distribution, 1995) (Arabic).

35 Aburish, *Arafat: From Defender to Dictator*, p. 323.

36 Tawfiq Abu Bakr, *The Process of the Political Settlement, 1977–1994: Dialogues and Testimonies* (Amman: The Center for Strategic Studies in Jenin, 1998), p. 13 (Arabic).

37 Ibid., p. 10.

38 Sayegh, *September 13*, p. 31.

39 Sakher Habash, *Historical Adventurism and Constraints of National Security* (Fatah Office for Thought and Research, 1998), p. 5 (Arabic).

40 See Khaled al-Hassan, *Lest the Leadership Become a Dictatorship: From My Own Experience* (unpublished) (Arabic).

41 Sayegh, *September 13*, p. 121.

42 Aburish, *Arafat: From Defender to Dictator*, p. 325.

43 Qasim, *The Road to Defeat*, p. 72.
44 Al-Sharif, *In the Wake of the Entity*, p. 326.
45 As'ad Abd el-Rahman, "The Palestinian Struggle in the Context of the PLO", *Palestinian Encyclopedia* II, vol. 5 (1990), p. 249 (Arabic).
46 Sayegh, *September 13*, p. 119.
47 Ibid., p. 126.
48 Al-Sharif, *In the Wake of the Entity*, p. 320.
49 Sayegh, *September 13*, p. 123.
50 Ibid., p. 126.
51 Azat Abd el-Hadi, "The Problem of Elections to National Institutions and Calls for Change", in *The National Institutions: The Elections and the Authority* (Ramallah: Muwatan – The Palestinian Center for Democracy Studies, 1994), pp. 14–15 (Arabic).
52 Geoffrey Aronson, *Creating Facts: Israel, Palestinians, and the West Bank* (Washington, D.C.: Institute for Palestine Studies, 1987), p. 239.
53 Ziad Abu Amru, *Civil Society and the Transition to Democracy in Palestine* (Ramallah: Muwaten – The Palestinian Center for Democracy Studies, 1995), p. 68 (Arabic).
54 Ali Ahmad Abdallah, *The Situation of the Palestinian Press in the West Bank* (PLO Cultural Department, 1989), p. 38 (Arabic).
55 Ali al-Khalili, "The Renewed Problematic of the Press under the Occupation", in *The Palestinian Press, President and Future* (Ramallah: Muwatan – The Palestinian Institute for Democracy Studies, 1993), pp. 35–6 (Arabic).
56 Ibid., pp. 39–40.
57 Ibid., pp. 41–2.
58 *Palestinian Encyclopedia* II, vol. 4, pp. 461–2.
59 Ali Ahmad Abdallah, *The Situation of the Palestinian Press*, pp. 72–3.
60 Ibid., p. 61.
61 For details, see ibid., pp. 103–20.
62 For additional information about the image and problems of the Palestinian press under the occupation, see the *Palestinian Encyclopedia* II, vol. 4, pp. 464–5 (Arabic).
63 Azat Abd el-Hadi, "Notes on the Form and Content of the Associations Law", Conference of the Arab–European Encounters on Democracy (Nablus: Najah University, May 10–13, 1997) (Arabic).
64 Abd el-Hadi, "Notes on the Form and Content", p. 21.
65 Ibid., pp. 21–2.
66 Rima Hamami, "The Nongovernmental Palestinian Organizations: The Professionalization of Politics in the Absence of Opposition", *Majlat a-Siyasa al-Falastiniya* 10 (Nablus: The Center for Palestinian Research and Studies, 1996), p. 95 (Arabic).
67 Abd el-Hadi, "Notes on the Form and Content", pp. 22–3.
68 Hamami, "The Nongovernmental Palestinian", p. 96.
69 Ibid., p. 96.
70 Abu Amru, *Civil Society and the Transition*, p. 60.
71 Azat Daragma, *The Women's Movement in Palestine, 1903–1991* (Jerusalem: Sia'a Office for Research Studies, 1991), p. 59 (Arabic).

72 Muna Rashmawi, *A Preface on the Palestinian Woman* (Ramallah: Al Haq Institute, 1986), pp. 25–6 (Arabic).
73 Abu Amru, *Civil Society and the Transition*, pp. 60–1.
74 Daragma, *The Women's Movement*, pp. 109–13.
75 Ibid., pp. 125–9.
76 For more details see ibid., pp. 115–36.
77 Abu Amru, *Civil Society and the Transition*, pp. 50–1.
78 Ibid., p. 53.
79 Ibid.
80 Shaher Said, *The Palestinian Labor Unions and the National Reconstruction* (Nablus, 1993), p. 9 (Arabic); Abu Amru, *Civil Society and the Transition*, p. 54 (Arabic).
81 Ibid., p. 54.
82 Muhammad Sharaka, "The Labor Movement and the Defense of the Right of Labor Organization in Palestine", The Arab–European Conference; Abu Amru, *Civil Society and the Transition*, p. 56.
83 Ibid., p. 66.
84 Ibid., p. 67.
85 Ibid.
86 Abd el-Hadi, "The Problem of Elections", p. 15.
87 Lisa Turaki, *Palestinian Society in the West Bank and Gaza District* (Acre: Dar al-Aswar, 1990), p. 55 (Arabic).
88 Majdi al-Malki, "Variables and Constants in the Image of the Palestinian Student Movement", *Majlat a-Siyasa al-Falastiniya* 11 (Nablus: The Center for Palestinian Research and Studies, 1996), pp. 100–1 (Arabic).
89 Abu Amru, *Civil Society and the Transition*, p. 56.
90 Ibid., p. 57.
91 For more information on the clashes between students at Bir Zeit and the Israeli army, see Aronson, *Creating Facts*, pp. 201–3.
92 Raja Shehada, *The Occupier's Law: Israel and the West Bank* (Beirut: The Institute for Palestinian Studies and Kuwait University, 1990), pp. 162–70 (Arabic).
93 Ibid.
94 Ibid., p. 87.
95 Ibid., p. 88.
96 Ibid., p. 132.
97 Ibid.
98 *Palestinian Encyclopedia* II, vol. 1, pp. 904–5.
99 Ibid.
100 Management Consultants Group International, *The Development of the Palestinian Chambers of Commerce and their Federation* (Amman, 1994), p. 20.
101 Ra'ad Abd el-Hamid, p. 86.
102 Abd el-Hadi, "The Problem of Elections", p. 21.
103 Management Consultants Group International, *The Development of the Palestinian*, pp. 3–4.
104 Ibid., pp. 13, 15.
105 Al-Budiri, "Democracy and the Experience", pp. 55–6.

106 Ibid., p. 58.
107 *Palestinian Encyclopedia* I, vol. 2, p. 27; Al-Budiri, "Democracy and the Experience", pp. 58–9.
108 Ibid., p. 59.
109 Ibid.
110 For more information on the role of the mayors as political leaders, see Aronson, *Creating Facts*, pp. 182, 204, 207, 254, and 308.
111 Al-Budiri, "Democracy and the Experience", pp. 58–9.
112 Ibid., p. 59.
113 See: Ali al-Jarbawi, *The Intifada and Political Leadership in the West Bank and Gaza District: A Study of the Political Elite* (Beirut: Dar al-Taliya, 1989) (Arabic); Bassam al-Salhi, *The Political and Religious Leadership in the Occupied Territories: Reality and Evolution, 1967–1991* (Jerusalem: Dar al-Quds Distribution and Marketing, 1993) (Arabic).

4 The Formal Structure of Powers in the Palestinian National Authority

1 As to the details of the elections and their circumstances, see chapter 5 on the elections.
2 See *The Declaration of Principles with Regard to the Temporary Independent Rule, Washington, September 13, 1993* (Jerusalem: The Jerusalem Media and Communication Center, 1944) (Arabic).
3 See Appendix 2 of the Agreement: The Gaza–Jericho First Agreement, 1994 (Jerusalem: The Jerusalem Media and Communication Center, 1944) (Arabic).
4 See chapter 5 on the elections.
5 The Internal Statutes of the Legislative Council (Appendix 3), sections 102 and 103.
6 Ibid., section 38.
7 Ibid., section 39.
8 Ibid., section 40.
9 Ibid., section 41.
10 Ibid., section 42.
11 Ibid., section 43.
12 Ibid., section 89.
13 Ibid., section 91.
14 Ibid., sections 5–11.
15 The Interim Agreement, section 6.
16 The Palestinian Legislative Council (conclusive summary of activities), 1966; p. 89 (hereafter: Palestinian Legislative Council).
17 Palestinian Legislative Council, p. 90.
18 Ibid., p. 90.
19 Ibid., p. 91.
20 Ibid., p. 91.
21 Ibid., p. 92.
22 Ibid., pp. 92–3.
23 Ibid., p. 93.
24 Ibid., pp. 94–6.

25 Ibid., p. 97.
26 Ibid., p. 98.
27 The Internal Statutes of the Legislative Council (Appendix 3), section 44.
28 Ibid., sections 45, 46, 47.
29 Ibid., section 47.
30 Ibid., section 48.
31 Ibid., section 49.
32 Ibid., section 50.
33 Ibid., section 51.
34 Ibid., sections 54 and 55.
35 Ibid., section 52.
36 Ibid., sections 57, 58, 59, 60, 61.
37 Ibid., section 63.
38 The Basic Law of the PNA (Appendix 2), section 64.
39 Ibid., section 44.
40 The Internal Statutes of the Legislative Council, section 69.
41 Ibid., section 74.
42 Ibid., section 70.
43 Ibid., section 71.
44 Ibid., section 72.
45 Ibid., section 74.
46 Ibid., section 74.
47 Ibid., section 74.
48 Ibid., section 73.
49 Ibid., section 68, and The Basic Law of the PNA, section 48.
50 Ibid., section 72.
51 The Internal Statutes of the Legislative Council, section 63.
52 Ibid., section 64.
53 Ibid., section 64.
54 Ibid., sections 65–6.
55 See further details in a special publication of the council: The Palestinian Legislative Council, 1996, and The Palestinian Legislative Council, No. 1, January 1997.
56 The Internal Statutes of the Legislative Council (Appendix 3), section 12.
57 Ibid., section 12.
58 Ibid., section 20.
59 Ibid., section 21.
60 Ibid., section 22.
61 Ibid., section 23.
62 Ibid., section 14.
63 Ibid., section 16.
64 Ibid., section 24.
65 Ibid., section 17.
66 Ibid., section 18.
67 Ibid., section 19.
68 Ibid., section 15.
69 Ibid., section 25.

70 Ibid., section 26.
71 Ibid., section 28.
72 Ibid., section 27.
73 Ibid., section 29.
74 Ibid., section 30.
75 Ibid., section 34.
76 Ibid., section 31.
77 Ibid., section 32.
78 Ibid., section 33.
79 Ibid., section 35.
80 Ibid., section 36.
81 Ibid., section 37.
82 Ibid., section 75.
83 Ibid., section 76.
84 Ibid., section 78.
85 Ibid., section 80.
86 Ibid., section 80.
87 Ibid., section 81.
88 Ibid., section 82.
89 Ibid., section 84.
90 Ibid., section 87.
91 Ibid., section 83.
92 Ibid., section 85.
93 Ibid., section 86.
94 Ibid., section 88.
95 See The Basic Lines of the Palestinian Government (Appendix 1).
96 See chapter 5 on the elections.
97 See the Basic Law of the Palestinian Authority (Appendix 2).
98 Ibid., section 51.
99 Ibid., section 52.
100 Ibid., section 54.
101 Ibid., section 55.
102 Ibid., section 56.
103 Ibid., section 57.
104 Ibid., section 59.
105 Ibid., section 60.
106 Ibid., fourth paragraph.
107 Ibid.
108 Interview with the director-general of the ministry, Jihad Hamdan, *el-Melad*, November 1, 1995, p. 7.
109 Interview with the director-general of the ministry, Mr. Bahajat el-Khaldi, ibid., p. 9.
110 See interview with the director for supervision in the ministry, Omar Abu-Owla, ibid., p. 12.
111 Interview with the director-general of the ministry, Dr. Mundar e-Shareef, ibid., p. 11.
112 Ibid., p. 8.

113 Ibid., p. 13.
114 Ibid., p. 7.
115 From an interview with Talal Abu Afifa, the director-general of the Ministry of Sport and Youth, ibid., p. 10.
116 See, ibid., p. 6.
117 From an interview with minister Hassan Tahboub, ibid., p. 9.
118 See ibid., p. 13.
119 See ibid., p. 8.
120 From an interview with Minister Yasser Amer, ibid., p. 9.
121 See ibid., p. 10.
122 Ibid., p. 10.
123 Ibid., p. 11.
124 Ibid., p. 11.
125 Ibid., p. 12.
126 See Ali el Safarini et al., *Towards a Renewed Building of the Judicial Authority in the West Bank and the Gaza Strip, the Technical Staff and Advisors* (Jeruaslem, 1994) (Arabic), Ahmed el-Khaladi, *Comparison with the Principal Components in the Law concerning the Independence of the Justice System* (Nablus: Palestinian Center for Research and Study, 1998) (Arabic).
127 See Ali el Safarini et al., *Towards a Renewed Building . . .*; el-Khaladi, *Comparison with the Principal.*
128 See Ali el Safarini et al., *Towards a Renewed Building . . .*
129 The Interim Agreement, Chapter 3, Clause 17.
130 Ibid., section 9.
131 Ibid.
132 Basic Law of the PNA (Appendix 2), section 5.
133 Ibid., section 5.
134 Proposed law (bill) of the judicial authority (Appendix 4), Part 1, Section 1.
135 Ibid., part 2, section 2.
136 Ibid., part 2, chapter 2, section 9.
137 Ibid., part 2, chapter 1, sections 3, 4, 6.
138 Ibid., part 3, chapter 5, section 60.
139 Ibid., part 2, chapter 1, section 5.
140 Ibid., part 2, chapter 1, section 8.
141 Ibid., part 3, chapter 5, section 60.
142 Ibid., part 2, chapter 1, section 8.
143 Ibid., part 3, chapter 1, section 67.
144 Ibid., part 3, chapter 3, section 73.
145 Ibid., part 3, chapter 3, section 74.
146 Ibid., part 3, chapter 3, section 75.
147 Ibid., part 3, chapter 3, section 76.
148 Ibid., part 3, chapter 5, section 60.

5 The First Palestinian General Elections

1 Moshe Ma'oz, *Palestinian Leadership in the West Bank* (London: Frank Cass, 1984); Emile Sahliyeh, *In Search of Leadership: West Bank Politics since 1967*

(Washington, D.C.: The Brookings Institute, 1988).

2 See: Raja Shehadi, *The Declaration of Principles and the Legal System in the West Bank* (Jerusalem: PASSIA, 1994).

3 See: positions of Haidar Abd Al-Shafi, the head of the Palestinian delegation to the Madrid negotiations, and of Dr. Khalil Shakaki, Chairman of the Institute for Palestinian Research and Studies in Nablus, as they were reported in *Al-Nas Wal-Entkhabat* (The People and the Elections, special weekly newspaper of Palestinian electoral affairs), December 9, 1995; see also the views of the minister of local government in the Palestinian Authority, Dr. Saab 'Arikat, in an interview in *Al-Nas Wal-Entkhabat*, December 23, 1995.

4 See, for example, the positions of members of the Palestinian opposition leadership in interviews in *Al-Nas Wal-Entkhabat*, December 30, 1995.

5 Guillermo O'Donnell, Phillip C. Schmitter, and Laurence Whitehead, eds, *Transition from Authoritarian Rule: Prospects for Democracy, Part 3* (Baltimore: Johns Hopkins University Press, 1986).

6 Richard Rose, "Is Choice Enough? Elections and Political Authority", in Hermet Rose and Mary Rouguie (eds), *Elections Without Choice* (London: Macmillan, 1978).

7 Ibid.

8 See: Nabil Kasis, *Palestinian–Israeli Agreements and the Elections* (Nablus: Center for Palestinian Research and Studies in Nablus, 1994) (Arabic).

9 See: published public opinion surveys conducted by the Center for Palestinian Research and Studies in Nablus, 1995, summarized in Khalil Shakaki, "The Peace Process, National Reconstruction and Transition to Democracy in Palestine", *Journal of Palestine Studies* XXV/2 (98) (1996): 5–20.

10 Ali al-Jarbawi, *Elections and the Palestinian Regime* (Jerusalem: Palestinian Academy for International Affairs, 1994), pp. 13–16 (Arabic); Raed Abdul Hamid, *Legal Aspects of Palestinian Elections* (Jerusalem: Israeli/ Palestinian Center for Research and Information, 1995).

11 Al-Jarbawi, *Elections and the Palestinian Regime*, pp. 6–13; Abdul Hamid, *Legal Aspects of Palestinian Elections*, pp. 106–11.

12 See: Israeli–Palestinian Interm Agreement on the West Bank and the Gaza Strip (Jerusalem: Ministry of Foreign Affairs, 1995).

13 Haider Abed Al-Shafi, *The Importance of the Election to the Future of the Palestinians* (Nablus: Center for Palestinian Research and Studies in Nablus, 1994) (Arabic).

14 The Palestinian Authority, *The Election Law* (Gaza: The Palestinian Authority, 1995) (Arabic).

15 Arend Lijphart, *Democracy in Plural Societies: A Comparative Exploration* (New Haven, CT: Yale University Press, 1977).

16 *Al-Nas Wal-EntKhabat*, December 9, 1995, and *al-Quds* (Jerusalem, a daily newspaper published in Arabic in East Jerusalem), November 25, 1995.

17 *Al-Nas Wal-EntKhabat*, December 9, 1995 and December 16, 1995.

18 *Al-Nas Wal-EntKhabat*, December 30, 1995.

19 See, for example, *Al-Senara* (a weekly newspaper published in Nazareth), January 19, 1996.

20 See the Palestinian daily papers like *al-Quds*, *al-Ayyam*, and *al-Bilad* of elec-

tion day, January 20, 1996.
21 *Al-Nas Wal-EntKhabat*, January 20, 1996.
22 The Institute for Palestinian Research and Studies, special announcement, January 20, 1996.
23 In Israel's first elections, for example, the proportion of voters was 86.9 percent.

6 The Centralization of Power and Political Conduct in the PNA

1 Interview with Samir Shehada, September 24, 1996.
2 See *Al-Milad* 1 (November 1995), p. 2.
3 Ibid.
4 Ibid., pp. 2–3; interview, September 24, 1996.
5 For details on the ministry, see above, chapter 4.
6 See PECDAR *Activity Report 1996*, p. 1.
7 Ibid., p. 2.
8 See PECDAR *Activity Report 1996*, pp. 3–54.
9 Interview with a senior employee of the Company, November 9, 1998.
10 See Interim Agreement, section 14.
11 Graham Usher, "The Politics of Internal Security: The PA's New Intelligence Services", *Journal of Palestine Studies* 25 (2) (1996): 21–34.
12 Ibid.
13 For example: On Friday, November 18, 1994, shots fired at demonstrators in Gaza city killed 14 persons and wounded around 200, when a force of 30 policemen wearing plastic armor and flak jackets surrounded the Palestine Mosque in the city and dismantled loudspeakers mounted on trucks. In another incident, a group of children hurled rocks at police. After shooting in the air the police resorted to live fire, which caused the death of 14 persons (report by the Palestinian Independent Association on the shooting of civilians by members of the General Security Service and Police). In another case, on February 27, 1996, a policeman from the Nur Shams camp fired at a vehicle with Israeli license plates. The bullet missed the Israeli vehicle and struck a citizen, Ra'ad Rasmi Muhammad Harsha, of Kafr Qufin, killing him (Al-Qanun, *Annual Report to the al-Qanun Association about the Infringement of Human Rights in Palestine*, 1996, p. 61).
14 For example, the killing of Yussuf Abu Sneima during the dispersal of demonstrators protesting over the expropriation of land for the establishment of an airport. When the security forces began surveying and grading the land, citizens gathered to prevent this and witnessed the killing of Abu Sneima. General Jebali said, however, that there had been no demonstration and that force had been used against Yussuf because he was armed (Report of the Palestinian Independent Association on the shooting of civilians by members of the General Security Service and Police, 1997).
15 The wounding of children and citizens in Jebalya as the result of shooting by the Palestinian police. The incident began when members of the Preventive Security agency were conducting a search of the home of Ahmad al-Gandur. They opened fire when he tried to escape. A number of civilians were wounded,

including Suheil al-Araj, age 19, and Aisha Abd el-Al, age 67, who was struck in the head. Also wounded were the child Tha'ar Rashoud and the infant Salem Zaqoul (ibid.).

16 For example: Hanan Qush'am, age 38, a resident of the village of Rammun near Ramallah and the mother of eight children, was killed on April 17, 1997, while on a visit to her brother Ra'ad and their family for *Id el-Adha*. At nine in the evening, as their car was traveling toward Ramallah on the way to Rammun, they came under automatic weapons fire. One of the bullets penetrated the vehicle and wounded Qush'am in the back, as well as other members of the family and a six-month-old infant. Qush'am was taken to the hospital in Ramallah, where she died of her wounds the next day (April 18, 1997). There was no official investigation and no one was punished (*Annual Report of the Palestinian Group*, 1997, pp. 2–3). In another case, on October 23, 1997, Salim Muhammad al-Sha'ar was killed after the driver of the car in which he was traveling refused to obey orders at a Palestinian roadblock. A witness for the Palestinian Group told the human rights inspector that the police had halted the vehicle and asked the driver to back up and stop where police were standing; when the driver refused they fired at the vehicle. In addition to killing al-Sha'ar, the shots wounded the driver, Hashem Ibrahim al-Sha'ar, in his left arm (ibid.). Security forces at a roadblock shot and wounded the Zuhadi Ereisha. The event began in the industrial zones when a member of the security forces started firing at a truck and Ereisha was wounded (Report of the Palestinian Independent Association on the shooting of civilians by members of the General Security Service and Police, 1997).

17 Playing with guns or the accidental discharge of a weapon resulted in a bullet fired from the rifle of a member of the National Security Force penetrating the entrance to the hospital in Beit Jala and causing the death of Ali Zaboun of Bethlehem (ibid.).

18 Ibid.

19 Report of the Palestinian Independent Association on the Elections, 1996.

20 A.J. from Jenin, who works in a café, received a written summons to report to the Criminal Investigation Division, where he was questioned about a family squabble with a female relative. He answered the investigators' questions. Later he was charged with selling hashish in the café. He was tortured in a variety of ways – such as being bound in a cramped position, having his legs spread apart, pressure on his back, and having his head covered with a sack – until he lost consciousness from the blows. According to what he heard, the interrogators were sentenced to 18 days in jail. A young man from Buruqin was questioned using the same methods by one of the interrogators from the first case, five months later, and the same methods of torture were used (*Hoquq al-Nas* 2, p. 13).

21 On March 5, 1996, the Ramallah police summoned J.S., a Red Cross worker, age 26, from Deir Ghassana, for questioning about the theft of windows from the hospital. When he arrived at the police station he was taken to a nearby building. He said: "They took me to the other side of the police building, alongside the Farandes school, and two policemen began to beat me with their fists. Later they were joined by four others. A lot of blood flowed from me. After

half an hour of continued beating I began to feel faint and that I could endure no more. Then I received a strong blow in the abdomen, which made me nauseous, so I fell and could not get back up. They took me to the interrogation room, where two men beat me some more. Then I was taken back to the room a third time and M. hit me with a truncheon on my right side and another policeman hit me hard on my back and after that jabbed his elbow into my neck. I felt everything go black and felt I was about to faint. The next evening I woke up and found myself in the intensive care unit of the Ramallah hospital" (ibid.).

Another case involved Ibrahim al-Awisi, age 25, of the village of Beitin, in the Ramallah district, who works in a car body shop. He was renting the house in which he lived from Haj Sharif al-Nis. When the lease was up, al-Nis asked him to vacate the premises. Al-Awisi requested an extension of two months. When that was up al-Nis went to the office of the Preventive Security service in Tayyibe to complain and both men went to the office. Al-Awisi promised to vacate the house within a week, but did not do so. At that point the security forces summoned him a second time, on October 4. Al-Awisi explained that he could not move out of the house because he had still not found a new place to rent. After an argument about the delay, the officer told him, "We are the court and we are the judges and you have 24 hours. If you don't leave we will throw you and all your belongings into the street." They put him in a small room. A few minutes later, three officers of the Preventive Security force entered the room and beat him all over his body, after which a fourth and fifth officer came and joined them. This lasted for five or ten minutes, until al-Awisi threw up and then fainted. "After that one of them came back and grabbed me by my hair and head from the front and jammed it against the wall and said he would bash my brains out and began to smash my head against the wall. Then another officer entered the room and jabbed his fingers in my eyes and said he would tear them out, until I screamed from the pain. Then he slapped me on both cheeks, right and left, and cursed me. Before I left the police station the officer told me he would throw me out of the house by force, with the law or without the law" (*Annual Report of the Palestinian Human Rights Monitoring Group*, 1997, p. 3).

Muhammad Najib Salah, age 27, from the village of Tayasir in the Jenin district, gave an affidavit to the attorney of the al-Qanun Association: "On November 23, 1997, when I was standing outside a store in my village, an Israeli military vehicle pulled up and the soldiers asked me why I was standing there, whether or not I was married, and whether I had a job. When I told them that I don't have a job because my permit to enter Israel had expired; they told me to go to Dotan, the office of the Israeli civil administration, and ask for Yitzhak to help me get a magnetic card." He added: "I did go on November 27, 1997, and asked for Yitzhak. They told me there was no one there by that name. I submitted a request for a magnetic card and received it in the normal way." He continued: "A few days later, on December 9, 1997, I was summoned by the Preventive Security apparatus in Tubas, where I met with the two interrogators, A.T. and S.Q., both of them from Tubas. They put me in a room where there were wooden truncheons and an electric heater and asked me about the Israeli military vehicle and about Yitzhak. I answered them, but evidently my answer did not satisfy them. Then A. slapped me in the face and S. hit me on the back and arms with a stick and broke my right wrist. After that they began to curse me and beat me with sticks on my penis. Then they told me to take off my shoes and clothes except for the shirt and then they beat me on my legs after they pushed me on the floor and stamped on my head. They didn't stop hitting me from nine in the morning until four in the afternoon. Then they let me go on condition that I return the next morning at 10. Before I left they asked me, laughing, whether my head and body were aching from the blows? The next day I went with a medical report on my condition and they told me to "Stick it up your ass, you're a liar. Nothing hurts you." They told me to go away and come back two hours later to get my identity card. When I came back they wrote a statement in my name and I asked them to read it to me, because I don't know how to read, and they said that it wasn't allowed. And they got me to sign the statement and papers and told me to stay at home" (*Hoquq al-Nas* 11, p. 57). Khaled Mahmud Hassin el-Alami, age 22, of Beit Omar in the Hebron region, an agricultural worker, was severely beaten by the police in the Nuba jail, fracturing his left leg (ibid. 9, p. 47).

22 For example, two policemen asked a cassette seller to lower the volume and he did so. After that they asked him for his identity card and he gave it to them. Then they asked him to accompany them to the police station and he refused because he didn't know where to leave his cart if he went with them. Then a man in civilian dress appeared and began to curse him and say "This is what we'll do to all the residents of Jenin." Then two civilians were arrested and beaten at length, including blows to the feet (ibid. 2, p. 13). In another case a woman from the al-Amari camp heard cries next to her house and went outside to see what was happening. She saw six policemen beating her son. She tried to help him but they hit her with their rifle butts more than once (ibid.).

23 For example, policemen confiscated a vehicle owned by the citizen Dr. Nafez Ala from the village of Einabus, alleging that the vehicle was stolen. But the citizen later saw his vehicle, with the number plates replaced by Palestinian Authority plates. A 1996 Audi was confiscated from the same man and is being used by the head of the Nablus police (ibid., p. 15).

24 For example: On August 3, 1997, Issam Ramzi was arrested after responding to a summons to come to the Dahariyya detention center in Hebron for interrogation by the Preventive Security service. When he arrived he was placed under arrest and not allowed to contact anyone for a week. His wife received a visiting permit from the Preventive Security service and met with him in the presence of the interrogators, a circumstance that did not allow him to speak about the charges against him. After that Ramzi was transferred to the prison of the General Intelligence Service in Jericho, where he was held for five months. During that period his wife was unable to visit him because she was pregnant. After she gave birth she visited him in March. Later Ramzi was transferred again, to the Jericho general prison, where the Authority gave him a permit for a regular weekly visit. His family was never notified when he was transferred from one prison to another and found out through unofficial channels. During one of the visits Ramzi told his wife that he was being accused of

tax evasion, on the basis of testimony by two people from Hebron. He added that during the first four days after he was arrested he was bound and beaten and treated brutally in order to get him to confess. His wife sent letters to Chairman Arafat and members of the Legislative Council and got in touch with many human rights organizations, but her letters went unanswered. Ramzi was never brought to trial nor were any official charges lodged against him (*Al-Raqeb* 4, p. 4).

In another case Muhammad Kamal Touqan, age 30, from Gaza, was summoned by Military Intelligence to appear on July 2, 1996. Since then he has been held by Military Intelligence without a detention order. No indictment has been presented and he was never brought before a judge. After six months in detention he was permitted biweekly visits for two months. After that the visiting permit was suspended. He was tortured during the first 65 days of detention in order to get him to confess to security-related offenses, but he refused. He is married and the father of four. His father died while he was in prison and he was not allowed to see him or attend his father's funeral (*Hoquq al-Nas* 9, pp. 26–7).

25   For example: Ahmad Fathi Hassan Ziyyad was arrested on May 27, 1995, after confessing to incest with his mother and sister, and collaborating with Israel. According to his mother Nazihah and sister Hanan the charges are false, but he has been in jail for more than two years. An officer of Force 17 arrested Ziyyad in May 1995 when he quarreled with another man. When the police concluded their investigation and released him, Major Kifah Birkat of Force 17 took him to the detention station of the General Intelligence Service. After being held for five days without interrogation he was bound and beaten to force him to confess, but Ziyyad refused to do so. After eight weeks Ziyyad signed a confession written in advance, as a result of being forced to watch three of his brothers being beaten by the interrogators. The testimony of Hanan Fathi Hassan Abu Rahma, age 21, Zayyad's sister, sheds light on his arrest. Her testimony was taken by the head of the Palestinian Human Rights Monitoring Group, Bassem Eid, on June 3, 1997: "My brother Ahmad Fathi Hassan Ziyyad was arrested by Force 17 at his father's house on Hisham's Palace Street, near the presidential palace in Jericho. My mother Nazihah used to keep going to the offices of the various security agencies in Jericho but they always told her they did not know the name. In March 1996 I myself appealed to the office of the *Ra'is* in Gaza, at a time when the *Ra'is* was out of Palestine, and explained the situation to the employees there. They gave me a letter to Tewfik Tirawi. I don't know what was written in it. I went to Tirawi's office in Jericho. After he read the letter he gave me a letter for the prison. In this way I visited Ahmad in March 1997, that is, 10 months after he was arrested. Ahmad told me about the torture and beatings and said that as a result he had confessed to collaboration with Israel and incest with his mother and sisters. Later there were regular visits, once a week. But Ahmad is still being held in the Jericho prison. Until today no indictment has been submitted and Ahmad has not been brought before a judge since he was arrested. In April 1997 the family requested a meeting with the Jericho district attorney, whose name is Daud. I was one of those summoned by Daud, who questioned me about the

accusations against Ahmad and his confession. I rejected all the accusations and confessions. My parents and brothers were also questioned. After that the district attorney told me that he was passing on the case to the attorney-general, Khaled al-Qudra, to investigate the charges and present an indictment. But still nothing has happened. We tried to hire an attorney from Jericho, but after he read the file evidently he declined to represent him in court, because no indictment was presented. Every day my mother sends Ahmad food and clothes and money. This is difficult for the family and we don't know what to do in order to solve the problem" (*Al-Raqeb* 4, p. 4).

26 Adel Abu Seif was arrested in June 1994 and released on December 6, 1996. A resident of the Nuseirat camp in the Gaza district, he completed his studies at the school for blind of al-Azhar University. He is blind as a result of a fever he suffered when he was two years old. Before the founding of the Authority, Abu Seif was told that his blindness could be treated surgically; he contacted volunteer groups to help him fund the trip to Russia for treatment. Shortly thereafter the Authority was set up and he traveled to Jericho on his way abroad for the operation. He was arrested there by Military Intelligence, who accused him of collecting the money for hostile organizations and of traveling for this purpose. In a meeting between Abu Seif and the attorney-general, Khaled al-Qudra, the latter accused him of collaboration with Israel. When his father said that his son was not that kind of person, al-Qudra accused the father of collaboration and threatened to have him arrested. In the end he agreed to interrogate Abu Seif after he had spent months in detention. Some 30 months after his arrest he was released without any charges being lodged against him. His situation was very difficult because of the loss of his money and papers. He was a blind man without family or friends in Jericho, in addition to the difficulty of getting back to Gaza. After a while he was able to travel to Nazareth and marry, but his father continued to defend his son's rights and told his story to *Sawt al-Haq we-al-Huriyya*, an Arabic-language newspaper published inside Israel, which published it (ibid.).

27 For example, the security forces arrested 11 Palestinian citizens within three hours of their release. On August 15 the attorney-general issued orders for the immediate release of these individuals after they had been held for months without legal proceedings against them. What concerns Palestinian human rights organizations even more is that the arrests involved persons who are supposed to implement the law because of their duty to follow the instructions of the attorney-general, including Colonel Muhammad al-Tanani, the governor of the Gaza prison and head of the Palestinian Prison Service (*Third Annual Report of the Palestinian Independent Association*, 1997, p. 215).

In another case, after the Supreme Court ordered the release of Sheikh Mahmud Masalah, on the evening of December 9, 1997, the General Intelligence Service took him from the prison on a ride through the streets of Ramallah and el-Bireh in a car belonging to the service, which was supposed to implement the decision of the Palestinian Supreme Court of November 30, 1997, ordering his release. In their unique way they returned him to prison as if they had released and then re-arrested him (*Hoquq al-Nas* 11, p. 11).

28 From an article by Dr. Irvin Cottler in *Al-Raqeb* 3 (June 1997), p. 4.

29 Ibid., p. 2.
30 Ibid.; *Annual Report of the Palestinian Independent Association for Civil Rights*, 1997, pp. 112–13.
31 *Al-Raqeb* 3 (June 1997), p. 2; *Annual Report of the Palestinian Independent Association for Civil Rights*, 1997, pp. 112–13.
32 *Al-Raqeb* 3, p. 2.
33 Ibid.
34 Ibid.; *Annual Report*, 1997, pp. 112 and 113.
35 *Al-Raqeb* 3, p. 2; *Annual Report*, 1997, pp. 112–13; *First Annual Report of al-Qanun for 1996*, p. 53.
36 *Al-Raqeb* 3, p. 20; *Annual Report*, 1997, pp. 112–13.
37 *First Annual Report of al-Qanun*, p. 53.
38 *Al-Raqeb* 3, p. 2.
39 Ibid.
40 *Al-Raqeb* 3, p. 2.
41 Ibid.
42 *Annual Report*, 1997, pp. 112–13.
43 For example, a 14-year-old boy was tortured at the police station in Gaza city when his father brought him there after someone accused him of trying to rob him. In the Gaza Magistrate's Court, the father noticed a swelling above the boy's left eye and his general poor health as a result of being beaten. After that he was sent to the al-Rabi'a Institute for Social Rehabilitation, where he found his son unconscious, lying motionless in his room. At the hospital the boy was found to be suffering a high fever, a swelling above his left eye, and weakness. An examination revealed that there was a mass on the brain, under the meninges, along with weakness in his hands and feet and aphasia (*Annual Report of the Palestinian Independent Association*, 1996, pp. 93–4).
44 From the *Report of the Palestinian Independent Association on the Use of Torture by the Palestinian Security Forces*, 1996.
45 *Al-Raqeb* 3, pp. 6–7.
46 *Al-Raqeb* 5, pp. 2, 3, 5, 8–10.
47 Ibid.
48 Ibid.
49 Ibid.
50 Ibid.
51 Ibid.
52 *Al-Quds* (daily newspaper), August 8, 1996.
53 *Al-Raqeb* 5, pp. 2, 3, 5, 8–10.
54 Ibid.
55 Ibid.
56 Ibid.
57 *Annual Report of the Palestinian Human Rights Monitoring Group*, "Death in Palestinian Prisons", p. 2.
58 *Report of the Independent Association* for 1997, p. 189; *Annual Report of the Palestinian Human Rights Monitoring Group*, 1997, p. 2; *Al-Raqeb* 5, pp. 2, 3, 5, 8–10.
59 *Annual Report of al-Qanun*, 1997, pp. 64 and 65.

60 *Annual Report of the Palestinian Human Rights Monitoring Group*, 1997.
61 Ibid., p. 66.
62 *Annual Report of the Palestinian Human Rights Monitoring Group*, 1997, p. 2.
63 *Hoquq al-Nas* 13 (1998), pp. 4–6.
64 *Annual Report of al-Qanun*, 1997, p. 63; *Al-Raqeb* 5, pp. 2, 3, 5, 8–10.
65 *Annual Report of al-Qanun*, 1997, p. 65.
66 Ibid.
67 A press release by the Palestinian Human Rights Monitoring Group, August 10, 1998.
68 A press release by the Palestinian Human Rights Monitoring Group, October 4, 1999.
69 A press release by the Palestinian Human Rights Monitoring Group, December 15, 1999.
70 A press release by the Palestinian Human Rights Monitoring Group, June 7, 2000.
71 Ibid., p. 68.
72 *Al-Raqeb* 2, p. 10.
73 *Al-Quds*, February 2, 1997.
74 Several examples can be given: There were 36 security prisoners held for between one and three years in the Ramallah prison and not brought to trial, as mentioned in a letter they sent to Chairman Arafat (*Hoquq al-Nas* 13, 1998, p. 58).

   Israel accused Hamas of carrying out two attacks against Israel, on July 30 and September 4, 1997. The Authority arrested 80 Hamas members in the West Bank and 60 in the Gaza Strip. Thirteen of the West Bank detainees were tortured in the Dahariyya prison and released after two months. Another 42 were sent to the prison. At the end of November these prisoners held a six-day hunger strike to protest at their illegal detention (*Annual Report of the Palestinian Human Rights Monitoring Group*, 1997, p. 10).

   On February 18, 1997, the Palestinian security forces arrested 27 members of the Popular Front for the Liberation of Palestine – General Command (the organization of Ahmad Jibril), from the Hebron, Bethlehem, Ramallah, Nablus, Jenin, and Tulkarm regions, and held them in custody for several months. At the end of the year, two were still being held in the prison – Ghassam al-At'out and Mursi Bahalaq – without being indicted or brought to trial or even brought before the attorney-general. Those arrested included attorney Husam Arafat, who was released in Ramallah in July (*Annual Report of al-Qanun*, 1997, p. 102; *Annual Report of the Palestinian Human Rights Monitoring Group*, 1997, p. 10). For more examples see: *Al-Raqeb* 4; *Hoquq al-Nas* 12; *Annual Report of al-Qanun*, 1997.

   The case of the students from Bir Zeit University is one of the best-known events. In March 1996 the Palestinian security service arrested seven students from Bir Zeit University and locked them up in Ramallah prison on a charge of participation in illegal Hamas activities. No official indictments were filed and they were not questioned. A suit was filed against the attorney-general and Chairman Arafat as acting interior minister, after the two Ramallah district prosecutors, civilian and military, emphasized that they were not responsible for the arrests. The Supreme Court handed down its opinion on June 26, requiring the prosecutors to clarify the reasons for the students' arrest and continued detention. The Supreme Court issued its final judgment on August 18, 1996, calling for the immediate release of the students, noting the illegality of the arrest and that the Authority had not made proper use of its powers. But the students were not released until a decision by Chairman Arafat on October 7, 1996, to release 25 prisoners, including the seven students from Bir Zeit (*Al-Raqeb* 4, 1997, p. 6).

75   *Annual Report of al-Qanun*, 1997, pp. 106 and 107.

76   Ibid., 1995, pp. 57–60.

77   The incident at a-Najah University took place on March 30, 1996, when a force from the Palestinian security services invaded the campus in Nablus during a press conference being given by all the student factions, under the heading, "Free the prisoners in Israeli and Palestinian prisons". Before the representative of the Fatah movement had finished speaking, rumors reached the Student Council that the security services had entered the campus to arrest some of the students. A member of the student council announced this over the loudspeakers. After that the presidential security force, Force 17, the police, the riot squad, and security personnel in civilian dress invaded the campus and began to beat male and female students, resulting in injury to 17 students. The injuries included fractured limbs and cuts, fainting, and nervous collapse. An estimated 150–200 security personnel took part (ibid., 1997, pp. 57–60).

78   On Friday, August 2, 1996, disturbances began in Tulkarm when a group of women came to visit prisoners in the local prison. While they were there, several prisoners were transferred because of their poor health – the result of a hunger strike. When the women began to protest at this action, the Palestinian security forces pushed them, knocking one of the women to the ground. After that a group of teenage boys began to throw rocks and firebombs; the soldiers responded with heavy gunfire. After the afternoon prayer a number of residents gathered outside the building. The soldiers climbed to the roof of the building, following the orders of the governor of Tulkarm. Meanwhile, 66 prisoners cried out "Allah Hu Akhbar" and forced open the prison gates. Most of them fled outside. Later a large group from the various security forces went out into the street and swung their truncheons and fired in the air, paying no heed to the presence of persons on the balconies and roofs of nearby buildings. Subsequently the Palestinian National Authority declared Tulkarm a closed military zone and summoned reinforcements from Nablus and Jenin. In the following days there was a flurry of arrests of residents and political activists, who were transferred to the Juneid prison. Ibrahim Abdallah Ashtiwi Hodeida, age 44, of Tulkarm, was killed by a bullet that entered his back (ibid.).

79   The police fired at random during the incident at the Nablus Stadium, on September 23, 1996, during a soccer match between the al-Halal al-Muqdasi and Tulkarm Youth Center teams, after a fight erupted between the Tulkarm players and the referees. During the quarrel a large force from the riot squad of the Palestinian police intervened to protect the referees. Spectators began to throw empty bottles, but remained in the stands and did not climb down onto

the field. Without warning the police began to shoot indiscriminately from a distance of 15 to 20 meters, wounding three citizens – Hani Muhammad Suwan of Nablus, wounded in the chest, Nahi Issa Iyad, wounded in his left shoulder, and Salim Mustafa Abu Sanab, age 34, wounded in his head. Abu Sanab later died of his wounds in the Ramallah hospital (ibid.).

80 *Hoquq al-Nas* 13.
81 For example: Shots were fired at Dr. Abd el-Satar Kassem near a-Najah University on August 20, 1995, four weeks after the publication in *al-Watan* of his article, "Democracy in the Shadow of the Chairman". The day after the article was published he received an anonymous letter warning him to take precautionary measures because he was liable to be attacked, as indeed happened four weeks later. In Dr. Kassem's opinion, his assailant intended to threaten but not kill him. The bullets were fired from close range and struck his right arm. In another event, a correspondent for the Reuters news agency received a phone call from General Ghazi Jebali, advising him to stop "talking" so as not to cause a scandal to the Palestinian Authority. If not, they would smash his head. This came in the wake of the bloody events at the Palestine Mosque in Gaza on Nov. 18, 1994 (Khaled al-Omariya in *Al-Raqeb* 1).

Dr. Ayub Othman, a lecturer in the Faculty of Humanities and English Language Department at Al-Azhar University, was arrested after publishing an article about corruption, under the title "Long Live Justice", in the weekly *al-Balad*. The Criminal Investigation Division arrested him on May 30, 1997, and released him the next day. The same unit arrested the newspaper's editor, Maher Farraj, after investigating the article and newspaper, and released him the same day (*Annual Report of the Palestinian Human Rights Monitoring Group*, 1997, pp. 6–7; *Annual Report of al-Qanun*, 1997, p. 73).

82 *Al-Raqeb* 1.
83 For example: Four weeks after Arafat arrived in Gaza, on July 28, 1994, the Preventive Security service banned the distribution of *al-Nahar* daily newspaper for a month. The head of Preventive Security in the West Bank charged that the newspaper had connections with the Jordanian regime and that the PNA would not allow the existence of a rival authority in the areas over which it had jurisdiction (*Freedom of the Press and Expression*, al-Qanun Association, 1997, pp. 41–2). Also confiscated were *al-Quds*, *al-Nahar*, and *al-Aqsa* for four days; they were not allowed into the Gaza district on the pretext that they had failed to comply with the Authority's instructions with regard to the number of participants in an Islamic Festival. The officials responsible refused to clarify the reasons; the Press Association denounced the decision, but quietly (ibid.).

There are dozens of additional cases of infringement of the freedom of expression and information. See, ibid. and the *Annual Report of the Palestinian Human Rights Monitoring Group*, 1997, and the *Annual Report of al-Qanun*, 1997.

84 For example: Jibril Rajoub, the head of the Preventive Security service in the West Bank, confiscated the identity card of a journalist whom he encountered in a restaurant in Ramallah when the latter asked Rajoub for an interview. The

journalist had broken the story of the secret meeting between Rajoub and the Israeli chief-of-staff, General Amnon Lipkin-Shahak, in an Arabic-language paper published abroad. Although the journalist's well-placed connections in the Authority (a member of the Legislative Council, an official in the General Intelligence Service, and a personal advisor to Chairman Arafat) assured him that his interview would not last for more than an hour, he was arrested and tortured brutally by members of the Preventive Security force in Jericho. During the journalist's questioning Rajoub told him that if he got in touch with Chairman Arafat and complained, he would be killed, and that Arafat would reply, "Inshallah". The journalist was released after three days in detention (*Annual Report of the Palestinian Human Rights Monitoring Group*, 1997).

85   For example: On Wednesday, September 24, 1997, about 20 armed men arrived at the building of the Information and Culture Center in Nuseirat, identified themselves as presidential security agents, and asked about the activities of the center for about two hours. They refused to present personal identification or official orders. In the end they issued an order closing the Center and took the keys to the office. In a letter that the chairman of the board of the Center, Dr. Abd el-Rahman al-Jamaal, sent to al-Qanun, he wrote that he was astonished the next day to read, in the announcement of the Center's closure in the daily newspapers, that the grounds for the closure were its affiliation with Hamas, when in fact it was a center with a cultural and educational vocation, fully legal and approved by the Ministry of Culture and the Ministry of the Interior (*Annual Report of al-Qanun*, 1997, p. 71).

The Palestinian security services broke in and sealed without warning the building of the Gaza newspaper *al-Rasalah* on September 4, 1997, although there had been no official notification by the Authority or charges made against the paper by any official source. The security forces brought one of the employees to the newspaper's offices and forced him to unlock the door, after which they began searching the premises and confiscated material indiscriminately. After that they locked the door and posted a sign to the effect that the building had been sealed by order of the police and entry was prohibited. There was no signature or reference number on the notice. Dr. Ghazi Hamed, the editor-in-chief of the newspaper, emphasized that no official closure order had been received or explanation of the reasons for it, and that the paper is not affiliated with Hamas (ibid., p. 72; *Annual Report of the Palestinian Human Rights Monitoring Group*, 1997).

86   For example, in 1996 journalist Samir Hamato was detained for seven months, but no charges were brought against him and he was never even interrogated. The reason for his incarceration is still a mystery. He says, "I do not know the reasons for my arrest or the reasons for my release" (*Al-Raqeb* 3, p. 3). In another case, the journalist Maher el-Alami, the secretary of *al-Quds*, was detained for six days at the order of Chairman Arafat for publishing a report about the Chairman on p. 8 of the newspaper instead of on p. 1, as the Chairman's office had "suggested". He was held at the headquarters of the Preventive Security service in the Aqabat Jabbar camp in Jericho, and his friends and colleagues were not allowed to visit him. No newspaper, not even *al-Quds*, had the courage to write about his arrest or condemn it and demand

his release. The Palestinian press also passed over the fact that el-Alami was released and refused even to publish paid advertisements about his release (ibid.).

On March 12, 1998, the criminal police in Ramallah, at the order of General Ghazi Jebali, chief of the Palestinian police, arrested attorney Shawqi al-Issa, the executive director of the *al-Qanun* Association and editorial director of the magazine *Hoquq al-Nas*, the monthly published by the Association, and its editor-in-chief, the journalist Samih Muhsen, on account of an article in issue 31 of the magazine that criticized statements made by General Jebali during an interview broadcast on Israeli television. The interrogation of the two included accusations of slandering General Jebali. Their detention lasted from 11 o'clock Thursday morning until 10 o'clock at night. They were not allowed to speak with an attorney. They were asked to sign a commitment to refrain from writing articles against the Authority. The two editors denied the charges and refused to sign (*Hoquq al-Nas* 14, p. 10).

87 For example: In December 1997, Military Intelligence in Jericho prevented the distribution of issue 10 of the magazine *Hoquq al-Nas* because it contained a story about the torture of citizens by an officer of the force (*Annual Report of al-Qanun*, 1997, p. 74). The Communications Ministry requires private tele-vision stations to broadcast at least five hours a week about Authority affairs (ibid., p. 76). Newspapers that reflect the views of Hamas and the Islamic Jihad were closed in 1996 after the suicide bombings in Israel (*Al-Raqeb* 3, p. 3).

In February and March 1996, the Jenin local paper was closed and its editor, Imad Abu Zohara, was detained briefly; he was threatened with arrest again in November 1996 "should it prove necessary" (ibid.). The pro-Jordanian *al-Nahar* closed for financial reasons on January 1, 1997; the Authority had repressed the newspaper, causing problems in distribution and a loss of adver-tisers, which led to the financial crunch (ibid.).

88 For example, on November 28, 1996, the General Intelligence Service confis-cated books at the Jordan Bridge that the Israelis permitted to enter. These books were about the *Intifada*, the Arab–Israeli conflict, and the leadership of the Hamas movement. All were published by an Islamic publishing company in Jordan. In correspondence between the Palestinian Human Rights Monitoring Group and the Communications Ministry, the former requested legal justification for the actions of the security forces. Hani al-Masri, the official in charge of print publications in the Communications Ministry, replied that he had sent a letter to the General Intelligence Service asking it to return the confiscated books to their owners, but the latter refused, on the grounds that the books contained incitement and that in the absence of the rule of law the security forces decided the limits of freedom of opinion and expres-sion, despite the existence of the civilian authority. Some of the books written by Professor Edward Said were confiscated and their sale banned in 1996. The Palestinian National Authority has denied the existence of a ban on the sale of books by Professor Said, but it is difficult to find them in the bookstores (ibid.).

89 *Hoquq al-Nas* 5 (July 1997), pp. 17–20.

90 See *al-Waqa'a al-Falistiniya*. Sometimes Palestinian legislation promotes this phenomenon. For example, section 10 of the Civil Defense Law provides for

the establishment of a Supreme Council for Civil Defense and mentions the possibility of the appointment of more than one deputy minister. Several government ministries have double names; these include the Ministry of Trade and Economics and the Ministry of Planning and International Cooperation. In these ministries there are functionaries for each section, such as the appointment of Dr. Amin Haddah as director-general for economics and of Samir Halileh as director-general for trade (decision No. 94/34, *al-Waqa'a al-Falistiniya* 1, p. 54); and the appointment of Amin Bidun as director for international cooperation (decision 94/214, ibid. 3, p. 77); and of Dr. Abd el-Malik Jabbar as the advisor for planning affairs (decision 94/129, ibid. 2, p. 105).

91 See decision 97/49, ibid. 18, p. 7; decision 97/74, ibid. 19, p. 6; decisions 97/91, 97/92, 97/95, and 97/97, ibid. 20, pp. 35, 36, 40, and 42.

92 For example, the appointment of one assistant to the deputy minister in the Ministry of Education for the West Bank and of another for the Gaza district (see decisions 95/288 and 95/289, ibid. 11, pp. 48 and 49); the appointment of Dr. Muhammad al-Nahal as director of the Gaza office of the trade directorate in the Ministry of Trade and Economics and of Dr. Musa al-Seman to the parallel post for the West Bank (decision 94/33, ibid. 1, p. 53).

93 See decisions 95/272–282 (ibid. 9, pp. 58–68), decisions 95/288–290 (ibid. 11, pp. 48–50), decision 95/305 (ibid., p. 65), decisions 96/80, 96/82, 96/83, and 96/88–90 (ibid. 14, pp. 73, 75, 76, 81–3), and decisions 96/117–124 (ibid. 15, pp. 34–41). See also *al-Quds*, February 26, 1997, p. 8, about the appointment of engineer Husam el-Alul, a member of the board of directors of the Engineers' Association in the Gaza district, as director-general in the Office of National Institutions in the office of the chairman, retroactive to July 1996.

94 An example of this is decision 94/33 (ibid. 1, p. 53), naming directors for the trade offices in the West Bank and Gaza Strip, and worded so that each appointee would assume his post the moment he returned from Tunis.

95 See, for example: decision 96/43 (ibid. 12, p. 65), retroactively amending the appointment of Rana Hakim Balawi as second director of the Ministry of Local Government, so that the appointment of the daughter of Hakim Balawi, known for his closeness to Arafat, is effective as of October 16, 1995, even though not made until February 16, 1996. Note that Hakim Balawi represents the National Security Authority, which is directly subordinate to the Chairman, in accordance with decision 94/84 (ibid. 2, p. 59), in addition to his position in the Fatah movement and membership of the Palestinian Legislative Council.

Decision 96/97 (ibid. 14, p. 90) promoted Ibla, the daughter of Finance Minister Muhammad Zuhadi al-Nashashibi, to the rank of director-general in the Ministry of Finance retroactively: although issued on July 22, 1996, it was considered to be effective as of August 1, 1995.

The concentration of power through jobs and appointments sometimes involves close supporters who have been accused of corruption and dismissed from their jobs, but are rewarded with other positions. See decision 97/62 (ibid. 18, p. 22), the appointment of Fakhri al-Jebali (the brother of Ghazi Jebali) as director-general in the Ministry of Planning and International Cooperation, after Fakhri was dismissed as director of the war against drugs in Nablus because of his involvement in drug-dealing. Similarly, Mazen Anan was appointed to the Maritime Company after his dismissal as head of the Central Bureau of Statistics in Gaza because of corruption.

Decision 95/171 (ibid., 7, p. 24) named Fakhri Shukureh as advisor to the Chairman on security affairs; Shukureh later became a member of the legislative council. Also attracting attention is decision 95/223 (ibid. 7, p. 78), in which the *Ra'is* appointed Farouq Abu al-Rob as director-general of the legislative council. In addition to the oddity of the fact that the director-general of the legislature was appointed by the head of the executive branch, the decision was made on September 10, 1995, that is, before the election of the council itself on January 20, 1996.

96   See, for example, *al-Quds*, August 5, 6, 7, 8, 1998; *Fasal al-Muqal*, August 7, 1998.

97   Some of the advisors with titles include: attorney Ibrahim Abu Daqa, advisor to the Chairman on human rights affairs, decision 94/12 (ibid. 1, p. 24); Abd el-Fatah Ghanem, advisor to the Chairman for refugee camp affairs, decision 94/29 (ibid. 1, p. 49); Najib Mustafa al-Ahmad, advisor to the Chairman for general affairs, decision 94/57 (ibid. 1, p. 77); Samir Amar, advisor to the Chairman on special education, decision 94/91 (ibid. 2, p. 67); Jarir Nueiman al-Qudwah, advisor to the Chairman on education, decision 94/106 (ibid. 2, p. 82); Muhammad al-Amlah, advisor to the Chairman for national security affairs, decision 94/119 (ibid. 2, p. 95); Fakhri Shukureh, advisor to the Chairman for security affairs, decision 95/171 (ibid. 7, p. 24); Farid al-Quttab, military advisor in the President's office, decision 95/310 (ibid. 7, p. 70); Marwan Kanafani, media advisor to the Chairman, decision 94/147 (ibid. 3, p. 10); Muhammad Abu al-Leil, director-general for cultural and labor affairs in the office of the Chairman, decision 94/223 (ibid. 3, p. 86); Khaled al-Jundi, advisor on unions in the President's office, decision 96/109 (ibid. 15, p. 26); Faez Abu Rahme, legal advisor; Feisal Hamdi al Husseini, legal advisor in the President's office, decision 97/96 (ibid. 20, p. 41); Muhammad Burhan Rashid, economic advisor in the office of the Chairman, decision 94/48 (ibid. 1, p. 68); Muhammad Jarar al-Qudwah, special economic and financial advisor, decision 95/109 (ibid. 6, p. 41); Afif Saloum, advisor on banking and monetary affairs, decision 94/23 (ibid. 3, p. 46); Sheikh Muhammad Awad, advisor on religious affairs, decision 94/162 (ibid. 3, p. 25); Muhammad Ahmad Khalil, advisor on village and urban affairs, decision 94/24 (ibid. 3, p. 37); Tahsin al-Fares, advisor on agricultural affairs, decision 95/247 (ibid. 9, p. 43); Akram Abu Kamil, advisor for health affairs, decision 96/60 (ibid. 13, p. 11); Eith Abu Eith, advisor on clan affairs, decision 94/161 (ibid. 3, p. 23); Ruhi Fatwah, director of the public communications department in the office of the Chairman, decision 94/202 (ibid. 3, p. 65); Nabil Amar, advisor to the Chairman and supervisor of the Broadcasting and Television Authority (he is also a member of the legislative council), decision 96/162 (ibid. 15, p. 79).

98   Among the advisors without defined positions or titles are: Nabil Abu Rudeineh, decision 94/50 (ibid. 1, p. 70); Fahd Adel al-Raman, decision 94/78 (ibid. 2, p. 52); Issam al-Salah, decision 94/152 (ibid. 3, p. 15); Said Kenaan,

decision 95/206 (ibid. 7, p. 61), and his reappointment as advisor to the Chairman with the rank of director-general, decision 96/156 (ibid. 215, p. 73); Feisal al-Hourani, decision 95/300 (ibid. 11, p. 60); Ali Amar, decision 95/308 (ibid. 11, p. 68); Muhammad al-Hamurani, decision 96/7 (ibid. 11, p. 79); Salah Rafat of the FIDA party, decision 96/37 (ibid. 12, p. 57); Salah al-Masri, decision 96/147 (ibid. 15, p. 64); Faaq Wurad, decision 96/171 (ibid. 15, p. 88); and Faez al-Aswad of the Islamic Jihad (ibid. 17, p. 29).

99 Director-generals in the office of the Chairman include: Shawqat Issa Mustafa, decision 95/8 (ibid. 3, p. 99); Omar Said, decision 95/23 (ibid. 6, p. 85); Abd el-Fatah al-Jayussi, decision 95/156 (ibid. 6, p. 88); Kheiri al-Aridi, decision 95/227 (ibid. 9, p. 13); Said Abu Ali, decision 95/253 (ibid. 9, p. 39); Hassin Abu al-Awla, decision 95/298 (ibid. 11, p. 58); Said al-Qudrah, decision 96/16 (ibid. 11, p. 88); Ali al-Zajari, decision 96/56 (ibid. 13, p. 7); Jerais al-Atrash, decision 96/118 (ibid. 15, p. 35); Shadiyah al-Halu, decision 96/141 (ibid. 15, p. 58); Walim Najib Nasser, decision 97/64 (ibid. 18, p. 24); Khaled al-Yazji, decision 95/210 (ibid. 7, p. 55); Khalil Safi, decision 95/211 (ibid. 7, p. 66); Hanan al-Wazir, decision 95/226 (ibid. 7, p. 81).

100 Among those with clearly defined positions in the office of the Chairman are Samir Shehada, director-general of the Office of National Institutions in the office of the President, decision 95/146; and Sabri Jeryis, director-general of the research center in the office of the Chairman, decision 95/181 (ibid. 34, p. 34).

101 The two resigned their ministerial positions in August 1998 after the expansion of the government by the addition of new ministers, following the criticism by the Palestinian Legislative Council of the corruption revealed by the Comptroller's Report.

102 Interview conducted in his office in Ramallah on January 10, 1998.

103 *Al-Iyam*, January 1, 1998.

104 See *al-Quds*, December 30, 1997.

105 For example: the appointment of a *Mukhtar* for the Abu Sneina family in Hebron (*al-Hayyat al-Jadida*, December 15, 1997, p. 4), for the a-Sharif family in Gaza (*al-Quds*, December 24, 1997, p. 5), for the Hajjaj family and for the Talebani family (*al-Quds*, December 28, 1997, p. 1), and for the Saqiq family in Gaza (*al-Quds*, December 29, 1997, p. 1). Dozens of other examples could be offered.

106 The legislative council did not approve publication of this report, but it was published by mistake in the August 1997 issue of its magazine, whose distribution was immediately banned. The report associates prominent names with this phenomenon, including Nabil Sha'ath; Ahmad Qreia (Abu Ala); Khaled Salam (Muhammad Rashid), the economic advisor to the Chairman of the Authority; Muhammad Eshtayyeh, the director of PECDAR; Ramzi Khoury, the director of the office of the Chairman; and Dr. Maher al-Kurd, the deputy minister of trade and economics. Among the companies are the Maritime Company, owned by Ramzi Khoury and Hashem Abu Nida, another economic advisor to Chairman Arafat, behind whom are Suha Arafat, and Nabil Sha'ath, who owns another large firm, Tim, which holds concessions for "the development of human resources" for all ministries. There are also the

Palestinian Company for Economic Development, the Palestinian Company for Commercial Services, and others.

107 For a detailed investigation of the share of these close associates of Yasser Arafat in the concentration of economic power, see the following reports and articles: the Comptroller's Report; the Report of the Economic Committee of the Legislative Council, May 14, 1997; "Corruption in Gaza", an article by David Hirst in the *Guardian*, April 27, 1997; "The Man who Swallowed Gaza", an article by Ronen Bergman and David Renner in *Ha'aretz*, April 4, 1997; the *Magazine of Human Rights*, published by the al-Qanun Association in Jerusalem, No. 4 (June 1997), pp. 19–30; and the Comptroller's Report 1996, section on the Ministry of Labor.

108 Comptroller's Report 1997, section on the Ministry of Health.

109 Report of the Special Committee appointed by the Legislative Council, 1997, pp. 13–14.

110 Ibid., p. 35.

111 Ibid.

112 Ibid., p. 34.

7 Conclusion: Contradictions within Palestinian Democracy

1 Abd el-Rahman, *The PLO: Its Roots.*

2 Moshe Ma'oz, *The Palestinian Leadership in the West Bank* (Tel Aviv: Reshafim, 1985) (Hebrew).

3 Hassassian, "Policy and Attitude Change"; Sahliyeh, "The PLO and the Politics"; Ziad Abu-Amru, *Islamic Fundamentalism in the West Bank and Gaza* (Bloomington and Indianapolis: Indiana University Press, 1994).

4 Hassassian, "Policy and Attitude Change".

5 Independent Palestinian Association for Citizens' Rights, *Fourth Annual Report*, p. 68.

6 Ibid.

7 Al-Qanun Association, *Human Rights Journal* 15 (May 1998): 38.

8 *Shihan* (Jordan), November 22, 1997.

9 Independent Palestinian Association for Citizens' Rights, *Fourth Annual Report*, p. 98.

10 Ibid., *Third Annual Report*, p. 41.

11 Ibid., *Fourth Annual Report*, p. 58.

12 Ibid., *Third Annual Report*, p. 57.

13 Ibid.

14 Ibid., p. 144.

15 Omar Hamail, "Parliamentary Questions: An Active Technique for Oversight", *Journal of the Legislative Council* 2 (1999): 15.

16 See Independent Palestinian Association for Citizens' Rights, *Third Annual Report*, p. 54. In this context I can also mention the repeated failure of the justice minister to appear before the legislative council to answer questions about the non-implementation of court rulings (*Human Rights Journal*, August 1997: 49), the failure of the finance minister to meet with the Control Committee in the spoiled flour affair, the lack of cooperation by the supply

minister in the same case, and the refusal to provide information to the Committee (report of the Control and Economic Freedom Committee of the Palestinian Legislative Council, March 5, 1997).

17 Independent Palestinian Association for Citizens' Rights, *Fourth Annual Report*, p. 57.

18 See the al-Qanun Association, *Human Rights Journal* 19 (September 1998): 4–54.

19 Independent Palestinian Association for Citizens' Rights, *Third Annual Report*, p. 53.

20 *Human Rights Journal* 18 (August 1998): 49.

21 *Al-Sabil* (Jordan), May 23, 1998.

22 *Human Rights Journal* 18 (August 1998): 49.

23 Independent Palestinian Association for Citizens' Rights, *Third Annual Report*, p. 55.

24 Salah Rafat, "The Palestinian Legislative Council", *Palestinian Politics* 17 (Winter 1998): 94–9 (Arabic).

25 Independent Palestinian Association for Citizens' Rights, *Fourth Annual Report*, p. 69.

26 Al-Qanun, *Annual Report on the Situation of Justice in the Territories of the Palestinian National Authority*, 1998.

27 Ibid.

28 Ibid.

29 Ibid., pp. 17–34.

30 See: The Basic Law of the Palestinian National Authority (Appendix 2), section 2.

Index